Wole Soyinka Revisited

Twayne's World Authors Series
African Literature

Bernth Lindfors, Editor
University of Texas at Austin

TWAS 833

WOLE SOYINKA
Photograph by Jim Zietz © 1987 by Jim Zietz

Wole Soyinka Revisited

Derek Wright

Northern Territory University

Twayne Publishers • New York
Maxwell Macmillan Canada • Toronto
Maxwell Macmillan International • New York   Singapore   Oxford   Sydney

Wole Soyinka Revisited
Derek Wright

Copyright © 1993 by Twayne Publishers
All rights reserved.

Twayne Publishers   Maxwell Macmillan Canada, Inc.
Macmillan Publishing Company   1200 Eglinton Avenue East
866 Third Avenue   Suite 200
New York, New York 10022   Don Mills, Ontario M3C 3N1

Library of Congress Cataloging-in-Publication Data

Wright, Derek.
    Wole Soyinka revisted / Derek Wright.
       p.   cm. — (Twayne's world authors series ; TWAS 833)
    (Twayne's world authors series. African literature)
    Includes bibliographical references and index.
    ISBN 0-8057-8279-6 (alk. paper)
    1. Soyinka, Wole—Criticism and interpretation. 2. Nigeria in
literature. I. Title. II. Series. III. Series: Twayne's world
authors series. African literature.
PR9387.9.S6Z97   1993
822—dc20
                                                    92-24088
                                                    CIP

The paper used in this publication meets the minimum requirements
of American National Standard for Information Sciences—Permanence
of Paper for Printed Library Materials. ANSI Z3948-1984.∞™

10 9 8 7 6 5 4 3 2 1 (hc)

Printed in the United States of America

For my mother and my father

Contents

Preface

In his poem *Ogun Abibiman* Soyinka refers to his patron deity as "Him of the seven paths," and the writer has proved no less versatile than his god. Soyinka's writing talents alone are at least sevenfold: playwright, poet, novelist, autobiographer, critic, translator, and editor. To these vocations might be added an equal number of extraliterary talents: actor and director on stage and in film, theater manager, academic, political activist, recording artist, and dress designer, to name but a few. It was primarily as a dramatist and man-of-the-theater, however, that Soyinka won international fame, and it is in these roles that he features most prominently in the following pages. In keeping with the focus on his towering dramatic achievement, more attention than is usual in monographs on this author has been devoted to Yoruba dramatic traditions, to ritual and festival dramaturgy, and to the dramatic theory that he extrapolates from them. Inevitably in a short study of an author of over 30 works, it has not been possible to give every work equal notice. His smaller and slighter output in poetry and fiction, partly because of the dictates of space, have been dealt with in a more cursory manner. Soyinka's voluminous criticism, which might be the subject of another book, has little place in a study of his creative works and, except in the case of the dramatic theory, has been touched upon only in passing and in a brief concluding chapter.

Thanks are due to a number of people and institutions for aid in the composition of this book: to Bernth Lindfors and James Gibbs for generously providing me with copies of Soyinka's unpublished plays and revues and with secondary material that was difficult of access; to James Gibbs and Hans Zell for the timely provision of useful information; to the Northern Territory University for a semester's study leave, during which half of the book was written; to the interlibrary loan staff of the Myilly Point Campus branch of the university library for their rapid acquisition of some invaluable material; to Betty Oliver for her careful reading of the text and many helpful suggestions; and to Renate Mohrbach-Wright for her constructive support and advice throughout the project. Finally, I would like to remember two teachers of time past: Professors D. J. Gordon and Ian Fletcher, who knew nothing of Africa but who, 20 years ago at the University of Reading, taught me to love literature for itself alone.

Acknowledgments

I am grateful to the following publishers for permission to quote extracts from the works of Wole Soyinka:

Oxford University Press for *Collected Plays*, vol. 1 (1973) and *Collected Plays*, vol. 2 (1974). ©1973, 1974 by Wole Soyinka. Reprinted by permission of Oxford University Press.

Cambridge University Press for *Myth, Literature, and the African World* (1976).

Methuen Publishers for *Six Plays* (1984); *Idanre and Other Poems* (1967); *A Shuttle in the Crypt* (1972); *Isara* (1990); *Madmen and Specialists* (1971); *The Bacchae* (1973); *Jero's Metamorphosis* (1974); and *A Play of Giants* (1984).

Rex Collings Ltd. for *A Shuttle in the Crypt* (1972); *The Man Died* (1972); *Season of Anomy* (1973); *Ogun Abibiman* (1976); *Aké* (1981); and *Opera Wonyosi* (1981).

Farrar, Straus & Giroux, Inc. for excerpts from *Idanre and Other Poems*, copyright © 1967 by Wole Soyinka; *Madmen and Specialists*, copyright © 1971 by Wole Soyinka; *A Shuttle in the Crypt*, copyright © 1972 by Wole Soyinka. Reprinted by permission of Hill and Wang, a division of Farrar, Straus & Giroux, Inc.

Random House, Inc. for *Aké* (1982); *Mandela's Earth* (1988); and *Isara* (1989). © 1982, 1988, 1989 by Wole Soyinka.

New Horn Press for *Art, Dialogue, and Outrage: Essays on Literature and Culture* (1988).

W. W. Norton & Company for *The Bacchae* (1974), and *Death and the King's Horseman* (1975).

André Deutsch Ltd. for *The Interpreters* (1965), and *Mandela's Earth* (1989).

Holmes & Meier for *The Interpreters* (1972).

The *Southern Review* and the photographer Jim Zietz for the photograph of Wole Soyinka.

Efforts to trace other copyright holders have not been successful; responses and relevant information will be welcome.

List of Abbreviations

Chronology

1964   Produces satirical revue "The New Republican," a revision of "The Republican," with new material. *Five Plays* published.

1965   *The Road* published and produced in Commonwealth Arts Festival at Theatre Royal, Stratford East, London. Radio plays *Camwood on the Leaves* and "The Detainee" broadcast on BBC Overseas Service. Produces the satirical revue *Before the Blackout* and directs *Kongi's Harvest* in Lagos. *The Interpreters* published. Arrested in October in connection with a pirate broadcast by a masked intruder who holds up a Western Region radio station after Chief Akintola's rigged election victory. Acquitted in December.

1965–1967 Senior Lecturer in English, University of Lagos.

1966   Produces *Kongi's Harvest* at Dakar Festival of Negro Arts, Senegal. London productions of *The Trials of Brother Jero* (Hampstead Theatre Club) and *The Lion and the Jewel* (Royal Court).

1967   *Kongi's Harvest* and *Idanre and Other Poems* published. Receives, with Tom Stoppard, the John Whiting Drama Award in London. Off-Broadway productions of *The Trials of Brother Jero* and *The Strong Breed* at Greenwich Mews Theater, New York. Appointed chair of Drama Department, University of Ibadan. Detained, in October, by the federal military government after writing letters to the press opposing the civil war, and trying to form the Third Force to avert civil war, and visiting the Biafran leader Colonel Ojukwu in Enugu. In prison for two years and two months.

1968   Receives Jock Campbell–New Statesman Literary Award, London. *The Forest of a Thousand Daemons,* Soyinka's translation of D. O. Fagunwa's Yoruba novel *Ogboju ode ninu Igbo Irunmale,* published. *Kongi's Harvest* produced by Negro Ensemble Company, St. Mark's Theater, New York.

1969   *Three Short Plays* (new edition of *Three Plays*) and *Poems from Prison* published. Released from detention in October. Takes up position as head of Theatre Arts Department, University of Ibadan.

1969–1970 Directs Ibadan and Ife productions of *Kongi's Harvest.*

1970   Produces *Madmen and Specialists* at the Eugene O'Neill Theater Center, Waterford, Connecticut. Plays part of Kongi in Calpenny Films production of *Kongi's Harvest.* Literary editor of Orisun Acting Editions.

1971   *Before the Blackout* published. Produces *Madmen and Specialists* in Ibadan. *Madmen and Specialists* published. Plays part of Lumumba in Joan Littlewood's Paris production of Conor Cruise O'Brien's play *Murderous Angels* (1969).

1972   *A Shuttle in the Crypt* and *The Man Died* published. Resigns from academic position at Ibadan. Produces extracts from *A Dance of the Forests* in Paris.

1973   Visiting professor of English at University of Sheffield and overseas fellow at Churchill College, Cambridge University. *Collected Plays,* vol. 1, *Season of Anomy, Camwood on the Leaves,* and *Jero's Metamorphosis* published. *The Bacchae of Euripides* published and performed by the National Theatre at the Old Vic, London. Visiting lecturer, University of Washington.

1974   *Collected Plays,* vol. 2 published.

1974–1976   Editor of *Transition/Ch'Indaba* in Accra, Ghana.

1975   *Death and the King's Horseman* published. Edits *Poems of Black Africa.* Secretary-general of Union of Writers of African Peoples.

1976   Visiting professor, Institute of African Studies, University of Ghana. Professor of comparative literature and dramatic arts, University of Ife. Produces *Death and the King's Horseman* at Ife. *Myth, Literature, and the African World* and *Ogun Abibiman* published.

1977   Administrator of FESTAC (International Festival of Negro Arts and Culture), Lagos. Directs *Opera Wonyosi* at Ife.

1978   Forms University of Ife Guerrilla Theatre Unit. Produces satirical revue "Before the Blow-Out" at Ife.

1979   Joins People's Redemption party (which collapses soon afterward).

1980   Visiting professor, Yale University.

1981   *Opera Wonyosi* and *Aké* published. Produces satirical revue "Rice Unlimited."

1982 Radio play "Die Still Rev. Dr. Godspeak" broadcast on BBC African Service.

1983 Produces *Requiem for a Futurologist* and satirical revue "Priority Projects." Long-playing record *Unlimited Liability Company* released.

1984 *A Play of Giants* and *Six Plays* published. Film *Blues for a Prodigal* released. Produces *The Road* at Goodman Theater, Chicago.

1985 *Requiem for a Futurologist* published. Produces *A Play of Giants* at Yale Repertory Theater. Retires from academic post at University of Ife.

1986 Awarded Nobel Prize for Literature and Order of Commander of the Federal Republic of Nigeria.

1987 Produces *Death and the King's Horseman* at Lincoln Theater Center, New York. Leads seminars at Louisiana State University.

1988 *Art, Dialogue, and Outrage* and *Mandela's Earth and Other Poems* published.

1989 *Isara* published. Awarded honorary doctorates in literature from Yale University, University of Montpellier, France, University of Lagos, and University of Bayreuth, and the Order of La Légion d'Honneur (France) and the title of Akogun (Isara).

1990 Awarded the title of Akinlatun (Egbaland) and the Order of the Republic of Italy.

Glossary of Yoruba and Other African Terms and Names

Aafin: Alake's palace

Abibiman (Akan):   The world's black peoples

abiku: Spirit child who is repeatedly born and dies to the same mother

Adimu: Carrier in Eyo purification rite

agemo: Ritual religious cult of flesh dissolution among the Ijebu Yoruba, or dissolution-phase of rite

akogun: Carrier in Yoruba New Year Festival

Aladura: Breakaway, revivalist Christian sect

Alafin: Oyo king

Alagemo: Masquerade of spirits in *agemo* cult, or masquerader; wearer of spirit mask. Soyinka, on some occasions, uses *agemo* and *alagemo* interchangeably.

Alake: Local king in Abeokuta

Alarinjo: Traveling troupe of performing masqueraders; part of splinter movement away from *egungun* masquerades in Oyo court funeral obsequies in seventeenth century

Alashe: Priest of *agemo;* one who uses *Ashe* (word) for blessings, curses, or protective spells.

Alawada: Comic folk theater

Amagba (Ijaw):   Purification rite of carrier at New Year in Niger Delta

Ampe: Children's game which involves taking up mirror positions; literally, "Do as I do, we are the same."

apala: Nightclub band

Apo (Akan):   New Year Festival

Ashe: Power of unwritten word; quality in human personality that makes words, once uttered, come true

babalawo:	High priest who performs communal libation in *Olokun* festival; Ifa oracle priest who practices divination
Bale:	Chief or Oba
been to:	One who has been overseas, usually to Britain or Europe, for higher education
bolekaja:	Passenger lorry or "mammy wagon," usually gaily painted and decorated with slogans; words used (literally, "come down and fight") by drivers' touts competing for custom and adopted by critics of "Decolonization" school, notably Chinweizu et al.
egungun:	Masquerade of the dead; of ancestral spirits
Eshu-Elegba:	Confuser and trickster god; principle of chance, uncertainty, chaos, of disruption and disorder
Esumare:	Rainbow god
etutu:	Medicinal or placatory rites
folumo:	*Egungun* masqueraders used for specific purpose of annual purification of community in Ijebu-Igbo New Year festivals
glee:	Entrance song or ritualistic chant performed by chief actor and chorus at beginning of Yoruba folk opera, in which the audience is given gist or moral of play; a distant cousin to the European "glee," an unaccompanied musical composition for three or more voices
ijala:	Songs and chants of Yoruba hunters; salutes to lineage
ijuba:	Ceremonial opening in *Alarinjo* masque theater, including a pledge and salute to lineage (equivalent of *glee* in folk opera)
jero (Hausa):	Prison slang for criminal
Kadiye:	Village priest in Niger Delta region
Oba:	Paramount chief, traditional ruler
Obatala:	Creator god
Odemo:	Titled elder and leader of Isara

odu:	Ritual incantatory poems of Ifa oracle, used in divination
ogboni:	Ancient priestly conclave of elders; powerful secret society and executive cult
Ogun:	God of metals and the road; explorer and god of transition
Olodumare:	Supreme deity
Oloja:	Lord of the market, a position held by the *agemo* priest
Olokun:	Lord of the Sea or Spirit of the Lagoon worshipped in *Olokun* festivals in southern Yoruba states
ori:	Physical head or inner force or soul controlling actions and guiding personal destiny
oriki:	Ritual praise chants or songs
orile:	Salute to lineage
Orisa-nla:	Original unified, collective godhead; principal deity
orisha:	Individual gods formed from fragmentation of Orisa-nla
oro:	Reincarnated spirits of dead, often associated with natural phenomena such as wind, rivers, mountains, or forests
Oro:	God of punishment; also secret cult of elders with punitive task of carrying out sentences
Orunmila:	God of Ifa oracle; sky god; god of wisdom, divination, and preordination
osugbo:	Meeting house of council of elders in *ogboni* cult
oyinbos:	White men
panga (Zulu):	Broad-bladed machete
petro-naira:	Oil dollar
Sango:	God of thunder and lightning
Shopona:	God of smallpox
Tai Solarin:	A long-serving campaigner for justice and reform in Nigeria. During the week of Soyinka's 1977 Ife production of *Opera Wonyosi* he collected a much-publicized, decomposing corpse from a Lagos street

and presented it, in a symbolic protest, to the city council. Soyinka made use of the event in his production of the *Opera*.

wonyosi: Ragged-looking, expensive lace worn by affluent Nigerians during oil boom of 1970s

Chapter 1
Soyinka and the Yoruba Worldview

Wole Soyinka was born to Yoruba parents in 1934 and grew up in the Western Nigerian city of Abeokuta, beside the River Ogun. He received his primary education at the local Christian mission school, where his father was headmaster, and his secondary schooling at the more Yoruba-oriented and nationalistically minded Abeokuta Grammar School and at Government College, Ibadan. He went on in 1952 to the recently opened University College at Ibadan and from there to the University of Leeds, where his English studies included a course on world drama taught by the influential Shakespearean critic G. Wilson Knight. After graduating from Leeds in 1957, Soyinka spent 18 months as a play reader at the Royal Court Theatre in London, where he came into contact with the English dramatic revival of the late 1950s (John Osborne, John Arden, Arnold Wesker, and Harold Pinter) as well as with traditional English drama and the new avant-garde influences, such as Samuel Beckett and Bertolt Brecht, that were arriving from the Continent. Two of his early plays, *The Swamp Dwellers* (1963) and *The Lion and the Jewel* (1963), were performed in London at this time.

Soyinka's career as a writer and man of the theater was not fully launched, however, until his return to Nigeria in the year of independence, 1960, at which time he threw himself with immense vigor and zest into the nation's dramatic, cultural, and political life. During the next seven years, while holding various academic appointments at Nigerian universities, he established two theater companies, the 1960 Masks and the Orisun Theatre, to promote his own and other African plays and to achieve two important theatrical goals: the vitalizing of Nigerian English-language theater, which hitherto had lacked a writer of real imaginative power capable of creating a convincingly familiar African English; and the forging of links between the traditional Yoruba performance idioms of festival masquerade-dramaturgy and traveling folk theater and the dialogic modes of European drama. These were years of tremendous professional achievement, including the publication of seven plays, a novel, and a volume of poems, and also of personal happiness: Soyinka, who had been briefly married to an English girl during his London period and had a son from that union, married Olayide Idowu in 1963, and three daughters and a son were subsequently born from this second marriage. But the seven years from independence to the civil war were also a time of deepening public crisis, of political violence, intimidation, and assassination. Although he was radicalized by his later civil war experience and did not even consider joining a political party until 1979, Soyinka's career as publicist, controversialist, and political activist began in the 1960s. He waged a fierce campaign in the Nigerian press against censorship, corruption, and repression; used his theater group to produce satiric political revues, often in buildings barricaded against armed thugs; and resigned from both his radio series, "Broke-Time Bar" (in 1961), and his lectureship at the University of Ife (in 1963) when political interference with the media and academic life began to threaten freedom of thought and expression. He was even arrested (and later acquitted) on a charge of holding up a radio station and substituting his own tape for Chief Samuel Akintola's victory speech after the rigged Western Region elections of 1965. Soyinka's political activities culminated in the 1967 peace initiatives—and notably the attempt to form the "Third Force" to avert the approaching civil conflict—which led to his detention by the federal forces for the duration of the war. Most of his 26 months in prison were spent virtually incommunicado, and he was in solitary confinement for 15 of them. The quartet of writings consisting of the play *Madmen and Specialists* (1971), the poems *A Shuttle in the Crypt* (1972), the novel *Season of Anomy* (1973), and the prison notes *The Man Died* (1972), was the bitter fruit of this experience.

Shortly after his release in October 1969, and with Lt. Col. Yakubu Gowon's victorious federal regime entrenched in power, Soyinka went into voluntary exile and spent the troubled years of Nigeria's postwar period in Ghana, England, and America, returning only after Gowon's fall in 1975. While in Ghana he used his editorship of the journal *Transition* to attack Africa's military dictatorships, particularly Gen. Idi Amin's in Uganda, and in the epic poem *Ogun Abibiman*, published in 1976, he issued a direct call to arms against South Africa. After the publication of the play *Death and the King's Horseman* (1975) and the critical essays *Myth, Literature, and the African World* (1976), the writer's literary and theatrical activities became more overtly political on the home front. In 1978, after the latest military government had refused permission for the staging of his *Opera Wonyosi* (1981) in Lagos, he formed the University of Ife Guerrilla Theatre Unit and in the following years used it to improvise revue performances in marketplaces and lorry parks, exposing and lambasting the racketeering, spoliation, secret murders, and army massacres that characterized the second Nigerian republic (1979–83). During this productive period, and up to his retirement in 1985, Soyinka was professor of comparative literature and dramatic arts at the University of Ife and was also a visiting professor at Yale and the University of Ghana. In 1986 his long literary career—covering over 20 stage and radio plays and revues, four volumes of poetry and three of autobiography, two novels, and many critical essays—was crowned with the award of the Nobel Prize for Literature.

Soyinka is a man of many parts and, in the country where he is now a household name, a protean figure, bafflingly contextualized by his many professional and popular identities. In addition to being Nigeria's and Africa's most prolific and successful playwright, he is also an innovative poet and novelist, a translator, and a critic. His criticism, seldom lucid and always difficult, recognizes no disciplinary or cultural boundaries, and his creative output has ranged across many modes and veins of writing, from the comic and satiric to the tragic, from the naturalistic to the metaphysical. He has been a tireless experimenter with new genres (most recently autobiography) and has never been afraid to explore alternative and more popular media, such as radio, television, phonograph records, and film, to reach a wider audience. In addition to his work as a writer, he has also been a demanding editor and an exacting director and theater manager; an accomplished actor, with a rich and mellow baritone; and a public man of affairs who has held the posts of secretary-general of the Union of Writers of African Peoples (1975), administrator of the International Festival of Negro Arts and Culture (FESTAC) (1977), president of the International Theatre Institute in Paris (1986), and chairman of the council of the Oyo State Road Safety Corps (1979). Soyinka's bewildering versatility has at times seemed to make him a rich mine of contradiction. It is never safe to assume that ideas he propounds in one context will be consistent with ideas on the same subject he expresses in a different one. Soyinka has not hesitated to use one of his many walks of life to further causes in another, as in his use of the launching of his autobiography *Aké* in 1981 to attack the neofeudalist depredations of the Alhaji Shehu Shagari government and of his Nobel acceptance speech for an assault on apartheid.

These multiple selves are, however, but tributaries of the same single flow. "One must never try to rigidify the divisions between one experience and another," Soyinka has protested, for in the Yoruba worldview, "all experiences flow into one another."[1] It is only the Western consumerist mentality that puts "in strict categories what are essentially fluid operations of the creative mind upon social and natural phenomena."[2] He is, as he insisted on the occasion of his 1973 lectures at the University of Washington, a humanist and human being first and foremost, and inclusive of all other selves.[3] Over the years he has been drawn into print, the recording studio, and theaters of both entertainment and politics by the same basic human concerns: a desperate commitment to human freedom and social justice and fierce opposition to all administrations, civil or military, that deny them; and a belief that the example of individual integrity and courage can direct communal action and effect social change. Moreover, Soyinka's life and work, no matter how diversified, are not divided, and he has had an uncanny habit of anticipating both himself and history in his writing, as in his poignant radio play "The Detainee," about the solitary imprisonment of a political idealist, broadcast in 1965, two years before his own incarceration, and in the uncompromisingly independent stand against war by the Warrior (who is accused of being an enemy spy, as Soyinka would be) in the play *A Dance of the Forests* (1963).[4]

Within this fluid interplay of functions and forms, however, there is at work a painstakingly precise critical and theoretic intellect. Soyinka hates to have his intellectual positions simplified or falsified and builds into each one fine distinctions and subtle qualifications that challenge the complacency of orthodox judgments and, in their refusal of ideology, have been the despair of dogmatists in both cultural and political arenas. He has, for example, in *Myth, Literature, and the African World*, conducted his own exercises in racial self-retrieval, the rehabilitation of an authentic African worldview, and the visionary reconstruction of the African past. But he has been especially careful to distance himself both from the exotic narcissism and idealized irrationalism of Negritude and from more recent cultural primitivists who, in their rush to "decolonize" African literature and purge it of "Euromodernist" elements, praise African poets for describing airplanes as "iron birds" (Soyinka dubs these pseudotraditionalists "Neo-Tarzanists").[5] Though he has professed to believe in "what goes on under the broad umbrella of a . . . secular socialist ideology,"[6] he has dissociated himself from unproductive and self-serving academic "Leftocrats" and theoreticians who "merely protect themselves behind a whole barrage of terminologies which bear no relation to the immediate needs of society" (Agetua, 41). Soyinka knows only too well that, in the context of political crisis, literature and life, artist and citizen, cannot be separated, that commitment spills over beyond the printed page into political activism; for "the man dies in all who keep silent in the face of tyranny" (*TMD*, 13). Yet he has steadfastly refused, in defiance of radical critics at home and abroad, to use his plays as political platforms; he considers that "politics [is] first of all a citizen's duty," that the artist's role is primarily a visionary one, and he has rejected "the romantic idea of the writer as a political combatant."[7]

Within the strictly literary domain, he has been alert from the outset to the danger that his early call for "universal" standards of criticism might be mistaken for an invitation to read his plays purely in terms of Western styles and sources. Soyinka is the most eclectic and syncretic of writers. He admits to having been influenced by everything he has read and refuses to "preach the cutting off of any source of knowledge: Oriental, European, African, Polynesian, or whatever."[8] Accordingly, he has adapted dramatic texts and ideas by Euripides, Swift, and Brecht and has openly admired the last's "complete freedom with the medium of theatre" (Duerden and Pieterse, 172). Predictably, foreign critics have been all too ready to wall his works into Western literary debtor's prisons (usually alongside scraps of John Millington Synge, Shakespeare, and Eugene O'Neill) and, more recently, Nigerian commentators have complained of his overreliance on Western notions and forms. But Soyinka's works are really artistic hybrids of mixed Yoruba and European parentage, blending African themes, imagery, and performance idioms with Western techniques and stylistic influences. *The Road* (1965) combines absurdist dialogue with the masquerade spectacle of festival and the slapstick satire of the Yoruba Alawada or comic folk theater. In *The Lion and the Jewel* conventional motifs twisted from English Jacobean and Restoration comedy and the masked comedy of the commedia dell'arte—namely, of ancient deceit foiling young love—join hands with the idioms of the Yoruba masque (in the closing bridal masque a child is revealed strapped to the dancer's back to indicate Sidi's conception by the aging village chief). In *The Swamp Dwellers* Soyinka applies the poetic naturalism of John Millington Synge and Sean O'Casey to an African peasant society and tackles the parallel problem of finding equivalent English idioms for utterances from another language and culture. His adaptation of *The Bacchae of Euripides* (1973) and the novel *Season of Anomy*

mix Greek and Yoruba mythology, and *Madmen and Specialists* underpins
a demonic, Swiftian satire with Yoruba songs and incantatory chants.

Soyinka has written: "I cannot claim a transparency of communication
even from the sculpture, music and poetry of my own people the Yoruba,
but the aesthetic matrix is the fount of my own creative inspiration; it
influences my critical response to the creation of other cultures and
validates selective eclecticism as the right of every productive being"
(*ADO*, 329). Though he has spoken of the Yoruba world in which he
grew up as "one seamless existence" of Christian and Yoruba elements—
Bible stories and indigenous folkore[9]—the impression left by his account of his parsonage-based childhood in *Aké* (1981) is that, in his
upbringing as in his schooling, Christianity was a primary and Yoruba
religion a secondary influence, and that he came late to the latter, perhaps
with some of the fanaticism of the convert as well as the sharpened
objectivity of the outsider. It was not until his midtwenties, and after a
Western academic education, that Soyinka undertook any firsthand
study of indigenous ritual, religious, and dramatic forms. Nevertheless,
the Yoruba heritage has been famous throughout its diasporic history for
its quiet resilience and capacity for survival in foreign languages and
cultures, not to mention artistic forms and theories, and the remarkable
ease with which Soyinka "gave up Christianity" when the "first opportunity" arose (Gulledge, 511) evinces a deep and abiding substratum of
Yoruba values and thought. The essence of his art is not pure Yoruba but
a Yoruba-based eclecticism. The celebrative festivals that are so crucial to
farming peoples and punctuate the Yoruba agricultural year supply his
early plays with their atmospherics, moral symbolism, and structural
design (and Yoruba festivals are themselves unstable, eclectic forms,
constituted from diverse sources and constantly being modified by
individual additions that are then accepted by the whole community).
Though the tonality of Yoruba—a musical language chanted rather than
spoken—does not translate into English, its wealth of images, proverbs,
and folkloric motifs survives the transplantation to foreign forms in
Soyinka's work. His reading of Yoruba festival rites in his essay "The
Fourth Stage"—the metaphysical core of his dramatic theory—is an
idiosyncratic one; in addition to the acknowledged influence of Friedrich
Nietzsche, the ideas of Wilson Knight, with their emphasis on the total
theatricality of texts and the deep ceremonial and mythological properties of dramatic symbolism, are no doubt reflected in this essay. But
behind the basic arguments are concepts of being that are familiar and

essential to the Yoruba worldview. The remainder of this chapter will be devoted to this worldview and Soyinka's position in relation to it.

If Yoruba religious beliefs and mythology appear to be riddled with contradictions, it is partly because Yorubaland in southwest Nigeria is not a cultural unity, with doctrinal uniformity or religious orthodoxy, but a region comprising a collection of cult practices, with many local variations, loosely organized around the Ifa oracle. The apparent confusion also owes something to a multipurpose pragmatism in Yoruba religious behavior, underlaid by a belief in the indeterminate, many-faceted nature of truth and its expression as a variety of emanations from a single irreducible essence. Thus praise-songs, famous for their capacity to sustain a plurality of meanings, mix affection with abuse and, in their singling out of the extraordinary, allude to the god's undesirable as well as his desirable qualities and to the callousness that is a concomitant of the hero's courage. Rival eschatologies of a heavenly afterlife and bodily reincarnation may be simultaneously entertained, for the desire to become a revered ancestor and the hope of being reborn into the lineage, though arising from apparently contradictory conceptions of the life after death, express the same essential need for a desirable spiritual existence. The *orisha*, or individual gods, may be conceived either as deified ancestors or as nature forces, and as minions or manifestations of the supreme being Olodumare, or as all of these, as need and convenience dictate. Whatever their form, they are regarded as materializations of the same divine energy source: they are all shards of the original godhead, and all humans carry a fragment of an orisha that determines their own essence and makes them responsive to that particular god. Underlying Yoruba pragmatism is a deep conviction of the fundamental unity of all being and the interpenetration of all earthly substance, what Soyinka calls "integrated essentiality" or "the animist interfusion of all matter and consciousness" (*MLAW*, 51, 145).[10]

The totalist worldview of the Yoruba has no difficulty in conceiving of lightning both as a stream of electrons and as an expression of the god Sango's will, or of smallpox as a microscopic virus and the work of the god Shopona, and instinctively absorbs science and technology into religion and mythology, treating phenomena that are radically dissimilar to the European mind as part of the same fabric of existence. "In tragedy, lightning is a messenger," writes George Steiner in *The Death of Tragedy* (1961). "But it can no longer be so once Benjamin Franklin (the incarnation of the new rational man) has flown a kite to it."[11] Yet in

traditional societies like the Yoruba, where ritual has not lost touch but
has kept pace with technology, this is not the case. In his response to
Steiner, Soyinka opposes to the compartmentalist dialectics of European
thought a unitary, "matrical" African consciousness that simultaneously
affirms valid autochthonous insights and the desire to keep in step with
the march of scientific thought and technological progress: "The assimilative wisdom of African metaphysics recognizes no difference in essence
between the mere means of tapping the power of lightning—whether it
is by ritual sacrifice, through the purgative will of the community
unleashing its justice on the criminal, or through the agency of Franklin's revolutionary gadget. . . . For cultures which pay more than
lip-service to the protean complexity of the universe of which man is
himself a reflection, this European habit of world-redefinition appears
both wasteful and truth-defeating" (*MLAW*, 49). For the Western
thinker the world has been fundamentally altered and the state of
knowledge redefined, including the notion of what is alterable; for the
Yoruba the empirical challenge to the numinous has not undermined it
but has merely been absorbed into its indivisible metaphysic. Not
surprisingly, Soyinka has come in for a certain amount of criticism from
Western rationalists and materialists for whom this is not complexity
but confusion, not protean multifacetedness but a grand homogenizing
simplicity, an absorption of discrete knowledge into a mystifying monotony of numen and essence recommended for its "infinitely stressed
spirituality" (*MLAW*, 146).[12] By the tenets of this elastic worldview,
modern man, conceived by Soyinka in the image of the god Ogun, is "a
singly comprehended essence" and not, according to his early essay "And
after the Narcissist?" a subject for individuating dissection: "There is no
separation . . . of the scientist from the artist in him, of the explorer
from the warrior, the warrior from the artist, and so on. The face and
essence are the same."[13] Much in this conflict of worldviews hinges on
the question of world redefinition, to which Soyinka's holistic, noncom-
posite order is fiercely resistant. As an alternative to the murderous
redefinition of knowledge that has demanded the liquidation of millions
in European history, the Yoruba, argues Soyinka, "instead of chopping
off one another's heads over the question of whether electricity is caused
by a movement of electrons or by a frown on Sango's face, simply promote
Sango to the honorific role of the Demiurge of Electricity. . . . Sango
(Dispenser of Lightning) now chairmans the Electricity Corporation,
Ogun (God of Iron) is the primal motor mechanic" (*ADO*, 9, 310). The
African belief in "essence" makes for hospitable accommodation and

continuity, the Western materialist belief in "existence" for a narrow compartmentalism, conflict, and intolerance of new phenomena. But this then begs the question of whether Africa's more flexible and less wasteful habit of world definition is really definition at all and whether the real choice is not between Europe's dubious redefinition of knowledge and Africa's virtual nondefinition—between a hair-splitting empiricism on the one hand and, on the other, a bland accommodation that conceals an effective annihilation of differences behind a superficial toleration of them. The Western pragmatist points out that the world does not stand still but, for good or ill, *is* constantly being redefined, and simply to incorporate new technologies and medicines into existing mythologies of Sango, Ogun, and Shopona is not to explain the workings or to define the nature of electricity, motor technology, and preventive vaccination.

There can be no truce between these conflicting worldviews, the complexities of which merit more detailed discussion than there is space for here. Suffice it to say for present purposes that in the single, undivided reality of Yoruba religious, social, and commercial life the accessories of the modern world are constantly drawn into the embrace of cosmic essences so that the numinous and the mundane are never very far apart. Thus Ifa religious divination uses the nuts of the oil palm, a traditional mainstay of Yoruba economic life, and in an order where everything is holistically an aspect of something else, even the crippled and mentally retarded become expressions of divine weakness (of the creator god Obatala whose hand slipped when he was drunk). Religious essence is reflected in an art and a technology that are infinite in radius, and access to it can be gained from any point: "A blacksmith's poker, an egungun dance, an Ifa prognostic verse, or a royal stool may simultaneously express the history of its makers, their concept of beauty, their propitiation of unseen forces, a statement of cosmic relativity *and* a mode of experiencing all of these, of harmonising them with the challenge of existence" (*ADO*, 108). All sacrifice, whether at the literal level of ritual or the psychological level of redemptive creative processes, and all power, whether for artistic creation or political control, derive from the same undifferentiated primal energy sources. Thus for Soyinka the political power drive is merely a negative manifestation of what in its essence is the energy of creation and renewal, prone to occasional destructive excesses.

Superficial differences and oppositions in the Yoruba worldview are bound at a deeper level by a structure of complementarities in which all elements are contained in and are outgrowths from their opposites. In ritual forms the value of something is established by reference to its opposite (health by disease, order by chaos); libation and prayer safeguard the living by honoring the dead; and blood spilled in sacrifice is the blood of new life, not death. In religious metaphysics Orunmila, the god of the Ifa oracle and principle of preordained order, is outwardly opposed to Eshu-Elegba, the principle of chance, uncertainty, and chaos. Yet Eshu is assistant of Orunmila, and his face is carved upon the Ifa divination tray; human relationships with the oracle are a complex mix of choice and chance, freedom and fate,[14] and there exists within Eshu's famed capriciousness a core of predictability insofar as certain punishments are sure to follow particular offenses to him. Thus in conflating Eshu with Oro, the spirit of punishment, and creating a character called "Eshuoro" in *A Dance of the Forests*, Soyinka perhaps brings out and magnifies the latent characteristics of the god. Orunmila and Eshu are not contradictory but complementary forces, containing their opposites within themselves, and this principle of antinomy runs through Soyinka's thought, whether he is discussing African cuisine or the violently destructive acts of creation that release the seed of being in cosmogonic myths. It has been said that "the Yoruba world does not know of totally opposing forces" (Awolalu, 28). Soyinka argues that societies that still live in a close relationship with nature are governed by a "metaphysics of the irreducible: knowledge of birth and death as the human cycle; the wind as a moving, felling, cleansing, destroying, winnowing force; the duality of the knife as blood-letter and creative implement" (*MLAW*, 53). These warring dualities are to be found everywhere in the Yoruba cycle of existence. During the violent storms and harvest rains Sango's fertile electricity is conducted by Ogun's iron staffs into the womb of earth and is there discharged to be released into new crops, thus tapping and harnessing potentially destructive cosmic energies to check their hostile expression and ensure the violent regeneration of nature. Soyinka's adopted personal god, the ultimate chthonic deity Ogun, epitomizes the duality. As the god of iron he ransacks the earth for metals, which are in turn used to harvest it for food, and he pacifies it, homeopathically, with its own constituents: "from earth itself he extracted elements for the subjugation of chthonic chaos" (*MLAW*, 146). The earth too is double, providing both iron for Ogun's wars and healing herbs that, as the two Earth Mothers in *Madmen and Specialists* explain, are themselves ambiguous and can serve as either poison or medicine.[15]

In traditional Yoruba thought existence is conceived as a seamless continuum and, more particularly, as a religious circuit of passage through a world of ancestor-spirits, into which this world's dying are reborn and from which outgoing spirits become the material world's new births. In this unbroken life-death cycle, represented by the figure of the snake eternally eating its tail (worn around the neck of Ogun worshipers), the unborn turn in a wheel of dependency with elders and ancestors who exercise power over new births. (Like many West African peoples, the Yoruba live very close to their dead and do not herd them off into anonymous cemeteries but bury them in family compounds.) The continuum consists of three interlocking stages—the living, the dead, and the unborn—and insofar as each contains within it manifestations of the others, they exist contemporaneously, without periodicity. There are, however, gaps in the continuum, spaces between worlds and existences, and these gaps, collectively, constitute what Soyinka calls in his essay of that name, "the fourth stage" (*MLAW*, 140–60). This dark middle area, alternatively termed the "chthonic realm," "primordial marsh," and "transitional gulf," is an inchoate chaos, a "storehouse for creative and destructive essences" (*MLAW*, 2) in which are to be found all the raw unfinished things that exist halfway between states. In this twilight zone or fourth dimension many of Soyinka's plays are set: *The Strong Breed* (1963) in the space between the old and new years, *A Dance of the Forests* in the turmoil of a national rite of passage from colonialism to independence, and *The Road*, in a no-man's-land that hangs between traditional and modern cultures, rival religious beliefs and language registers, and this world and the next.

It is the aforementioned principle of complementarity, by which things generate from within themselves the energy to embrace their opposites, that carries life across the gaps in the continuum—between the living and unborn, childhood and maturity, old age and spirithood—and the dynamic of this process is ritual. The gods are custodians of these gulfs, so rites of transition that tap the energies of the "chthonic realm" to ease the passage between worlds are offered to them. As these same rituals are performed on behalf of the communities the gods guard, communities that are repositories of religious beliefs about the universe, they acquire both communal and cosmic dimensions, diminishing not only the chasms between and within worlds but also those between gods and men. In a note to the director of his adaptation of *The Bacchae* Soyinka wrote, "Ritual equates the divine (superhuman) dimension with the communal will, fusing the social with the spiritual" (*ADO*, 71). Though these terms are dramatically equatable only through the rather artificial

link between religious ecstasy and political revolution in this play, the
idea of ritual as the meeting point of divine and human, sacred and
profane, spiritual and social, dominates Soyinka's metaphysical theory.
Ogun, the communally minded, daring pathfinder deity who first
bridged the abyss between gods and men so that the former could return
as a group to earth, is himself the god of transition, the archetypal crosser
of boundaries. It was his crossing that repaired the shattered godhead by
reuniting man and his divine essence, and it is this cataclysmic event that
is reenacted at the human level in festivals by men, who are themselves
shards of the original fragmentation. Thus Soyinka, in his highly personal reading of Yoruba myth and ritual, is able to see transition not only
as an esoteric religious experience but as a unilateral, all-pervasive
phenomenon. He finds something of Ogun in all dangerous passages and
all crises of change and confrontation, whether of nations at the brink of
creation or a major upheaval or of the individual at the edge of a personal
unknown: "What constitutes [man's] sense of strife, of conflict and
resolution . . . of coping even with the contemporary world, day to
day mundane experience, is always related to this experience of passing
from one world to another. . . . [H]e represents it by the area of
transition."[16] For Soyinka the rites of the gods are "a projection of man's
conflict with forces which challenge his efforts to harmonise with his
environment" (*MLAW*, 1), and all struggles of the human will with
forces inimical to the self, all experiences of exploration and risk, are
conceived in terms of the Ogunian paradigm of transition from one
dimension of reality to another. When man "is stripped of excrescences,
when disasters and conflicts have crushed [him] . . . it is at such
moments that transitional memory takes over and intimations rack him
of that intense parallel of his progress through the gulf of transition"
(*MLAW*, 149). Man, in extremis, is again Ogun; his life, transition.

The general concept of transition is central to Yoruba life. Like many
West African societies, the Yoruba view excessive stability as undesirable because it induces stagnation and entropy, and therefore they have
devised checks to restrict power and keep anything from lasting too
long.[17] By these means the Yoruba prevent the petrifaction that follows
from the preservation of dead things and ensure a continuous flux of
self-renewal. The assimilation of changeful and even alien influences has
always been a principle of social life and aesthetics. Houses are built of
mud, carvings are left unprotected from termites, and nothing in religious, cultural, and artistic life is static. Yoruba art and religion have long
been famous for their capacity to accrete and absorb new forms and ideas

without being subverted by them and for expanding identity beyond the point where most value systems would have lost theirs.

Soyinka subscribes to an appropriately mobile and eclectic concept of traditional culture and has always distrusted talk of "tradition" and "authentic African values" because these are not inert bodies of value or retrievable cultural curiosities but dynamic, cumulative wisdoms still in flux and being invigorated by new ideas: "We must not think that traditionalism means raffia skirts; in other words it's no longer possible for a purist literature for the simple reason that even our most traditional literature has never been purist" (Agetua, 35). The religious literature of Ifa wisdom is continual and collective; myths migrate, and gods evolve and are deposed as the orisha legends are refashioned to rationalize or even influence historical changes as they arise. Soyinka's own *A Dance of the Forests*, in its visionary rereading of mythology to suit the changing communal needs of Nigeria on the brink of independence, is a part of this additive process, and his plays are full of characters who revitalize tradition by a visionary reapprehension of it. Oral poetry and ritual chants, aware that they are always being overtaken by time, are continually modified and created anew in performance. Much in the mode of this tradition, Soyinka builds time capsules into the scenes of political comment in his plays in the form of instructions to future directors to vary speeches to fit new historical contexts or to replace them entirely with more topical material if occasion demands.[18] Art must move with the current and be perpetually in transition, not become petrified in the past.

Likewise, in Yoruba cosmology, a constant input of transitional energy is required to regenerate the universe and prevent its precarious equilibrium from settling into a sterile and stagnant harmony. This energy, in Soyinka's visionary reading in "The Fourth Stage," is supplied by an unceasing, alternating cycle of disruption and reparation, a dialectic of infraction and restoration ruled by the principle of complementarity. In Western traditions of tragedy derived from Greek drama, where the gods are estranged and incomprehensible and have taken to killing us for their sport, man is an innocent victim and his sufferings are as irreparable as they are undeserved. In the humanistic symbiotics of Yoruba theology, however, the gods yearn for reunification with the humans who first conceived them and are tied to humanity by a common fallibility and reciprocal needs: to become complete they need to reexperience the human in themselves—as man needs to recapture his divine essence—and they need human endorsement of their creative acts to maintain their spiritual status. Humanistic as well as anthropomorphic in their conception, the gods are error-prone and humanly accountable for their transgressions. Accordingly, they are given the opportunity to make amends to mankind for their hubristic infractions of nature, committed when at their most human, by means of the rituals that provide humans with access to their cosmic powers. In Soyinka's account in "The Fourth Stage" it is the total cycle of actions, the antithetical interflow of disturbance and conciliation, that provides the conduit of vital transitional energy necessary to recharge the universe and keep it in motion (*MLAW*, 18–19). Some of this dangerous energy that regulates the cosmos is available to all inhabitants of the "fourth stage" between worlds. It is encountered, for example, by neophytes in the liminal or transitional phase of traditional rites of passage, when they belong to no stable, clearly defined state but, as people who have died out of one identity and have not yet been born into another, are caught, in Victor Turner's phrase, "betwixt and between."[19]

Soyinka's plays seem to invest special value in figures whom the Yoruba regard as imperfect or between states—for example, idiots, cripples, albinos. These correspond to the neophyte's ritual lack of definition and, from their liminal positions on the edge of society, become sources of abnormal vision and supernatural power. They are half-human and half-divine, and have a sacred link with the creator god Obatala whose weaknesses and imperfections they are living testimony of. Soyinka has said that these ambiguous beings, neither one thing nor the other, partake in their daily lives of the special anarchic, dangerous energy of transition that exists in the space lying between worlds and are ready-made symbols of the transitional process (Morell, 118). Thus in *A Dance of the Forests* the *abiku* (spirit child, called the Half-Child in the play) who constantly crosses from the unborn to the living and from the living to the dead represents the new nation's perilous rite of passage into an unknown future at the time of independence; the mentally retarded man-boy Ifada in *The Strong Breed* stands for the transitional turmoil in the space between years; and the deformed man-god Murano in *The Road* embraces a whole zone of trapped, tormented spirits hanging between worlds. (The albino Lazarus performs a similar function in the novel *The Interpreters* [1965].) Ogun, who is perpetually between identities and sometimes between two opposed things at once, is the epitome of this doubleness. By turns peaceful and violent, reclusive and gregarious, Ogun in his founding of the kingdom of Ire inaugurates a world in which he cannot settle, for the energies unleashed in him are such that no humans can live with them. Therefore he can serve society only by removing himself from it and can redeem it only to the extent that he is unlike it: the pattern, which will be repeated in Soyinka's use of the carrier archetype, is of an absence and estrangement that sharpen awareness and foster the energy of renewal.

Ogun exemplifies the Yoruba dynamic of complementary, mutually determinative opposites. He represents the complete cycle of death and creation, in which dissolution and decay are accompanied by fertility, creation employs violently destructive energies, and even slaughter may be conducive to new growth. Ogun is the blood-besotted war god who in a drunken delirium slaughtered his own men; but he is also the protector of the orphans his wars make. As god of the road he is a force for progress, but he is also the greedy scavenger preying upon the wrecks that it daily provides. In Soyinka's account the iron in Ogun's nature is complemented by the peaceful symbolism of the palm, "the aggressive ore" by the palm's "fertility invocations," even as his violent error is associated with its wine (*MLAW*, 31–32). Ogun, moreover, was himself torn apart by cosmic winds in his crossing of the transitional gulf and triumphantly reconstituted from his own disintegration, which therefore became a condition of a more complete and enlightened restitution. Devastation and despair are necessary preludes to renewal and reconstruction: in Ogun forces must first collide before they can cohere, and the earth must be ravaged to be restored. This warring duality, the lesson of Ogun, is present throughout Soyinka's work, from his early essay on African cooking, founded on the "masocho-hedonistic cycle" in which "pain becomes pleasure which is in turn stimulated by pain,"[20] to his comments on Ogun's liberal enjoyment, as a test of his will, of the palm wine that unleashes his murderous instincts (*MLAW*, 159), to the closing remark of his Nobel speech, that "the humanistic conversion even of the most terrible knowledge can improve the quality of life for mankind."[21] For Soyinka the duality is inescapable, and it is the Elesin's tragedy in *Death and the King's Horseman*, the play of purest transition, that he shirks the transition from self-willed destruction to new health, the passage in which the creative-destructive conflict will be fruitfully resolved, and settles instead for the easy, unalloyed option and mono-principle of fertility, as embodied in the young girl whom he carries from her bridal bed.

How reliable are Soyinka's metaphysical essays as a statement of the values and thought expressed in Yoruba mythology? Even if we allow for the poetic license of the dramatist that conflates existing gods and invents new ones (as in *A Dance of the Forests*), the essayist's translation of myth into a private religion of essences remains a highly idiosyncratic and narrowly selective exercise. (We hear from Soyinka nothing, for example, of Olodumare, supreme diety, or Orunmila, god of wisdom.) Soyinka's mythology of the fourth stage is, by his own admission, a private articulation of something merely implicit in the tripartite Yoruba metaphysic (Morell, 117–18), and the "personal element to-wards one's diety" of which he has recently spoken seems in his elastic, eclectic Ogun to be abnormally developed (Gulledge, 513). Though ranked only fourth or fifth in the Yoruba pantheon—he is usually preceded by Olodumare, Obatala, and Oduduwa—Ogun, as the iron god, is the most demanding, assertive, and pervasive of the deities. His identification with all metals—whether in weapons or scalpels, hammers or farming implements, in knives for carving or for sacrifice—has made him a perpetually expanding, evolving divinity, the god of war and healing as well as the patron of blacksmiths, farmers, sculptors, and hunters (and more recently, of motor mechanics). As the forger of earth's ore into steel for the crossing of the chthonic chaos between the gods' world and ours, he is, like Milton's Satan, the first scientist, artist, and Promethean pyrotechnologist.

The god of transition cannot be expected to stand still, and Ogun has enjoyed a varied and mobile interpretation in Yorubaland. Soyinka, however, stretches Ogun's versatility even beyond the usual limits—for example, in his eagerness to infuse Ogun with regenerative powers he makes him additionally a god of the harvest, thus giving undue emphasis to a seldom mentioned fertility dimension—and the result is a character much more multifaceted and amorphous than the divinity who in the legend descended with a company of gods at Ile-Ife, one bearing little resemblance to the god who has emerged from the work of Yoruba scholars.[22] Soyinka's Ogun, as we have seen, is a somewhat abstract embodiment of humanity's conflicting, warring impulses, held in a tense equilibrium; this characterization has certain negative repercussions when removed from the purely conceptual level. There is, for instance, a point in the essay "And after the Narcissist?" where the god's perfect balance of "crude energies" and "humane creativity," brute technology and contemplative aesthetics, begins to blur into a bland, featureless monotony, a point where the complementarity of the oppositions be-come so strong that they effectively cease to be oppositions (60). One of Ogun's *ijalas* (hunting songs) runs: "Ogun kills on the right and . . . kills on the left. / Ogun kills the thief and the owner of stolen

goods. / Ogun kills the owner of the house."[23] The energy of Soyinka's
Ogun tends finally to be as undifferentiated as it is undifferentiating and
is not easily contained in any existing set of definitions (as the men of Ire,
to their peril, discovered of its original). Indeed, Soyinka's mythography
seems at times to enact the god's own inability to particularize and his
subsequent failure to understand, to be able to mark off one human being
or experience from another. Ogun is many things in many places in
Soyinka's work—a conventional, Greek-style deity in *A Dance of the
Forests*, pure primal essence in the poem *Idanre* (1967), a symbolic figure
in a painting in *The Interpreters*, and a force for political revolution in *Ogun
Abibiman*—and it is hard to recognize the same god in these several
permutations. Soyinka writes tellingly: "The gods are accommodating
and embrace within their eternal presences manifestations which are
seemingly foreign or contradictory. . . . Ogun, by incorporating
within himself so many seemingly contradictory attributes, represents
the closest conception to the original oneness of Orisa-nla" (*MLAW*, 31,
155). In his effort to make Ogun cover the whole range of human
endeavor and the totality of human experience, Soyinka has in effect
regathered the entire godhead representing them, but the god's symbolic
carapace is spread so thinly and is so diluted by diversity that it seems
always about to dissolve. When nothing is excluded, everything becomes
of equal—and therefore nothing of any—importance, and the attempted
all-inclusive oneness becomes a union of nothing.

In "And after the Narcissist?" Soyinka somewhat gratuitously offers
Ogun as a complex, dynamic myth to serve as antidote to the easy
narcissism of Negritudinist myths. Many have wondered, however,
whether Ogun is not merely a rival narcissism and private eccentricity on
Soyinka's part—that is, another intellectual fabrication, ultimately, one
more polemical counterconstruct to Western mythologies in which
Soyinka outdoes the West at its syncretic best by incorporating scraps of
Nietzsche, Blake, Dionysius, Zagreus, and Prometheus in order to
transcend them.[24] To other commentators the narrow creative-
destructive cycle of Ogun to which Soyinka has virtually reduced the
whole corpus of Yoruba myth gives his vision of history too pessimistic
and "tragic" a slant and is locked into a fundamentally reactionary
worldview. More radical critics have questioned the ultimate relevance of
notions of primal essences to the contemporary Nigerian situation and
have found the metaphysical orientation of the work inconsistent with its
author's social and political activism.[25] It is true, on the first score, that
when Soyinka construes the endless interchange of violation and repara-

tion in the Yoruba universe in historical terms, the resulting history innately tends toward cyclic repetition and a rather bleak kind of behavioral essentialism that recycles the perennial cruelties and follies of human nature. (Hence, in *A Dance of the Forests* corrupt people from the past are no different when reincarnated in the present.)[26] Cyclic patterns often have fatalistic resonances, especially when reinforced by preordained structures such as ritual, and Soyinka has not helped matters by an added and disturbing complacency in his morally neutral, albeit remotely abstract, picture of cosmic disintegration and restitution: "Offences even against nature may be part of the exaction by deeper nature from humanity of acts which alone can open up the deeper springs of man and bring about a constant rejuvenation of the human spirit. Nature in turn benefits by such broken taboos, just as the cosmos does by demands made upon its will by man's cosmic affronts" (*MLAW*, 156). Evil and its complementary reparation are alike necessary for the fruitful upheaval and rejuvenation that they engineer: they are both part of the nature of things, so no moral obloquy attaches to them. Soyinka's answer, which has not satisfied all his critics, has been that his is not a self-indulgent or perversely celebrative brand of pessimism but the positive and creative kind that consists of "a very square, sharp look" at reality at its worst as a prelude to reconstruction (Agetua, 39). Thus the apparent defeatism of a play like *Madmen and Specialists* only arises when the path to constructive action is temporarily blocked; in its violent exorcism of negative impulses and destructive energies, that defeatism negotiates the path's reopening. Expressions of pessimism, Soyinka insists, do not mean acceptance and do not preclude challenge and action as "the ultimate expression of will" (Jeyifo 1973, 63).

On the second score, Soyinka has always seen the artist as primarily "the voice of vision" in his society (*ADO*, 20)—Ogun is a seer and maker as well as a doer. Although he accepts that the combination of political fervor with the artistic vocation may sometimes be inevitable, Soyinka has refused to make one a condition of the other. The question of ultimate relevance, however, remains. Even sympathetic commentators have made much of the idealizing, synthesizing cast of mind that, with its gaze fixed on the spiritual dimension of the human condition, habitually substitutes mythic for historic reality (Irele, 210; Moore 1980, 217–18); hostile critics have regarded the obsessive rendering of human follies and lusts in terms of occult essences or clashes of cosmic wills as a retreat from historical experience into metaphysical fantasy (Nkosi 1981, 190–91). For both of these groups, history and society are simplistically mythologized in Soyinka's works. History is distilled into a series of behavioral essences, making everything the fault of the inherent failings of "human nature," not the determinations of complex social and political forces; evil is depicted as metaphysical in origin.[27] Society becomes a monolithic bloc that exists merely to be rescued from the abuses of power by the lone challenge of a mythic Ogunian savior and is not itself viewed as being made up of rival groups and interests who are themselves involved in the abuse. Whether the mythic aspiration is reactionary or revolutionary, pessimistic or utopian, there is no analytic portrait, argue Soyinka's detractors, of the social canvas on which it is predicated.[28] Part of the problem is that, as already noted, Soyinka directly equates the communal with the divine will through the medium of ritual and so leaps from the communal to the cosmic without allowing for any sociopolitical dimension between the two: having transcended the abyss, Ogun moves, in Soyinka's words, "from the plane of the individual to a communal experience and also to a cosmic experience" (Katrak, 20). Additionally, as will become clear in the next chapter, the blurring in Soyinka's dramatic theory of the distinctions between ritual and drama, communicants and community, and secret and national societies, tends to telescope social into ritual processes.

If Soyinka has fallen victim to radical historicist criticism, it must be conceded that he has to some extent invited such criticism by his somewhat erratic attempts to remove Ogun from the purely conceptual realm of essence and give him some practical application or analogue in the contemporary world. Soyinka's gods are of uncertain status, a mixture of external agency and human essence that is nevertheless always endowed with awesome power; in recent interviews he has defended his gods as "creative metaphors" (Gulledge, 512) and "expressions of human will, human strength, a superhuman aspect of human energy, of collective being."[29] But the mythopoetic mind tends to regard myth not so much as symbolically representing reality as being identical with it, so it is not surprising that Soyinka stated in earlier interviews that Ogun is "the reality of nature," "the reality of man," and "the Promethean reality of our existence" (Agetua, 39), or that the question "What is the will of Ogun?" preoccupies the Yoruba mind (*MLAW*, 156). Ogun, because of his links with iron, has naturally been seized upon by modern scholars as a relevant cultural aid to technological transition, bridging the gap between a relatively simple past and a complex present (Barnes, 29–30). Yet Ogun also represents certain dangerous, lawless, and barbaric energies that are not easily controlled once unleashed; these forces, though

not incompatible with modern technology, are harder to reconcile with
social progress and enlightenment. Significantly, Soyinka's own artistic
control and authentic tone tend to falter whenever he attempts to
socialize and historicize Ogun by fusing him with some contemporary
revolutionary force: with Chaka in the unengaging, unconvincing anti-
apartheid rhetoric of *Ogun Abibiman*; with Dionysius in the ritual esoterics of
The Bacchae, where political revolution, aided by magical supernatural
power, is conceived only in rarefied spiritual terms; and with Fidel
Castro, who, in some romantically inept critical comparisons, is seen to
transcend his own annihilation in the style of Ogun (*MLAW*, 54; *SP*,
xvii–iii; *ADO*, 119). Myth is not politically innocent or exempt from
historical determination, and the sociology of the god does not quite fit
him for the role of revolutionary challenger of contemporary Africa's
social and political evils. Ogun, as James Booth has observed, is a feudal
warrior god, a product of an aristocratic and patriarchal warrior society,
and in his alternating negative and positive input, first as butcher and
then as deified protector of his people, he is really more like Cuchulain
than Prometheus.[30] His legendary slaughtering of his own men gave
him a fortuitous relevance during the fratricidal carnage of the Nigerian
civil war, but in the eyes of a younger generation of Yoruba writers and
critics he has no continuing application to the needs of modern Nigeria.
It is perhaps significant that Soyinka's example in the cultivation of
traditional deities has not been widely followed.

There are many different currents in Soyinka's thought; to the "mac-
rocosmist" and mythopoetic essentialist who has attracted the animus of
both Western and African critics—the Soyinka of "Idanre" and the
metaphysical essays—must be added the historical particularist of the
comedies and satiric revues and the miniaturist of the autobiographies.
There are perhaps two principal and opposing strains throughout
Soyinka's work that tend, respectively, towards heterogeneity and ho-
mogeneity. On the one hand, his work vigorously celebrates versatility
and is responsive to the naturally eclectic and paradoxical in human
experience, as in the village chief Baroka's defense of "rich decay" and
distrust of "the spotted wolf of sameness" in *The Lion and the Jewel* (CP2,
47–48), in the diversification of the world by Atunda's fragmentation of
the godhead in "Idanre," and in Soyinka's recent polemics against all
reductivists of literary experience, from neotraditionalists to Marxists.
As if to compensate, however, for the Atunda-like historical atomization
of African culture with an Ogunian regathering of the shattered godhead, Soyinka's mythopoetic writings, from "The Fourth Stage" to *Ogun*

Abibiman, have another, opposing tendency: to unify the whole of reality through a universalist, essentialist concept of myth that seizes upon the perennial and immutable in human experience, and to draw the most heterogeneous phenomena into an all-embracing cosmic oneness—which, like most onenesses, tends to be a sameness. What realism particularizes, differentiates, and renders diverse and discrete, myth generalizes, harmonizes, and unites; thriving on unexpected imaginative associations and recurrences, myth obscures and dissolves the rational boundaries that analysis defines. The tension between these two conflicting currents produces what Biodun Jeyifo in his introduction to Soyinka's collected essays has described as a self-cancelling "aporetic" quality in Soyinka's criticism (*ADO*, xxvi). Even the celebrated philosophic accommodativeness of Yoruba culture and belief, though it would seem to lean most heavily upon the essentialism that is paramount in Soyinka's thought, takes on something of this duality in its critical interpretation. In the commentary to his 1963 film *Culture in Transition*, for example, Soyinka insists that "tradition is now, and is born of every experience, not buried in the stillness of antiquity," leaving the African artist free "to reinterpret ancient idioms through a unique personal pattern in the contemporary experience."[31] When, as on this occasion, his context is cultural transition, Soyinka emphasizes the dynamic reinterpretation of the past in the light of the present and the diversification and redefinition of the old by new and even alien influences. The accent is somewhat different, however, in the metaphysical context, where he is concerned with more numinous kinds of transition. Here all newness is overenergetically assimilated, to the point of conversion, into a preexisting order and dynamism tends to be subsumed into a continuing stasis: from a Western viewpoint, the system seems to absorb differentness only by doing away with it.

Soyinka opts in these latter writings for an all-inclusive cosmic absolutism or mystical holism that effortlessly absorbs science and technology into the animist metaphysics of existing myth—he speaks of "the mystic creativity of science" (*MLAW*, 157)—and leads to a conflative cross-referencing from one order of experience to another. Whatever one makes of Soyinka's metaphysics, the gains that accrue to his creative work from this inspired and often unsettling practice—the atmospheric power and haunting sense of the numinous that derive from a belief in contiguous, parallel worlds, negotiable by transitional crossings—cannot be denied. On the minus side, the usual difficulties attend the concrete realization of abstractions. This is not a problem when Soyinka's mode of composition is metaphysical lyricism, as in "Idanre" and parts of *The Interpreters*. But when he attempts the physical transposition of the cosmic cycle of infraction and reparation to the stage, in the form of the Eshuoro-Ogun rivalry in *A Dance of the Forests*, the result is a baffling multiplicity of living and reincarnated humans, gods and spirits, agencies and essences, and a cumbersome cosmic algebra that finally collapses in total confusion. These practical difficulties will become more evident when Soyinka's theory of drama, in which the metaphysic of transition again figures strongly, is placed beside his creative practice.

Chapter 2
Yoruba Theater: Ritual, Tragedy, and Dramatic Theory

Drama is the most primal mode of artistic expression; mediated by no pigment, print, or lens, it communicates directly through the raw material of the pulsating human body, its rhythmic movement, sounds, and presence. Soyinka's Yoruba world has always been rich in these elements. It was not until the end of World War II that Yorubaland officially received its first professional folk theater, fashioned by Hubert Ogunde out of the broad Western cultural matrix of Bible drama and colonial concert party. But in reality the Yoruba chiefdoms had had their own indigenous theater for centuries in the form of the festivals and ceremonies that still punctuate Yoruba life. In ceremonial masques where personality transformations were conjured by costume, and vocal projections and distortions by masks, the effect was a powerful combination of the consecrated and the comic, involving both ecstatic possession and satiric entertainment, solemn and acrobatic dance. It is in one such masquerade, the *egungun* procession of the dead, that the roots of traditional Yoruba drama are conventionally located.[1]

Yoruba religious festivals, like the Great Dionysia in ancient Athens, are apt to turn into social occasions, and divine worship to be subsumed into a humanistic celebration of life, though with the important difference that such strict categorizations of the sacred and secular do not come readily to the Yoruba mind. Yoruba metaphysics, it has been noticed, is famous for its warring complementary dualities and has a special capacity for making extremes generate their opposites, with the design of containing conflict and maintaining harmony through balance and release instead of by repression. This spirit of complementarity is forcefully expressed by the egungun, in which the cultic and the festive, the sacred and satiric, coexist. Out of awesome funeral rites, in which the masks of the dead are brought forth into the community, emerge the opposing

forces of ribaldry and ridicule, the regulating agents that sustain the
social equilibrium by exposing the failings and follies of authority for the
purpose of entertainment. The spirits of the ancestors—or a god if he is
the patron of the festival—materialize through the masks and movements of the dancers and, by means of a very basic question-and-answer
routine too skeletal to be called dialogue, proceed to advise or instruct, to
bless or berate their descendants or worshipers, thereby strengthening
their bonds with the living community. The members of the community, by turns, placate and entertain the spirits in a two-part ceremony
that follows the welcoming of the dead with a burlesque of the living. In
the occult or magical part of the ceremony a select circle of initiates is
drawn into ecstatic communion with the masked celebrant when, by
means of a trance, the power of the god or spirit enters into him. At this
stage he becomes "possessed" in the sense that he totally identifies with
the supernatural presence. Though there has been a kind of role change
here, it has not happened through the pretense of "acting" in the
Western sense, since what has been substituted for the individual's
ordinary personality is not another human persona but the character of
the spirit, for which the human identity has vacated itself. (Thus in
Soyinka's own egungun play, *The Road*, the masked celebrant, Murano,
though he retains his outward form, is really no longer Murano but the
god Ogun, who in this bizarre instance is trapped in transition.) In
Aristotelian terms, the egungun is not the representation of an action but
the action itself: the mask, nonimitative in the cultic phase, has *presented*
a superhuman reality, not *represented* a human one. But in the secular
entertainment that emerges as a kind of comic counterdiscourse to the
sacral rites—performed in public, it has a clearer performer-audience
division—belief gives way to something closer to the willing suspension
of disbelief in the Western convention. The masked dancer, now unpos-
sessed, metamorphoses himself into the living targets he caricatures
through the conscious assumption of the appropriate voice, manner, and
gait and by the use of specifically imitative masks. The performance is
mainly on the level of a noninteractive mono-drama, and in the manner
of most outdoor pageant theater from medieval to modern times, it
retains large elements of the merely presentational, of display rather than
play, or of "play" in the purely recreational sense of fun, pranks, and
games. Yet it was this ordering of creative energies into deliberate and
sustained acts of impersonation that seemed in the broad (though by no
means unanimous) consensus of critical opinion to point the masquerade
along the way toward the secular, illusionist theater of entertainment,

thus effecting the eventual transformation of magical drama into dramatic art, religion into theater, cult into culture.[2]

The ritual bipartism featured in the model of the egungun runs deep in Yoruba thinking about drama. On the one hand there is the secular masquerader, his grotesquely imitative mask a link between himself, his role, and his audience; on the other hand is the religious celebrant, his abstractly expressive mask a sign of the bond between man and spirit. The former, like the Greek *hypokrites*, studies and dons his mask in the hope of finding himself in the role; the latter hopes to lose himself, to be dissolved in the personality of the invading god or spirit, and to approximate to its otherworldly being through the dance of possession. The masquerade reveler imparts a kind of psychological therapy, liberating stifled collective emotions through satiric caricature performed before a spectator audience; the votary transmits a much more dangerous and traumatic catharsis to a small chorus of communicants who participate in his religious ecstasy and are made privy to its esoteric symbolism. It has been argued by Nigerian writers and critics that the egungun is the model, in its bifocal vision of festival dramaturgy, for the two kinds of drama in Soyinka's own theater: the popular and the hermetic, satiric comedy and metaphysical tragedy, ritual as both a universal and an esoteric idiom.[3] It is a crudely compartmentalized model of the kind mistrusted by Soyinka himself, but he has at different times in his theoretical writings traced Yoruba drama to its dual components. Writing in the persona of cultural historian in his essay "Theatre in African Traditional Cultures," he derives Yoruba theater, dramaturgically, from the pseudoillusionist modes and primitive satiric mimesis of the secular masquerade (*ADO*, 191).[4] Meanwhile, in the altogether more metaphysical perspective of *Myth, Literature, and the African World*, and more particularly, in the essay "The Fourth Stage," he "extrudes" a concept of tragic drama—more a distillation of essences than a derivation of particulars—from the consecrated component or cultic "mysteries" of Ogun rites. The bipartite model of the egungun, whatever its limitations as dramatic paradigm, is thus of seminal importance in Soyinka's critical as in his creative practice, and I will have occasion to return to it in my discussion of the more esoteric of his ritual dramas.

Faced at the outset in *Myth, Literature, and the African World* with the "perennial question of whether ritual can be called drama, at what moment a religious or mythic celebration can be considered transformed into drama" (*MLAW*, 6), Soyinka affects a strong antihistorical bias, favoring the African's "irreducible truths" and "fundamental, unchang-

ing relationships between himself and society and within the larger
context of the observable universe" over Western "period dialectics"
(*MLAW*, 38). It appears at first that we are being invited into a realm of
timeless essences where ritual, insofar as it has always contained the
inherent possibility of drama within itself, is eternally drama and drama
ritual. Certainly, Soyinka is not concerned in this context about investi-
gating the dynamics of ritual's physical displacement from its primordial
habitat in sacred grove or shrine, first to festival contexts and from thence
to the alienatory setting of the modern theater. But the apparently glib
metaphysics mask deeper historical perceptions. Fundamentally, Soyinka is antievolutionist in his dramatic thinking (he humorously caricatures western thinking about drama as a steam engine shunting short
distances between historical stations to pick up successive cargoes of
ritual, naturalism, and surrealism), and he is concerned that "ritual" (like
"African") should not be seen as existing, at one end of the scale, in
negative conjunction with the developed literary form of "drama" (like
"European") at the other.[5] He has in fact, in his cultural polemics,
seriously doubted whether it is correct to see the nondialogic masquerade
dramaturgy of festivals, after the Western fashion, as a primitive ingre-
dient of modern drama, an embryonic "predrama" or historical halfway
house in a direct line of descent between religion and theater.[6] Indeed,
after evaluating the festival's prodigal resources and communal involvement, its artistic stylization of events and vivid intensification of
everyday reality, he has pondered whether contemporary theater does not
really represent a contraction, rather than an expansion, from its supposed origins (*ADO*, 194–95). Soyinka's argument, in the more theoretical context of *Myth, Literature, and the African World*, is that the question
of dividing lines is only a problem for cultures that have divorced drama
from its ritual roots and need to reestablish points of demarcation in
order, by diverse artificial methods, to recover them. (He instances Jean
Genet's plays and Peter Brook's *Orghast* [1971].) The implication is that
dividing lines are not a problem—and can be no more than an academic
issue—for cultures in which ritual roots are still visibly present. There is
historical substance in this idea. In the pluralistic setting of contemporary Yoruba drama, for example, the oldest autochthonous, hieratic
forms of ritual theater coexist, as in a cultural time warp, with the
sophisticated dramaturgy of the modern literary theater. Thus it is still
possible for a modern audience for one of Duro Ladipo's dynastic Yoruba
plays or for an English-language play like *A Dance of the Forests* to identify
the various stylized and hybridized borrowings from ancient legends,

folk motifs, ritual practices, and masquerade dramaturgy and to measure them against their "pure" originals, still extant in festival form.

In the circular, holistic maze of Yoruba religious art, where ritual constantly enacts myth lore, there are many natural points of contact between masquerade, folk theater, and drama in English.[7] There are no theatrical thoroughbreds along this cultural spectrum, only a succession of mongrelized, concurrently advancing and fruitfully interacting modes. In a 1975 discussion Soyinka described his own theater as an attempt to combine the festival-folk hybrids of Hubert Ogunde and Ladipo with the more technically sophisticated literary drama (Morell, 100), and even in his earliest interview, in 1962, he viewed as an inevitable step the incorporation of traditional masquerade idioms—ritual, dance, and mime—into the pattern of modern theater (Duerden and Pieterse, 170). The more culturally pure mythological folk theater of Ladipo, with which Soyinka's own theater company worked closely in the 1960s, improvised plays around ritual chants and songs, often with an eye to original festival forms. Ladipo's *Oba Koso* (1968) utilizes incantation and trance in much the same way as Soyinka's *Death and the King's Horseman*, which is in fact a reworking of historical material dealt with in Ladipo's earlier *Oba Waja* (1964). Given the broad interpenetrative continuity of theatrical developments in Yorubaland, it is not surprising to discover the illusion-conjuring technology of Western theater bringing out ritual dramaturgy's expressive drama in emotional power of a frightening intensity—as in the egungun sequences of *The Road*. Neither is it odd to find Soyinka, never an armchair dramatist, working in the same combined capacity of writer-actor-manager-director as the giants of the folk theater and adopting some of their production techniques. The hit-and-run style of Soyinka's 1970s guerrilla theater—the limited, cautious publicity and risk-taking political burlesque, the lightning presentation of what are effectively corporate creations, the minimal scripts and rehearsals, and the constant modifications in performance—are all in the best traditions of Ogunde's folk theater and of the Alarinjo traveling troupes with which Ogunde performed as a masquerader in his youth.[8]

The crosscurrents and continuities between Yoruba theatrical forms have, in fact, been palpably present in Soyinka's work from its early stages, notably in the festive mime of *The Lion and the Jewel*, the spectacular mummery at the end of *A Dance of the Forests*, and the ritual fury of the egungun at the climax of *The Road*. Nevertheless, the displacement of ritual effects and devices from their proper festival contexts to the autonomous dramatic ones of the plays is never a simple or direct affair. It has been noticed, for example, that Agboreko, the misnamed "Elder of the Sealed Lips" in *Dance*, functions as the traditional *babalawo*, the high priest who in the Olokun festival performs the communal libation to the spirits (represented here by the tree imp Murete) and who "grasps and unfolds the secret magic of words."[9] This is true enough, but in Soyinka's play the priest's ritual observances have been edged with irony. Agboreko's timid libations are thwarted by the caprice of gods who are themselves too full of human weaknesses to sustain much human faith, the sacrifices made expiate nothing, and the priest is a pompous charlatan, a garrulous windbag whose ponderous proverbs are only spasmodically relevant. Similarly, the processional dance of the Ondo Ogun Festival described by Oyin Ogunba (1978, 20) is the likely model for the Drivers' Festival of *The Road,* but Soyinka seems to have inverted the pattern, so that the interrupted rite that constitutes his play runs not from the dusk of one day to the dawn of another but between two twilights of the same day, ending with an abrupt finality in the gathering dark and with no hint of renewal, no glimmer of returning light. In *The Trials of Brother Jero* (1963) the eponymous antihero's starting address to the audience is reminiscent of the Yoruba folk opera's opening *glee* in which the gist and moral of the play are given, though with the ironic twist that here it is Jero who provides his own (and in his case, highly amoral) prologue. One of the possible festival models for the glee is the ceremonial opening of the Alarinjo mask drama, the *ijuba*, which contains a pledge, a salute by the troupe leader to his lineage and to the leader from whom he received his training, and limited self-praise (Adedeji 1978, 45). As in the other examples of ritual displacement given here, the traditional element is presented in the inverted form of parody. Jero, in a rather crude flashback, invokes the memory of the old prophet to whom he was apprenticed, but only to ridicule and revile him and then to lavish all of the praise upon himself for his clever deception and betrayal of his old master.

According to some sources, the Rockefeller research fellowship on which Soyinka returned to Nigeria in 1960 was awarded for the study and recording of traditional Nigerian festivals, but the degree of direct empirical input from this research into his early plays, such as *A Dance of the Forests,* remains imponderable and ultimately unimportant.[10] The intense rituality of his early drama is at once more dynamic and organic than the material normally derived from sober academic research and its inspiration is in the quick of experience: ritual is integral to a culture and worldview imbibed in childhood,[11] and is a generally pervasive influence in his work, not something easily pinned down to particulars. Moreover, Soyinka, in his ritual usages as in his other practices, is the most eclectic, idiosyncratic, and supremely inventive of writers. His work is steeped in Yoruba culture, but unfathomably so, to the extent that it has the power to transform that culture out of all recognition: his are the innovations of the deeply initiated, the improvisations of the maestro who has long dispensed with classical orthodoxies. His use of festival lore is therefore never merely nostalgic or antiquarian but is always reinterpretive and interpolative, usually in a highly individual manner and with an abundance of ironic barbs and twists. In *Kongi's Harvest* (1967) the New Yam Festival, which usually signifies renewal and new beginnings, is made to mark the end of an era, and the use of the egungun motif in *A Dance of the Forests* completely reverses the customary relationship between the living and the dead: the ancestors return not to judge but to be judged, in the vain hope that they will receive justice this time around, and instead of being honored with the customary salute to the lineage (the *orile*), they are chased away. Soyinka's imagination makes similarly cavalier play in this work around Yoruba ideas of reincarnation. In his ironic readaptation, he reincarnates not the good ancestors who have lived well on earth, as is customary in Yoruba eschatology (Awolalu, 60, 65), but the collaborators with and victims of horrific evil, on the apparent assumption that the former still have some sparks of decency and potential for redemption (though Adenebi proves a hopeless case), and in the hope that the latter will someday find the world ready to receive their goodness. In Soyinka's version it is not the evildoers who become the wandering, lonely, neglected spirits (Awolalu, 60) but the good whose spirits, more in keeping with Western Gothic tradition, are so tormented by the memory of their sufferings in their earthly lives that they can find no rest in the spirit world. Soyinka, it would seem, has little interest in reincarnation as a literal phenomenon—the blood by which the revenants are "linked . . . with four of the living generation"[12] does not refer to the literally reincarnated essence or blood of the lineage—and the idea has no value in the play except as part of a conglomerate metaphor. In the giant, radial image complex at the center of *Dance* three separate but intricately linked motifs—reincarnation, the egungun, and the New Year Festival in which certain egungun (the *folumo*) are often used for purposes of purification—converge to focus upon themes common to each of them: the returning dead, the confrontation of the present by the past, and the recall of the contemporary world to historical reality and to the abiding truths of the human situation.

Ritual, religious, and mythological elements are interesting and important in the plays only with regard to what Soyinka makes of them, notably the ways in which they are pressed as intellectual vehicles into the service of broad imaginative concepts. This does not mean that there are no specifically identifiable ritual features in the plays. Most noticeable among Soyinka's theatrical effects, after the mimes and masques of *The Lion and the Jewel*, are the ritualistic denouements of *The Road, Kongi's Harvest*, and *Madmen and Specialists*. Each of these includes that sudden quickening of tempo and whipping up of emotion into frenzied, trance-like states by a rising crescendo of hieratic chanting and drumming that is characteristic of the phenomena of possession and dispossession (or exorcism). There is also everywhere on the Soyinkan stage, but most intensely in the esoteric plays, that hallmark of the ritual process: the sense of a suspension of ordinary reality and of a deferment of or removal from the normal time order.[13] *A Dance of the Forests*, with its multiple, recurrent action, radial symbolism, and characters who move strangely about in (and in and out of) time, has the fluid, free-ranging form of the festival, in which there is always the feeling of events taking place within the context of a larger, cosmic time scale. Yet these are all general drawings upon the ritual heritage. With the possible exception of *The Road*, Soyinka's plays are not ritual-specific in the sense that their ceremonies can be pinned down to precise forms in contemporary geographic or ethnic settings. The carrier rite in *The Strong Breed* combines variant features from different forms of the rite as practiced both inside and outside of Yorubaland, and in *The Bacchae* the rite is mixed up with Greek lore. In the New Yam Festival of *Kongi's Harvest* Soyinka is more concerned with the atmospherics of excited preparation than with the details of the ritual event itself. *A Dance of the Forests*, which Oyin Ogunba, despairing of derivation, has aptly called "a special Wole Soyinka festival,"[14] is an extraordinary ritual and mythological concoction, its roots everywhere and nowhere. In the area of ritual the primary interest is not in the features of any particular festival but in the general *idea* of the festival, in its imaginative possibilities (for communal celebration, purification, and regeneration), and in what it can be made to represent in the troubled transitional period of modern African history. The ceremonies and masquerades that feature even in those plays that I later characterize as "ritual-intensive," as against "ritual-inclusive," are not naturalistic, photographic reproductions of their originals but poetic conceptions, reworkings of ritual through metaphor into art. Some evaluation will now be made of this elastic, visionary concept of ritual and of the ultimate relevance both of Western tragic forms and mythologies to Soyinka's ritual metaphysics and of the metaphysics to his dramatic practice.

Ritual, whether expressed in a universal or esoteric idiom, is the dynamo of Soyinkan drama; it is not only the principal source of the dramatic power and excitement of his work but the mainspring of his ambivalent vision. Ritual ambiguity informs the mixture of violent climax and quiet close in the plays' open-ended finales, either through the general pattern of redemptive sacrifice—death gets things born—or, more particularly, in the form of the New Year Festival, which looks transitionally both backward and forward and confuses ends and beginnings. In the ambience of festival drama short-term recurrence is complemented by long-term revaluation. The repetition of ritual acts, which will always have to be done again, is balanced by the New Year's stock-taking mood, the reassessment and retrospection that may be prologue to some lasting regenerative change. If repetitiveness licenses a pessimistic view of history as locked into a doomed cycle of pollutive evils, retrospection sanctions an impulse toward messianic deliverance. New Year ritual reserves a place in the deterministic scheme for the creative act of the special individual—often a visionary or artist figure in Soyinka's metaphoric treatment—or for an act of the revived collective will, which is capable of decisively breaking the exhausted cycle of pollution and purification, guilt and expiation, and, as with the intervention of Athena and Apollo at the endings of Aeschylus's *The Oresteia* and Sophocles' *Oedipus at Colonus*, calling a halt to suffering. The ambiguity is, of course, also present in the erratic nature of Soyinka's adopted deity Ogun. "This god is a cycle," Soyinka has said, "the complete cycle of destruction and creativity" (Morell, 121). Ogun, though he represents the exceptional individualism that is able to break the "tragic" cycle of repetition, is yet himself one of its alternating components and part of the matrix of forces that he challenges, and through contingency (as in the unplanned death of the road accident) he constantly fractures the continuum that he helps to maintain. In *A Dance of the Forests* the contradiction is resolved by having Demoke, Ogun's own artist, break the cycle of horrors caused by his patron deity's interminable metaphysical vendetta with Eshuoro. In the tangled metaphysics of "The Fourth Stage" the fatalistic acceptance of the cosmic cycle of infraction and reparation is countered by the assertive challenge of Ogun's combative will, which yet keeps the cycle intact; the prevailing note of any play, tragic or otherwise, depends in theory on the point of the cycle at which it comes out, whether at the disturbance or the resolution, at the upturn (as in *The Bacchae*) or at the downturn (as in *Madmen and Specialists*) of the wheel.

Soyinka's idiosyncratic contribution to Yoruba mythology's structure of complementarities is to combine Ogun with Obatala, the god who is "the embodiment of the suffering spirit of man . . . of the redemptive qualities of endurance and martyrdom" (*MLAW*, 152). In his theoretical account of the ritual and mythological archetypes of Yoruba drama, Soyinka conjoins the separate legends of Obatala's confinement and Ogun's transitional crossings, and in such a way that Ogun's energy is made to issue out of Obatala's enforced, captive inertia and is then reabsorbed into his harmony (a pattern repeated in the release of Dionysius's energy from Pentheus's imprisonment in *The Bacchae* and of Olunde's from Elesin's in *Death and the King's Horseman*).[15] "With the former [Obatala] immobilised, Ogun comes into his own and enjoys full ascendancy" (*MLAW*, 19). Ogun's dynamism is triggered by his opposite number's passivity, and conversely, the "quietist wisdom" represented by Obatala in Yoruba metaphysics can be achieved only after Ogun's task of will and the passage of the gods through the transitional gulf (*MLAW*, 145–46). As there are always further alternating phases of disturbance and conciliation, there is no final, absolute affirmation of the confrontational impulse over the human tendency toward complacency and inertia. Rather, the prevailing pattern in Soyinka's ritual dramas is one of rebellious chaos and disintegration, represented by Ogun, repeatedly accommodated by but never wholly resolved into the quiescent harmony represented by Obatala. Subsequently, some critics have stressed the Ogun element of the model and have endowed the god's emergence from his own annihilation with revolutionary propensities, and others have favored the Obatalan complement and have viewed Soyinka's dramatic ideas as expressions of fatalistic acceptance and resignation after the fashion of European tragedy.[16]

In fact, Soyinka makes significant departures from Western tragic models. In the calamitous Shakespearean model the hero, educated by his ruin too late to repair it, grows only to die, and the closing notes of communal redemption are not deeply felt but are perfunctory sops to the idea of social continuance and conventional notions of justice, howled out by the prevailing desolation. Pulling against the power of the death-ended drama, the ritual trappings of vegetation motifs, slain gods, and regenerated nature form only a weak undertow. In Yoruba ritual drama, however, as to a lesser extent in Greek drama, these motifs are not subdued, secondary resonances but powerful primary encodings. In the Yoruba form suffering must be undergone and ritually performed not merely as a prelude to but as a condition of the restoration of communal prosperity, the earth's fertility, and the whole continuum of existence. If the logic of Western tragedy leans toward the retributive, that of its Yoruba ritual counterpart is more directly sacrificial: it is what the community makes of the protagonist's martyrdom that is important.[17] Thus it has been observed that if there are Western equivalents of the Ogun-Obatala archetype, they are to be found in the tragic repertoire's more affirmative and progressive structures: notably, those unorthodox, open-ended "tragedies of reconciliation," Aeschylus's *The Eumenides* and Sophocles' *Oedipus at Colonus*, where the closing focus switches to the continuing community and the land blessed by the hero's death (Katrak, 34–35). In the Yoruba theoretical model the protagonist's disintegration may be followed by death or by a self-willed reconstitution, an "epilogue of reassemblage" that, Soyinka insists, "does not nullify the tragic experience" (Katrak, 19). Yet the hero's fate, and whether he does or does not achieve self-knowledge (Professor and Pentheus do not), finally matter less than that his ordeal injects a new strength into the communal lifeblood, either by bringing the community to self-knowledge or by the example of his exemplary moral courage in the face of adversity (Katrak, 19–20, 31–44). The beneficial follow-on effect for the community is at once more tangible and pervasive than in the Western individualist tragic tradition, for the ritual action does not end with the life of the hero or even with his usefulness as a cautionary or exemplary model, as in Sophocles' *Oedipus Rex*. Rather, it is removed, post-tragically, to communal and cosmic levels by his self-transcendence and apotheosis into public figurehead, abstract religious principle, legendary hero, or mythic archetype—suggesting to some that the real subject of Soyinka's ritual drama is religious salvation, conceived at an abstract metaphysical level and with more than a hint of the *Divine Comedy* paradigm, rather than the "social regeneration" and "revolutionary challenge" of which he speaks so much in his dramatic theory.[18]

    When all has been said about alternative "tragic" structures, however, certain reservations remain. The cycle of Soyinka's informing metaphysic, in which the joy of Obatalan resolution is always about to be plunged back into grief by Ogun, is a volatile, endlessly alternating continuum that contains within itself both change and recurrence, and the ritual that gives it expression constantly recharges the flux to prevent stagnation. And yet any cyclic order, even one that contains disturbance and is capable of self-violation, expresses a static worldview consistent with that required by tragedy; as Andrew Gurr and others have noted, Soyinka has a theoretical tendency in "The Fourth Stage" to see Ogun's disruptions merely as a prelude to returning harmony and to find an ultimate resolution in Obatala's quietist calm.[19] This serene, fatalistic wisdom, insofar as it explains why everything is eternally the way it is (a variant on justifying the ways of god to men), can be used to rationalize inertia in an unalterable cosmos; it is very close to the paralyzing knowledge of Hamlet, which seeks to understand the world as an alternative to changing it—or to change human consciousness of reality rather than reality itself—and so becomes a substitute for instead of a spur to action. Some commentators have found this "safety valve" or opiate element of the tragic worldview—more anodyne than antidote—to be consistent with ritual, which has been viewed as inherently change-resistant in its capacity for accommodating and sublimating disaster and containing rebellion within purely ceremonial limits.[20] It must be conceded, moreover, that the very primacy in ritual of a totalist organic mythology gives it conspicuous common ground with the inert worldview of Western tragedy. In this mythology, as in tragedy, society, nature, and supernature are each part of a single indivisible whole, with the result that misfortunes may radiate out from a stable human center to shake the cosmos from its course. "Ritual is a metaphor for the perennial," writes Soyinka. "Birth is a perennial event, so is death. So are courage, cowardice, fear, motion, rain, drought. . . . Ritual is the irreducible formal agent for event-disparate and time-separated actions of human beings in human society" (*ADO*, 120). Ritual reflects a fixed cosmic order and an unchangeable human lot, in which knowledge is an eternal adjustment to things as they are—an essentially tragic viewpoint that has been largely abandoned by Western modernism. It has been argued that tragedy dies in a curable world; that as soon as human ills, once only spiritually redeemable, become medically or technologically remediable, then hitherto mysterious phenomena such as incurable diseases and electrical energy become humanly correctable and controllable and immediately cease to be part of an inescapable fatalistic order (Steiner, 193–94, 290–98). Soyinka's response is that the lightning and metal gods are no less awesome or easier to placate in their most recent historical manifestations, and though medical science may have temporarily removed the aura of genetic doom from Ibsen's *Ghosts*, new resistant strains of the syphilitic virus (and, one might add, AIDS) always arise to restore the terror of the inexorable (*MLAW*, 46–49). Suffering and evil are not man-made, socially removable contingencies but, like death, are irreducible phenomena endemic to the human lot. Soyinka's "metaphysic of the irreducible" is a fundamentally tragic one in which the curative, changeful forces of history are constantly being absorbed into the numen of fate—the remediable assimilated into the realm of the irremediable instead of the other way round.

Soyinka's ritualistic conception of history as an infernal cycle of repeated follies, cruelties, and ignorance has already been noticed. The circuit can occasionally be broken at certain kinks in the cycle (the Möbius strip in *Idanre*); recurrence is never exact, but as the fate of the revenant spirits in *A Dance of the Forests* demonstrates, a pattern of ingrained similarity persists beneath variant historical statistics. "Unborn generations will, as we have done, eat up one another," says the Warrior in one of the play's many Shakespearean echoes (*CP1*, 49).[21] The cyclic rivalry of Ogun and Eshuoro expresses the same sense of nemesis as the feuding deities in Aeschylus, and the doom of repetition signified by Ogun's tail-devouring snake finds its Western equivalents in Lear's wheel of fire and Oedipus's circular journey to violate the source of his own conception. Eman of *The Strong Breed* is again Oedipus, struggling against an inescapable personal destiny but forced back into its fulfillment by a perverse twist of events and by deep compelling needs within his own character. Furthermore, as in Western tragedy, the play shifts from the social and political theater of action to the growth of the individual consciousness into self-knowledge. In his tragic form Soyinka tends to place social redemption not with the collective will but with the exemplary sacrificial suffering of the protagonist, who brings human society, in a sudden act of collective self-apprehension, to new exalted levels of communal consciousness. Soyinka relies heavily on ritual forms—such as the Ogun rite and the carrier in New Year festivals—that favor this precise pattern.

Finally, some words of warning about Soyinka's extraction of a ritual theory of drama from the Ogun Festival. A certain amount of critical confusion hinges on the term "ritual" in Soyinka's theoretical writings because its meaning shifts as it moves between contexts, particularly between ceremonial drama and stage drama. (The same is true of "revolution," which may refer to social regeneration, awakened consciousness, or the periodic recharging and seasonal turning of nature's cycle.) In the

Cambridge lectures of *Myth, Literature, and the African World* "ritual" refers throughout to the cultic esoterics of Ogun mysteries; in the Washington lecture, "Drama and the Idioms of Liberation," delivered to a largely black American audience, it is used in a more generic sociological sense (ritual is "a language of the masses" and "a universal idiom"), or it refers, dramaturgically, to the authenticating, self-sustaining power that a play derives from being grounded in an indigenous, grass-roots milieu or "self-apprehended world" (*ADO*, 53–60). "Ritual theater," as conceived in *Myth, Literature, and the African World*, is the outcome of the operation in the dramatic context of Soyinka's mystical essentialism— namely, of the philosophic outlook that conceives of ritual as the meeting point of the numinous and the mundane, of human and cosmic essences—and it gives rise to two basic areas of confusion. Firstly, Soyinka's account of Ogun rites awkwardly conflates the private circle of communicants surrounding the ritual celebrant and the larger community that is set to benefit from the act and on whose behalf it is performed (*MLAW*, 33–34, 142–44). "Community" in his ritual metaphysics begins as the local village community, which may participate *in toto* as communicants in the rite, but is then extended by metaphor to take in the collected communities that constitute the entire nation or society. Thus the logic of corporate recovery through religious communion in the Ogun mysteries gets mixed up with the revolutionary energies required for social transformation, and ritual subsequently acquires a spurious currency at levels where it would appear to have no place. Secondly, Soyinka proceeds to employ a markedly dramatical terminology that implicitly claims for the cultic experience something beyond the usual aesthetic boundaries of ritual. Ogun is seen as the "first actor" to whom the communicants are "chorus," and the turmoil of his transitional crossing is what "the modern tragic dramatist recreates through the medium of physical, contemporary action" (*MLAW*, 149). Soyinka begins by regarding the celebrant in the divine presence as an "actor-surrogate" and then, by means of a protean usage of the vocabulary of acting, progresses to an analogy with his distant descendant: "The tragic hero stands to his contemporary reality as the ritual protagonist on the edge of the transitional gulf" (*MLAW*, 36). He next makes a striking synthesis of the stage actor in the modern European theater, alone on a darkened stage, with the Ogunian celebrant or "protagonist" about to confront "the dangerous area of transformation" (*MLAW*, 41–42). The actor afraid of blacking out and the celebrant paralleling himself with the deity on the brink of annihilation are both suspended in a moment of supreme aloneness, about to take the dangerous plunge into the self that will give it energies for the forging of a new identity. Each of these parallel encounters with infinity, claims Soyinka, "involves a loss of individuation, a self-submergence in universal essence" (*MLAW*, 42). The telescoping of acts of artistic and spiritual communion that follows conflates, on the one hand, the risk-taking, psyche-probing "Ogunian" actor and the god-possessed celebrant and, on the other, rival formal and metaphysical conceptions of theater as, respectively, "a physical area for simulated events" and a "contraction of the cosmic envelope" (*MLAW*, 39–41).[22]

There is a problem with this visionary, Ogunian conception of the actor as permanently in extremis, throwing caution to the cosmic winds: his habitual presentation as an agent in a liturgical rite creates a basic uncertainty as to whether the ritual celebrant is being conceived in merely analogic terms or a more literal link between cultic rites (the drama of the gods) and theater (the drama of men) is being claimed; that is, whether ritual is being likened to drama or *is* that thing. "The actor in the ritual drama operates in the same way," we are told, as Ogun in his titanic archetypal struggle (*MLAW*, 30). Analogy in Soyinka's prose has a habit of slipping into direct association and thence into identification. Even allowing for the complex interweavings and hybridization of religious and theatrical forms in the Yoruba world, a rite is not instant drama, nor ritual movement ballet, and elsewhere Soyinka has been at pains to point this out.[23] My own tentative distinctions, in the following chapters, between Soyinka's "ritual-inclusive" and "ritual-intensive" dramas are made in light of the understanding that all of these plays are ritual metaphors, not rites proper; that a play is about reality, whereas a rite is its own reality; that in the last analysis, all plays are ritual-imitative, and not even the sacrifice of live goats on stage can disguise this.[24] Soyinka's vigorous antimimetic stance, his insistence that Ogun's "spiritual reassemblage does not require a copying of actuality" and is not "a reflection or illusion of reality" (*MLAW*, 142, 160), are more meaningful in the ritual than in the theatrical context. The subtitle of "The Fourth Stage" promises to locate the origins of Yoruba tragedy in "The Mysteries of Ogun," but in spite of its dramaturgical terminology, the essay in fact sheds little light on the mysteries of "ritual drama" and is finally not an exploration of dramaturgy or any aspect of theater but a flight of metaphysical lyricism that has as its real subject religious ecstasy.

Soyinka's reading of ritual as the drama of transition is in itself a narrowly selective one. Not all rites enact transition (the purification rite in *The Strong Breed* is merely separative and cathartic), and not all transition is Ogunian (in *Death and the King's Horseman* it takes the form of ritual suicide, and in the New Year Festival plays it is a purely calendrical phenomenon). Ritual does more than enact myths, and there are other myths besides the myth of Ogun for it to enact; the tendency of Soyinka's critical "monomythopoeia" is to make Ogun stand for the whole of Yoruba myth and rituality. And yet, in the more genuinely "universal idiom" of the plays themselves, ritual is as slippery and multifaceted a property as its metaphysical interpretation in "The Fourth Stage" is narrow. On Soyinka's stage traditional ritual practices may be positive or negative, beneficial or exploitative, repressive or subversive in the uses to which they lend themselves and the interpretations put upon them, and they are defined by these extraneous elements. They may sanctify evasion, brutality, or corrupt inertia (*The Strong Breed, The Swamp Dwellers*) or license melodramatic moral gestures and merely symbolic confrontations that do nothing physically about evil (*Kongi's Harvest*); they may maintain the flux of change from one generation to the next (*Horseman*) or be mobilized from tools of reactionary oppression into instruments of insurrection (*The Bacchae*). Ritual, in Soyinka's own words, may be used in his plays to "question accepted History (*A Dance of the Forests*) . . . for ideological statements (*The Bacchae*) . . . and to 'epochalise' History for its mythopoeic resourcefulness (*Death and the King's Horseman*)" (*ADO*, 126). Moreover, only in a small number of plays, notably *The Road*, is there any strong suggestion that the theatrical element in ritual makes it inherently dramatic and that the relationship between ritual and drama is any less arbitrary than that between any play and its subject. Ritual elements and effects in the plays are not dramaturgically consistent and may at times be intrusively overtheatrical or simply untheatrical. In the thematically overloaded *Dance* they are poorly integrated with verbal expression, and mime and dance are allowed to make off with meanings not delivered in the dialogue. Or ritual elements may be entirely at odds with dramatic clarity: in *Kongi's Harvest* the moral debate is submerged in festival spectacle and the protagonists' functions in the mystique of the masque are more impressive than the characters themselves. Ritual may even be used to impose unconvincing resolutions upon plays, as in *The Bacchae*, where revolution is presented as taking place through quasi-ritual processes and the logic of events is made more purely religious than political.

Since its publication as a coda to *Myth, Literature, and the African*

World, "The Fourth Stage" has been conceived in Soyinka criticism as something of a sacred text and the primary works as themselves "Ogun mysteries" whose secrets the essay alone can unlock. This idea has led to a number of blanket mythographic readings of the plays that force them into the narrow conceptual framework of Ogunian challenge resolved into Obatalan wholeness; these analysts see only a protagonist experiencing estrangement and disintegration followed by a reconstitution that discharges a new energy or expanded awareness into the community.[25] At this level of abstraction anyone undergoing a crisis is likely to be dragged across an elastically metaphoric "transitional gulf," and the presence of Ogun detected in any fusion of contradictions or ambiguity of definition, or wherever metal or transitional phenomena are in evidence. But the small dent in the status quo made by Igwezu's futile gesture of protest at the end of *The Swamp Dwellers* hardly qualifies him for the Ogunian status that has been claimed for him,[26] and Kongi, Professor, and Dr. Bero are only partial Ogun figures, with the hubristic challenge and will to power abnormally developed and the redeeming sacrificial and creative characteristics left out. In *The Strong Breed* the imprisonment of Obatala may form a distant backdrop to the abduction of Ifada and its subsequent energizing of Eman as an Ogun-surrogate; but nothing is made in the text of the idiot's sacred link with Obatala, and the play operates perfectly well on levels that make no reference to mythic archetypes.[27] *The Bacchae* ends with an Ogunian revolutionary breakthrough and *The Strong Breed* with a hint of Obatalan resolution in the lingering sense of balanced alternatives, but most of the plays do not end in either of these ways. The wheel—if it is a wheel—comes to a halt at a different place in each play: on the edge of a yawning void in *Horseman*; in barely relieved despair in *The Swamp Dwellers*; at entrapment in an infernal cycle in *A Dance of the Forests*; and in the final holocaust of *Madmen and Specialists*, with the explosion of the very idea of redemptive and regenerative sacrifice. The resulting impression is not that these plays break off either at the upturn or downturn of an endlessly alternating cycle. Rather, as Annmarie Heywood has suggested, they merely break off, arbitrarily and inconclusively, at any point of conflict: with a revolver shot and in midchant in *Madmen*; with the jail door's iron clang in *Kongi*; and with an unresolved peroration in *The Road*.[28] Moreover, these abrupt terminations probably owe less to the structures of mythic archetypes than to specific ritual dynamics such as the utterances, during trance possession, of the egungun and the *oriki* (praise-chants) which merely pour out until cut off in midflow (Barber, 509).

In spite of Soyinka's theoretic harping on the sacrificial teleology of
Yoruba tragedy, in his own creative practice some doubt always surrounds the strengthening of the community's spiritual health or material
well-being by the protagonist's trauma or death. Professor and Pentheus
have to die because one preys upon life and the other denies it altogether.
And yet, though the ritual mystiques of the plays in which they appear
do much to disguise it, their riddance, by creating in each case a vacuum,
releases merely negative energies into their societies. The world is rid of
a parasite and a tyrant and restored, respectively, to sanity and liberty. It
is hard to imagine, however, the underworld of touts and thugs being
much changed by Professor's end, and there is no certainty that the new
order of Dionysius will be any less tyrannical in its way than Pentheus's
old one. In material terms, society is not regenerated by the deaths of
these figures but is simply better off without them; the pragmatic logic
of socioeconomics and politics is given primacy over the ritual one of
sacrifice. Meanwhile, in *Horseman* the closing impression is that no
Yoruba "world" or "universe" is left intact to benefit from the double
death, no future exists for the rite to admit passage into. The unprecedented role reversal of father and son leaves no successor to take up their
ritual task, and the world stumbles forward into a void. The feelings of
desolation and needless death that prevail at the end of this play seem to
have little to do with a pattern of beneficial tragedy built around the
Ogun archetype and are more like the conventional feelings at the end of
a Shakespearean tragedy or a play like Brecht's *Mother Courage* (1941),
where waste is perceived not as tragic or purposive, but as simply
wasteful.

Finally, Soyinka's relentlessly cosmic view of drama is too tenuously
abstract to imagine in theatrical terms. Plays are, after all, about people,
not primal essences projected into mythological beings; even in Greek
drama divine appearances are rare, and Racine's neoclassical deities are
but magnified human passions. Significantly, Ogun presides over only
one play and makes a single personal appearance on Soyinka's stage, for
he is never closely characterized in the theoretical writings but is rather
a matrix of essences, a crucible of creative and destructive energies. When
Soyinka does attempt a pristine cosmic drama of essence, representing
the whole of human and divine history (in *Dance*), the stage is simply not
big enough, and the numerous boundary crossings between different
orders of being, manageable in a metaphysical essay but perilous in
performance, create only multiple confusions of identity. In addition, the
abrupt switches to mythic registers and a rhetoric of "essence" in the

local effects of plays are also responsible for some of Soyinka's most inflated and pretentious writing, as when the love chat of Segi and Daodu in *Kongi* swings into the choric chant of Earth Mother and Spirit of Harvest and their sexuality suddenly begins to incorporate powers of natural and political regeneration (*CP2*, 97–99); or when Elesin casuistically defends his deathbed lust in terms of seeds, shoots, and stalks, as if he were not a man but an impersonal element in a seasonal cycle (*SP*, 160). These episodes lack transitional, stylistic modifiers to ease the passage from one frame to another—odd in a writer who speaks so much of transition—and one is unsure if the intended tone is celebratory or ironic. Perhaps, then, the mythographic lore of dismembered deities and chthonic gulfs has had too loud a voice in Soyinka criticism, disproportionate to its true importance. The metaphysics of transition, like Yeats's symbological system, is fitfully relevant to the work, and then mainly for esoteric nondrama texts such as "Idanre" or parts of *The Interpreters*. *The Road* and *Horseman* naturally benefit from some knowledge of it, but metaphysics translates badly onto the stage, and plays have to stand on their own feet if they are to have any viability at performance level. The paradoxical result is that a metaphysic sited in ritual and drama has come to lead a life almost independent of the plays, which often seem to go one way while it goes another. The following chapters will pursue some of the directions taken by that extraordinary, rich, and profound achievement; from here on the play's the thing.

Chapter 3

A Natural Idiom: Tragic Realism and Festive Comedy

The naturalistic idiom of the early plays gathered here—*Camwood on the Leaves, The Swamp Dwellers, The Trials of Brother Jero, Jero's Metamorphosis,* and *The Lion and the Jewel*—suffers minimal interference from the spectacle and intense ritualism of Yoruba festival theater. These plays are, of all Soyinka's work, perhaps the most accessible to Western audiences, approximating closest to the dialogue drama and well-made play of entertainment theater. Written just before or during the year of independence, they employ traditional comic-satiric and somber-tragic modes to explore cultural contrasts and confrontations in a crucial period of transition. The masque elements in *The Lion and the Jewel* behave in much the same way as their counterparts in the European musical, surrounding the play's conflicts with the general conviviality and concord of the comedy tradition. Although Soyinka subtitled his radio play *Camwood on the Leaves* "a rite of childhood passage" and expressed a wish to "utilize the idiom of the masquerade in auditory terms" (Duerden and Pieterse, 171), the play's rituality does not run deep into the texture of the writing but, through the backcloth of the egungun, merely notates in the personal psychology of the boy Isola a decisive break in religious and cultural conditions during the transition from colonialism to independence.

Camwood, broadcast in 1960 but not published until 1973, tells the story of the 16-year old Isola's traumatized childhood at the hands of his savagely repressive, puritanical father, the insecure Christian pastor of a still largely "pagan" parish. After being mercilessly beaten for taking part in an innocent egungun masquerade, Isola flees to the forest and, in the "chapel" of a clearing, builds an alternative world that nevertheless mirrors that of his home life: he projects upon a mother tortoise and a fearsome boa constrictor that dashes the tortoise's eggs against the rocks the identities of Moji, his timid and powerless mother, and Erinjobi, his brutal father. Here his childhood sweetheart Morounke becomes his lover; when her pregnancy is exposed Isola is accused of her abduction and becomes the victim of a campaign of lies orchestrated by her outraged father, the influential Olumorin. At the latter's behest, Isola is hunted down to his forest hideout by an angry mob, and though Erinjobi, somewhat mellowed by a night of prayer at his church, manages to deflect the mob, the identification between python and pastor becomes complete when the son, driven by persecution to madness and murder, confuses the two and at the play's climax shoots the father with the bullet intended for the snake.

The moral logic of *Camwood* is clear enough. The play is not a cautionary homiletic on the impiousness of filial rebellion: Isola's initial disobedience and defiance of his father are not conceived as the first faltering steps along a wayward course that culminates inevitably in parricide. Rather, the father's hatred and rejection of his son bring an equally unnatural fate down upon his own head. It is the self-righteous cruelty and blind intolerance of the parents, and their hysterical rage against all natural instinct, that harden their aptly named son's desperate isolation. In the process he is driven into the arms of traditional religion, and the point of the Yoruba dirge songs that punctuate the play's time shifts is not only to mourn the son who is already dead to them (camwood dye is used for funeral clothes) but to assert the more humane and life-respecting alternative order of native wisdom: "My back supports the child like a much blessed mother / This child is to you—your own flesh and blood" (*SP*, 139). The play is a penetrating psychological study of the neurotic effects of an alien, puritanical religion on the minds of the new African middle class—a class fearful for its exemplary position, obsessed with respectability, and brainwashed by colonial Christianity into despising the customs of its own people. Since this class has severed all connection with indigenous values, Erinjobi's traditional invocation of filial duty and parental authority carries no weight. He has himself initiated the Westernizing process that issues in the un-Yoruba-like total rebellion of his son, and in his failure to demonstrate any authoritative wisdom for his son to respect, he has forfeited the traditional rights of fatherhood (hence Isola's reference to him throughout by his Christian name or his office). It is significant that Isola seeks refuge from his father's murderous religion in the local egungun society. The second-generation Christians of the play are, after all, the direct inheritors of the evangelical, missionary brand of Victorian Christianity that, when exported to Africa in the late nineteenth century, fiercely suppressed the egungun societies in both their cultic and theatrical forms, and it was the egungun that consequently became the strongest and most organized weapon of resistance (Adedeji 1978, 33; *ADO*, 191–92). Dramaturgically, *Camwood* may not quite be the aural equivalent of an egungun masquerade that Soyinka had in mind, but its latterday anti-Christian polemic carries vestiges of the protest tradition of the Alarinjo theater, which is thought to have evolved from the egungun. Beyond the battle between paternal dogmatism and youthful rebellion lies a deeper conflict between Christian and African beliefs. The play does not, of course, advocate parricide as a solution to culture conflict but uses it symbolically to mark the departure of the new nation, on the brink of independence, from the emotional and cultural dependencies acquired with its colonial Christian inheritance. It is thus a national as well as a childhood rite of passage: with the killing of the father and all that he represents, the nation comes of age.

Much of Soyinka's mature work is foreshadowed in this early radio piece—Isola, as pathfinder and hounded rebel, is an embryonic Ogun and scapegoat figure—but his dramatic technique is not fully developed. The scene-fades in the flashbacks to Isola's traumatic childhood and to the earlier events of the day are too fast and frequent, even for a radio play,[1] and certain puzzles, such as the violent opposition of two Westernized, socially aspiring families to a union of their offspring, are left unexplained by the plot. The snake and tortoise, though powerful general images for a predatory, life-crushing religion and the younger generation's need to "go and come as they please" (*SP*, 128), are but the disturbed projections of Isola's private nightmares, the dark whimsies of his mental suffering and final madness,[2] and do not successfully blend with their human referents in the play. When a more exact correspondence between the two is attempted, as at the stage-managed climax, the result is a clumsy, telegraphic symbolism.

In Soyinka's other preindependence drama in the tragic mode, the more overtly naturalistic *The Swamp Dwellers* (1963), the authority challenged is that of traditional religion, and the challenge comes from an urban returnee, Igwezu, who is shocked into enlightenment by his misfortunes and by an alien religion (Islam, in the shape of a blind Hausa beggar fleeing a drought-stricken, locust-infested North). After eight months in the city, during which time he has lost both his wife and money to his prosperous twin brother and has pledged his farm as security for his debts, Igwezu returns to the parental home in the swamp to find his farm ruined by flood. Casting around for a culprit, he finds one in the Kadiye, the village priest who accepted Igwezu's sacrifice of a calf to the local deity, the Swamp Serpent, to secure a good harvest but who, it is suggested, has a habit of appropriating offerings for his own use. At this inauspicious time the corrupt priest, who is crassly insensitive to Igwezu's sorrows, demands to be shaved to mark the end of the rains. Spurred on by the radical questioning of the vagrant beggar, the enraged youth proceeds with a cross-examination in which the bloated Kadiye, at the mercy of his razor, is forced to listen to a few home truths and has his fraudulent extortion of produce exposed for those present to see. In one of Soyinka's characteristic open-ended finales, the terrified Kadiye scampers off to raise the village against his tormentor; Igwezu goes out into the night, either to return to the misery of the city or to be hunted down in the swamp; and the wandering beggar, who has mysteriously declared himself Igwezu's "bondsman," takes custody of his remaining land and looks forward to the regeneration of nature in the new agricultural year.

The play's prime target is self-serving religion, characterized by a morally pointless vow of abstinence from washing and shaving that neatly encapsulates the priest's indolence and accumulated corruption. The Kadiye, it is clear, is but a local symptom of that universal greed for wealth that in the rival swamp of the metropolis turns brother against brother and makes sons forget their parents. (The play was prompted by the discovery of oil in the Niger Delta and anticipates the destructive rapacity of Nigeria's short-lived oil boom.) But beyond these, the play calls into question the whole psychology of dependency fostered by obscurantist and fatalistic religions like the cult of the Swamp Serpent. Though his loss of money and wife is not immediately the Kadiye's fault, Igwezu is ultimately justified in attributing his overall failure to the habits of mind inculcated at home by religious customs such as that of reserving the most fertile land for the Serpent. The Kadiye's cult *is* responsible for the village's rationalization of failure and inertia, its patient reconciliation to its pains, and its discouragement of positive efforts at redress such as the land reclamation proposed by the more enterprising northern beggar. It is this fatalistic dependency that causes Igwezu to depart for the city as soon as the appropriate offerings have been made, leaving his untended farm under "the protection of the heavens" and forgetting that the land does not produce for those who neglect and abandon it; the same automatic faith that good harvests will be returned by official sacrifices leads him to pledge his farm as security for his urban debts. This curiously helpless, initiative-lacking figure, hitherto unable to accept responsibility for his own fortunes, must learn from the beggar how to challenge and take charge of his fate instead of merely awaiting and then railing against it. The beggar, the play's model

of self-reliance, renounces sluggish dependence on divine favor (he is
quick to recognize the Kadiye as part of this pattern) and resolves on
redeeming the land in defiance of Serpent, priest, and community.

But the radical skepticism of this play probes beyond the corrupt
confiscations of the profiteering priest and his opportunistic use of
superstition to keep the village at subsistence level. Indeed, the play is
unique in Soyinka's stage work in its placing of ritual practices, basely
exploitative in this instance, within a frame of prose realism that ratio-
nally interrogates and demystifies them. Soyinka uses the innocent
bewilderment of a man of simple animist faith over the nonreturns from
his sacrifices to question the validity of all sacrifice and its informing
metaphysic and to challenge the whole religious basis of life in the
village. Igwezu's despair issues in an iconoclastic atheism: "If I slew all
the cattle in the land and sacrificed every measure of goodness, would it
make any difference to our lives, Kadiye? . . . I know that the floods
can come again. That the swamp will continue to laugh at our endeav-
ours. I know that we can feed the Serpent of the Swamp and kiss the
Kadiye's feet—but the vapours will still rise and corrupt the tassels of the
corn" (*CP1*, 110). Men, not gods or nature, are to blame for human
misfortunes, and the telescoping of Serpent and priest by the imagery of
Igwezu's climactic speeches insists that there is no Serpent but the
Kadiye himself. Both are "gorged" and "sleepy-eyed" and "lie upon the
land," the pun coupling fraud with indolence, and the verbal play on
corrupt in the above speech parallels the priest's private consumption of
ritual offerings with the swamp's swallowing of crops: the moral corruption of one feeds the physical corruption of the other. By the end of the
play Igwezu knows that he has lost his own faith and so places his farm in
the hands of the blind believer whom misfortune has driven to action and
whose faith is not the blind, paralyzing hope of the fatalist but a current
of constructive energy and the foresight of the "seer."

Radical though Igwezu's questioning is, his defiance of the priest does
not make him the "slayer of serpents" of the beggar's eulogy, and the
protagonist-community pattern of the Ogun archetype is of little relevance here. He has exposed the false prophet, has briefly put perverted
power back in its place and proved it vulnerable, but the play ends not
with a communal casting off of superstition and a move toward land
reclamation but with a deeply conservative community rallying to the
support of its outraged priest. *The Swamp Dwellers* is essentially a familial,
domestic tragedy, and its subject is the attitudes and beliefs of Igwezu's
parents Alu and Makuri, the swamp dwellers of the title who occupy the

stage for most of the play. They are the real victims of the tragedy, and it is on their behalf, not the community's, that Igwezu vainly challenges the Kadiye's authority. Igwezu gives vicarious expression to Makuri's suppressed doubts about the priest and directs at its proper target the unspoken resentment that his parents deflect back upon one another in their futile bickerings. But because he does so without their consent and support, Igwezu's emancipated decision to do without the props of Serpent and Kadiye is his and his alone. Alu and Makuri represent a moribund traditional order, incapable of changing itself. They are too deeply sunk in spiritual lethargy, too deeply conditioned by the energy-sucking culture of the swamp to heed the voice of dissent and nurture the seed of doubt; though unable to reject their son, they side fearfully with traditional religious practice. The community is, finally, best served not by their religious quietism (giving in) or by their son's desertion (giving up), but by the infusion from outside of new, changeful energies, represented by the beggar, in whose hands Igwezu is a mere instrument. The blind man is no passive Obatalan figure (he rejects his prescribed place as one of "the afflicted of the gods") but is the catalyst of the youth's rebellious challenge. He feeds Igwezu the questions about the Kadiye that Igwezu then puts to the Kadiye himself, and his rational, constructive approach to both religion and the land represents the only hope for survival.

The Swamp Dwellers, written while its author was still an undergraduate and first performed in a London student production in 1958, shows signs of apprenticeship. Uncertain stagecraft results in a dizzying number of entrances and exits, and it is hard at times to resist the notion of the young Nigerian writer breaking the national scene down into capsule form, for the benefit of a London audience, through a series of deliberate mechanical contrasts: desert, savannah, and swamp; drought and flood; Muslim North and animist South; backward village and wicked metropolis. The Kadiye is a crude caricature of a village priest, too obviously a fraud and too ready-made a target for the hero's rebellion to allow for an even contest between tradition and modernity. Igwezu's entry in the last third of the play is too late for him to acquire the tragic proportions that Soyinka seems to have wanted for him, with the result that he is never more than an ineffectual sentimental hero making a melodramatic gesture of protest. Finally, *The Swamp Dwellers* suffers from some stylistic uncertainty. Soyinka opted in this play for a universal idiom—hence the many biblical echoes and the Serpent's built-in Judeo-Christian associations of predatory trickster and universal enemy—and for a mainly naturalistic language convention, a kind of poetic peasant realism in the style of Synge. The result, however, is an impeccable but flat and neutral English, disturbed by erratic bursts of poetic lyricism and ponderous proverbial cadences, in which no attempt is made to differentiate characters according to speech style. (In standard English the Ijaw peasant, inevitably, ceases to be a peasant.) Soyinka has not quite mastered his medium in this early one-acter, but in spite of its blemishes the single, continuous action of *The Swamp Dwellers* generates, within its narrow dimensions, a mood of dark foreboding and menace and a near-tragic power. The bareness of the language and the economy of action, the brooding atmospherics of the swamp noises, and the threadbare, subsistence-level set, broken only by the starkly alien symbol of the barber's swivel chair sent back from the city by Igwezu, combine to give a sense of man in extremity, conducting a futile struggle with an unpitying and devouring nature.

Religious charlatanism is again the subject in *The Trials of Brother Jero* (1963), only here the context is a comic one. The culprit is a messianic beach prophet of one of the Aladura or breakaway, revivalist Christian sects that were such a marked feature of the uncertain transition at the time of independence from a communalist to a consumerist society and from orthodox to hybridized religious forms. Brother Jeroboam, "a prophet by birth and by inclination" (*CP2*, 145), operates on the assumptions that dependency is the key to power and that he must therefore keep his congregation dissatisfied and insecure if he is to keep them at all. Thus he refuses to allow his gullible disciple Chume to beat his shrewish wife Amope because Chume's newly discovered independence would give him no further need of the prophet. Meanwhile, in his private life Brother Jero is hounded at the hut where he sleeps (on a featherbed, not on the beach as he tells Chume) by a termagant trader over a debt owed her for a velvet cape. What the audience knows from the start is that the trader and Chume's wife are one and the same person, and when the prophet tumbles this he decides to relinquish Chume's discipleship and, at a single stroke, revenge himself upon and rid himself of Amope by permitting Chume the desired punitive action. The plan backfires, however, when Chume learns from Amope herself the truth about Jero—that he has allowed his disciple to beat his wife purely for his own convenience—and, brandishing a cutlass, sets out in a vindictive rage for Jero's hut. The plays ends with a rather hasty and contrived stratagem: Jero ensnares a local member of parliament by prophetic promises of a ministry and then uses the influence of his new and powerful ally to have the unfortunate Chume packed off to a lunatic asylum. At the close the rogue hero has escaped paying his debt; he has humiliated his creditor and averted the wrath of his disaffected disciple; and with a politician now calling him "master," he has moved on to bigger game and into a new league where his deceptions may prove dangerous.

Soyinka's first Jero play, written over a weekend for an improvised stage in a university college dining hall and thereafter the most frequently performed of his works, is a broad satiric comedy and has all the staple ingredients of that genre: chance encounters, sudden reversals and concealed identities; the prolongation of comic suspense by the delayed recognition of hidden connections between lives; the farcical piling up of incidents, welded together in this play by Jero's choric soliloquies; and some vivid characterization, notably of the long-suffering husband and his wife's whining mock persecutions. Soyinka stretches his linguistic resources to new limits: Jero is a master of every kind of rhetoric, able to switch his style to suit his potential prey, and the play's English ranges from the archaic biblical incantation with which he numbs the intelligence of his congregation to the "animal jabber" of Chume's pidgin when the spirit takes him and he loses self-control. The play is also, incidentally, one of the most spectacular and noisy of Soyinka's stage works: in each of the African productions I have seen the theater was filled with shouting, rhythmic chanting, clapping, and drumming, rising at times to a deafening crescendo.

It is tempting, with the hindsight knowledge of Jero's reprise in the altogether bleaker *Jero's Metamorphosis* (1973), to make heavy weather of the moral satire in *Trials* and of its picaresque hero's predatory and criminal propensities.[3] Some serious matter has been discovered in the play, and one critic has even discerned mythic dimensions patterned on the confuser god Eshu-Elegba.[4] Soyinka has said, however, that his comedy is "a very light recital of human evils and foibles" (Duerden and Pieterse, 174). The satire on consumerism in the scene where the servant hijacks his master's prayer is tempered by the comic exuberance of Chume's pidgin: "If we dey walka today, give us our own bicycle tomorrow. . . . I say those who dey push bicycle, give the big car tomorrow" (*CP2*, 160). Moreover, the punishment of stupidity by the lunatic asylum, though unjust, is yet harmlessly contained within the broad bands of comedy and its whimsical sense of poetic justice. Soyinka has even encouraged audiences to discover "redeeming qualities" in his Falstaffian hero beyond the obvious theatrical ones (Morell, 89–90). The

wit and ingenuity of Jero's warped genius and his engaging candor are
the main sources of pleasure in performance, as in the trickster narratives
of West African folk tales about Ananse the Spider and the Tortoise
where the narrator often plays chorus to his own intrigues, using the
first-person voice to give particularly shocking effect to his frank admis-
sions of deceit. Furthermore, Jero is himself the perfect representative
and critic of his society, an accurate reflection of its aggressive materialism and misplaced religious devotion. The prophet is no more commercial and acquisitive in his acts than the prayers of his congregation: he
merely takes advantage of the extreme gullibility wrought by avarice and
ambition. In the process Jero becomes a vehicle of satire against the
society whose lusts he panders to and preys upon. Societies get the
prophets, and the leaders, they need and deserve. Wherever there is greed
for wealth or fantasies of status and power there will be a Jero diagnosing
the symptoms of the disease across the whole range of society (everyone
but the astute Amope is taken in) and trimming his techniques of
persuasion to fit the subject.

In the last scene, however, the satire takes an unexpected sinister turn,
and there has been some critical dissatisfaction with it. That the rogue
should escape and live to fight another day is true both to the spirit of the
Tortoise tales and to the feeling in the play that the gulls, in being
swindled, have received no less than their just deserts: the Jonsonian
moral vision is closer to *The Alchemist* than to *Volpone*. But the main
reason Jero is not served his comeuppance is that his author still has too
much need of him, in the play's final twist, as a vehicle of the satire to
allow him to become a victim of it. Jero's final crowning fraud not only
demonstrates that politicians are no less immune to guile than traders
and office boys but says something about the spiritual disorientation of
Nigeria's period of historical transition, in which even powerful and
educated members of the community resorted to superstition and supernatural aid—and thus placed influence in the hands of prophets—to gain
advancement in sophisticated modern social structures. Moreover, Soyinka has said that as independence approached he experienced instant
suspicion of the motives and intentions of the new legislators (*SP*, xiii), and
it seems that he manipulated the ending of his play to express his deep
concern about the nation's future leaders. The prophet's almost parodic
identification with the member of parliament issues a telling reminder
that politicians also manipulate through dependency; they also nourish
vain ambitions with empty promises and ambiguously worded prophecies that, like Jero's, are usually either intelligent guesses or undetectable

frauds. It is no accident that one of Jero's beach "penitents" believes that he will be prime minister of the as-yet-uncreated "Mid-North-East State," and we are clearly invited to see the division of the beach by the bogus prophets as a microcosm of the division of the national spoils by equally phony politicians. The ominous prophecies of a Ministry of War bestowed upon the foolish M.P. and of "the country plunged into strife" by "a mustering of men, gathered in the name of peace through strength" (*CP2*, 169)—all to prove true—deliberately darken the play and carry it into deeper waters than Soyinka had perhaps originally intended or knew how to get out of. The abrupt, makeshift ending, using Jero's powerful new disciple to get him out of his entanglement with his old one, may indicate that he did not quite know where to go next.

In Soyinka's most famous early play, *The Lion and the Jewel* (1963), the theme of reactionary authority challenged by youthful revolt is given its most provocative treatment, though the controversial material is camouflaged in a comedy of great wit and charm. At the start of the play the wily old Baroka, the Bale (chief) of the remote village of Ilujinle and "lion" of the title, has been outfaced by the fame bestowed upon Sidi, the village beauty and "jewel," by a glossy-magazine photographer and is growing wary of the rival attentions toward Sidi of Lakunle, an absurd, superficially Westernized young school-teacher who wants to turn the village into an ultramodern metropolis. Baroka therefore seeks to reassert his offended authority and enhance his sexual status by having Sidi join his harem of wives. Insulted by advances from a man three times her age, she rejects his proposal, whereupon the still virile Baroka lets it be known through Sadiku, his most senior wife, that he has recently become impotent. Allowing her vanity and vindictiveness to get the better of her wisdom, Sidi accepts an invitation to supper and goes off to the palace with a view to mocking the Bale's failing powers. That night in his bedchamber the inevitable happens, and Sidi, a maid no more, returns crestfallen to the village. The wretched Lakunle condescends to take up the "fallen woman," but in a surprising twist in the play's tail, Sidi rejects him in favor of the Bale, protesting that she could not wed "a watered-down . . . unripened man" after feeling "the perpetual youthful zest of the panther of the trees" (*CP2*, 57). As in the best comedy tradition, the play ends happily and harmoniously with no one left dissatisfied or empty-handed. The Bale has had his way with Sidi, who is in turn to become his favorite wife and mother to his heir, and in the closing bridal masque Lakunle, ever the object of sympathetic fun, quickly overcomes his disappointment and pursues a new madonna.

Sadiku's misconceived joy at Baroka's supposed emasculation at least
enables her to work off some of the sublimated sexual malice and
resentment aroused by the polygamous marriage system, and her power
and dominance as the "mother of brides" are not diminished but newly
enhanced by the addition of another wife to his menage.

Much critical discussion of the play has turned upon the subject of
"culture conflict" and the supposed opposition of "traditional" and
"modern" values, the genuine and false, and the assured and confused. In
fact, no one has a monopoly on genuine or authentic values in the play.
Both men woo Sidi with falsehoods: Lakunle with the foreign glamor of
beauty contests and cocktail parties; Baroka with the fraudulent promise
of her image on a postage stamp and appeals to her vanity that are not
very different from the blandishments of the Western photographer.
And both men are confused: Lakunle naively so in mistaking fashion for
progress, and Baroka willfully so in identifying what is good for the
village with what best suits his own purposes. "There is no clash of
cultures," Soyinka has said in a recent interview (Gibbs 1987, 79),
because Lakunle's undigested, ill-assimilated values signify only a
pseudo-Westernization, a travesty of a Western culture that is not, in
fact, represented in the play.[5] Lakunle's very peculiar idea of progress is
fueled by an attraction to the tawdry trimmings of Western
civilization—nightclubs, pinup photography, gaudy cosmetics—and is
supported by quotations from outmoded sources, notably pseudoscien-
tifically sexist ones long ago abandoned by his European originals.
But if Lakunle does not represent Western "progress," neither does the
Bale stand for pure tradition. Traditions have no inherent value for
Baroka but simply keep him in power; his "traditionalism" is a highly
selective and self-seeking affair. He is not averse to raking off the benefits
of modern ideas (though his use of modern technology is singularly
inept) or to committing highly "untraditional" acts such as deflowering
a virgin to render her ineligible for bride-price. Though he claims to hold
"the welfare of his people deep at heart" (CP2, 47), his selection of
desirable items from both old and new—polygamous hierarchies and
trade unions, mock wrestling contests and printing presses—is quite
whimsical and erratic; it depends upon what catches his fancy or supports
his authority and is not informed by any systematic worldview or body of
communal values. Baroka is modern or traditional as convenience dictates, and the same is true of everyone else in the play. Lakunle's
egalitarian modernism, as threadbare as his suit and fragile as his foreign
dinner plates, is only superficially opposed to Baroka's traditional elit-

ism. His remarks upon the Bale's wives leave no doubt that he would have settled comfortably into the latter's polygamous decadence had he been born into it, and his mixed motives are especially in evidence in his attitude to bride-price: making a virtue out of necessity, Lakunle affects to disdain what he really cannot afford to pay, and then, after Sidi's disgrace, rehabilitates it when he no longer has to. Sidi herself, though described in the opening stage directions as "a true village belle," readily adopts Lakunle's modern terminology to protest Baroka's regarding her as his "property" and conceives her self-worth through the fame afforded her by Western photography, a fame she then uses to advance her local status. No one in *The Lion and the Jewel* is consistently and disinterestedly modern or traditional in his or her thinking or behavior, and the result is that terms like "progress" and "tradition" have no meaning outside of the highly relative and pragmatic uses to which they are put by characters in the play.[6]

The Bale is a particular problem in this respect. In the seduction scene Baroka claims that he does not hate progress but only its nature, which "makes all roofs and faces look the same," and insists that somewhere among the bridges and "murderous roads," "between this moment and the reckless broom that will be wielded" in years to come, there must be left "virgin plots of lives, rich decay," and "the tang of vapour" rising undisturbed from "forgotten heaps of compost" (*CP2*, 47). This sounds at first like the last plea of an organic biochemical culture in the face of an invading technological one, and it is, of course, vintage Soyinka: most particularly, the suspicion of undiscriminating change "wielded" like a weapon and the somewhat anarchic, tradition-oriented concept of change, with its complementary interaction of old and new, continuity and innovation, decay and renewal (the "rust is ripeness" theme that runs throughout Soyinka's work). Nevertheless, the investment of Baroka with the play's richest poetry fails to disguise the fact that the author's own dynamic concept of tradition has no more than a theoretical and rhetorical presence in this scene. The truth is that Baroka's real policy is merely to leave things alone, to let them be, and thus to keep intact that very sameness—"the spotted wolf of sameness"—that he claims to be resisting. "The old must flow into the new, Sidi," Baroka goes on, "not blind itself or stand foolishly apart." Old wine thrives best in new bottles. Its "coarseness is mellowed down, and the rugged wine," he persuades, "acquires a full and rounded body" (*CP2*, 49). The sage aphorisms are, of course, vibrant with erotic meaning, and though the sexual innuendos are there to declare Baroka's intentions to the audience, and Sidi herself is lulled into submission by the sound rather than the sense of his words, the rhetoric is more than merely seductive. It literally seduces, and the solemnly proverbial philosophical flights have no autonomous, independent value: they are earthed, and negated, by the salacious pragmatism of speaker and context. Any concern that Baroka has for tradition is overridden by his enjoyment of Sidi's incomprehension and deception, and the devious loading of proverbs with sexual meanings to make a statement about the interaction of tradition and progress is symptomatic of his general identification of the public interest with his own. The speech is, in fact, sheer sophistry, and only a perversely allegorical reading of Baroka's sexual conquest could make it symbolic of an ancient, traditional Africa, deceptively weak in appearance but really inwardly powerful, revitalizing itself in its accommodation of young blood. Baroka does not accommodate Sidi but merely appropriates her for his harem (what else would a lion want with a jewel?), and given his rapid turnover of wives and capacity for deceit, it is unlikely that he will keep his promises of favoritism and personal postage stamps. (The stamp machine is a piece of useless junk, and he has no understanding of postal systems.) The Bale, more fox than lion and decadent rather than defunct, is not an idealized portrait of old Africa and its traditional wisdom; though Soyinka has conceded that he "represents a certain virile and therefore reproductive force in society," he has also insisted that "Baroka himself does not represent any culture [or] tradition as such" (Gibbs 1987, 80, 86). The idyllic life of his village may have much to recommend it (perhaps, romantically, too much), but its ruler has little beyond the sexual prowess and cunning instinct for self-preservation that are the ingredients of theater entertainment in the best rogue-comedy tradition.

The Lion and the Jewel, Soyinka has said, is not "a complex play" that "interrogates the march of history" in the manner of A Dance of the Forests (Gibbs 1987, 73). Of course, the play was written out of a specific historical situation, and the apparent siding of its young author with a reactionary chief makes it a testament to its times, particularly to the short-lived illusion, prior to independence, that some sort of alliance between traditional authority and the new Western-educated elites was still possible.[7] Soyinka may have deliberately loaded the case against the "progressives," presenting them only in travestied form, in order to make the polemical point that it was their ineffectuality and failure that, by default, allowed indolent and self-serving traditional rulers to hang on to power. The play is not history, however, but a piece of theater. Within the imagined comedic world of the play, Sidi rejects the half-formed values of the schoolteacher and prefers mule-headed conservatism to muddleheaded progress because, in the given context, the former appears to be the lesser of two evils; because Baroka is the more dignified, impressive, and authentic figure, and the play wishes to celebrate these qualities; and because he is at least solidly grounded in his roots, and though he may not know or care where his world is going, he knows where he belongs in it.

The central motif of *The Lion and the Jewel*, of the man feigning impotence to win a pretty maid, is universal: it can be found in classical comedy, the *Arabian Nights*, Jonson's *Volpone*, and William Wycherley's *The Country Wife*, as well as in Yoruba folklore. But the play's stylistic experimentation marks the confluence of two specific traditions, the Alarinjo mask theater and the European musical comedy. As with songs in the musical, the highly stylized comic masquerades that punctuate the action are set up deliberately by the dialogue; because they often involve sophisticated technical resources not normally a feature of village life, Soyinka makes no attempt to pass them off, naturalistically, as the homemade entertainments of villagers who enjoy making mimes. At least two of the masquerades, Baroka's diversion of the railroad and the history of his sex life and reputed impotence, are performed not by the characters but by troupes of professional mummers, and the persons portrayed—the old and young wives, the white stranger, and the village chief, first at the height of his powers and then in decline—correspond closely to the masked stereotypes of the Alarinjo tradition. There are, however, a great many complex and telling interweavings between the illusionist idiom of the drama and the "presentational" one of the masque-pageant. Sometimes, as in the mime of the photographer, the two modes may chime perfectly and yet be used to offset one another in the same sequence. Thus the real Baroka enters right on cue, perhaps to indicate that he is a consummate actor in real life. On the other hand, Lakunle is initially reluctant to take the foreigner's part, which identifies him with Western follies, but then, quite contradictorily, throws himself into the role with a zest and freedom from inhibition that suggest he is still deeply African beneath his pompous Western affectations. The masquerades' larger purposes, however, go beyond dramatic effects and narrative detail. Like most masquerades, they reenact and commemorate both remote and recent events that have passed into local legend and become part of the communal memory, and thus turn the verbal drama of a quartet of villagers into a drama of celebration involving the whole village. The events are distanced in space and time, taken impersonally into the community at large, and also lifted out of their circumstantial historical world and given the formalized, timeless air of fable (Ogunba 1975, 47). The masquerades ritualize experience, most noticeably in their ceremonial marking of sexual milestones: for example, Sadiku's menopausal mime of Baroka, which ironically coincides with his theft of Sidi's virginity, and the closing procession and bridal masque, with its anticipation of childbirth. The play is a festival drama that compresses the whole reproductive cycle into a single day, a comic rite of sexual passage that travels from the "Morning" of Lakunle's adolescent sentimental romance via the crossroads of "Noon" to the intrigues and betrayals of adult sexuality in "Night," and beyond to a new dawn, prefigured by the child in Sidi's womb.

Soyinka's closing stage directions recommend that the "festive air" be "fully persuasive," and the term "festive comedy," with its associations of *Twelfth Night* and *A Midsummer Night's Dream*, is a fitting one for *The Lion and the Jewel* and the first Jero play. These two plays are distinguished by their celebrative idiom, by their lightness of touch and disinterested joy in exuberant comic characterization, and by a quirky, independent-minded fidelity to experience that insists on keeping all options open and allows characters to outgrow bland stereotypes and simplistic formulas such as that of stagnant traditionalism versus progressive Westernization. When Soyinka went back to comedy after the tragic dramas of the 1960s and early 1970s, the result was the harsh, embittered satire of the second Jero play and *Opera Wonyosi*. The light-hearted dramatic entertainment of the early years is a mode to which, except in occasional revue sketches, he has not returned.

Chapter 4
Ritual Theater: A Universal Idiom

Soyinka has said that the task of the dramatist is to "find a language which expresses the right sources of thought and values, and merges them into a universal idiom such as ritual" (*ADO*, 60), and in the plays discussed in this chapter ritual has something of this universality. In *The Strong Breed* an annual purification rite of the Niger Delta is cross-referenced, albeit elusively, with the Christian Passion, and a xenophobic village society displays the same guilt-ridden hysteria, the readiness to sacrifice the stranger within, associated with modern nation-states. Soyinka's adaptation of *The Bacchae* is an exercise in comparative mythology that reinterprets Euripides' play in the light of Yoruba cosmology, and *Death and the King's Horseman* and *Kongi's Harvest* explore the relevance of indigenous ceremonial traditions in colonial and postcolonial political contexts, respectively. First and foremost, however, the rituality of these plays is deeply African. Each play depicts an interruption, involving a substitution, of an indigenous ritual sequence, and it is often through this very diversion and corruption of the rite from its proper course that it acquires a "universal" and largely spurious archetypal identity. Nowhere is this more in evidence than in the somber one-acter, *The Strong Breed* published in *Three Plays* in 1963.

The eponymous heroes of this play are the families of hereditary carriers who year after year ceremonially carry away from the community the accumulated pollutions of the past twelve months. Eman, who earlier in his life abruptly departed from his home in the middle of an initiation rite, has now totally absconded from his native village and ritual heredity following his wife's death (like his own mother's) in childbirth. He has found employment as a teacher and healer in another village and formed a relationship with Sunma, the daughter of the head man Jaguna, but as the New Year approaches in an atmosphere of great menace and foreboding, it transpires that he has not escaped his ritual duty. Because this village is unable to produce its own voluntary carriers, strangers are forced into the role, and Eman, because he harbors the only other resident stranger, the terrified idiot boy Ifada, finds himself pressed as a substitute into the familiar task. But the rite goes disastrously wrong when Eman, who has misunderstood its very different character in this version, panics and flees from its unexpected cruelties, and it ends with his pursuit through the village and his death in an animal trap on the path to the river. During the fatal pursuit episodes from the past flash through his mind and are enacted on the stage. In the final flashback Eman is symbolically confronted by his dead father, who warns him away from the river (now, of death) to which he carries the year's "evils" for the last time. At Eman's death Ifada consoles the broken Sunma while her pitiless father and his henchman Oroge are deserted by the remorse-stricken villagers.

Soyinka stated in his introduction to the film version of *The Strong Breed* that "the carrier is, in its original sense, the scapegoat" (Dundon, 21), and in the course of the play the figure of the scapegoat in its familiar Judeo-Christian form is seen to evolve, through the acquisition of corrupt accretions, from what appear to be variant models of the African carrier: the Yoruba *akogun*, the Eyo Adimu, and the Ijaw Amagba.[1] Though Eman, like the Christian Redeemer whose name his own is an abbreviation of, is a healer who suffers an arboreal crucifixion,[2] the play's Christian overtones are given no clinching finality. The vaguely archetypal, chronic illness of the sinister girl who dumps her effigy at Eman's doorstep and betrays him into the hands of his captors seems at times to signify incorrigible evil, or Original Sin (she refuses medical aid from Eman's clinic), yet Sunma insists that the surrounding wickedness, instanced in her father's vicious temper and the cowardly coercion of idiots as well as in the girl's treachery, is a peculiarly local and untypical phenomenon from which she and Eman are exempt (*CP1*, 121). Moreover, the African carrier is not specifically a sin carrier who, as in the Christian archetype, bears away the sins of the world by an abruptly sacrificial death. Traditional West African belief makes no allowance for unprovoked misfortunes, so the collective "ills" or "evils" shouldered by the carrier constitute the interdependent burdens of the community's sins and subsequent sorrows, often in the form of sickness. (In his discussion of the Eyo carrier Soyinka equates the year's "evils" with the burden of "unhappiness" and "disease" [Gates, 40].) Most important, in the original carrier rite the year's ills are projected, through cursing and touch, into the material object being carried, not violently alienated from the community and physically embodied in the person of the conveyor, as in the case of the scapegoat, and the carrier, though partly infected and stigmatized by his ordeal, is not slain like the latter but is allowed to return to the community. In Jaguna's perversion of the rite, however, the protagonist is made to suffer the scapegoat's defilement, mortification, and final immolation, which, in the carrier rite proper, are inflicted on the transported effigy.[3]

As in the twisted dialectic of the scapegoat, the expiator wholly exteriorizes his guilt onto the sacrificial offering and then defines this newly purified identity, antithetically, by reference to it, thus breaking the moral identification of the community with the ritual vehicle. The debased rite of the play thus denies all kinship with the iniquities entrusted to a stranger while itself being of their very essence, and even Sunma is not exempt from this abstract, mechanical process. Her sudden, willful, and gratuitous malevolence toward Ifada as the designated carrier—"It is almost as if you are forcing yourself to hate him," says Eman (*CP1*, 117)—has both a human and a ritual explanation: Sunma is hardening her heart toward one whom she can no longer help, and she is also going through the ritual motions and mechanics of insult and anathematization, the process of redefinition by dissociation that will rid her of her personal share in the collective guilt and purchase a token, theoretic innocence. In this most supremely selfish of ritual practices, not only do the villagers force an innocent to expiate their transgressions and undertake their ordeals for them but they have dispersed the customary single public effigy into a number of private effigies from which, as the sick girl warns Ifada, purely personal cures are sought. Their elders promote this general desire for merely mechanical relief in a spirit of cowardly expediency and self-preservation, and the local idiot, far from having any religious value as sacred to a god, becomes another scapegoat-expendable, a burden to the community who is therefore regarded, with cynical logic, as being best fitted to carry away the burden of its ills. A sense of normality is fleetingly restored by the flashbacks to Eman's father voluntarily carrying the ills to the river as an honorable service in a more traditional version of the rite. Meanwhile, in the present corrupt travesty the perversions, once initiated, multiply themselves: the unsuspecting stranger panics and takes refuge from the villagers' violence in their subsequently recontaminated houses, whereupon the higher price of his death is automatically demanded.

Appropriately for one who depicts a mechanical piacular rite emptied of all moral content, Soyinka is meticulously concerned in this play with the business of ritual mechanics and the excessively literal-minded habits of thinking that inform them. For example, according to the prevailing ritual values, Eman and Ifada are unwittingly contaminated and made "untouchable" as soon as they lay hands upon the sick girl's effigy (as in Eman's house when Ifada, as carrier, takes refuge there). Trapped in these mechanical mental habits, the villagers, once their elders have fixed upon Ifada as carrier, proceed to expropriate their ills to him and, by a paranoid logic, to see everything he does thereafter as evidence of his "evil" and as a justification of their behavior. Soyinka's purpose in these instances is neither to authenticate nor to ridicule ritual superstitions but to create the illusion of a wholly self-apprehended world, experienced from within, and to present its confusion of moral and ritual values in terms of its own customs and beliefs. *The Strong Breed* is one of the few plays by Soyinka to perfect a genuinely inside perspective. In this play the options are the rival moral codes and ritual traditions of different villages, relative only to one another, and no "enlightened" or "modern" external view, closer to the dramatist's own, is brought to bear critically upon them, as by Igwezu in *The Swamp Dwellers* or by Olunde in the later *Death and the King's Horseman*. (Eman comes not from the city or abroad but from another village.) The only critical self-apprehension is provided, ironically, by the cynical expediency of the ruling elders. So long as it does not become public knowledge, they are prepared to overlook a broken taboo (Ifada's entry into Eman's house and, in one of the flashbacks, the trespass into the male initiation grove of Eman's childhood sweetheart Omae), suggesting that they themselves do not believe wholeheartedly in the ritual but, to preserve their own interests, perfunctorily go through its morally meaningless motions. At the same time, the extreme, paranoid literalism of the villagers serves as a vehicle for Soyinka's own more rarefied moral symbolism. The mechanical business with the effigy, by identifying Eman with Ifada, anticipates the fulfillment of his ritual destiny, and Soyinka turns to symbolic advantage the idea that the ritual protagonist is also a literal carrier of infections that can be transmitted to others. In a society where no one is willing to bear responsibility, guilt remains trapped in the community, symbolized by the tainted effigy that, in a vicious circle of contagion, is passed around from person to person and avoided like a disease.

The ending of *The Strong Breed* is ambivalent, and the mood one of grimly guarded hope. Though Eman sacrifices himself in Christ-like fashion for an ungrateful community, the redemptive value and regenerative potential of his voluntary substitution for Ifada are thrown into doubt by his peculiar lack of both knowledge and volition. Soyinka has observed that, like the carrier in Eman's native village, the Eyo carrier "knows very well what is going to become of him" (Gates, 41). Yet it is clear from Eman's blithe references to "mummers and masquerades" and his failure to heed Sunma's warnings that he mistakes the nature of the approaching rite, in which the performer does not, in Jaguna's words, "carry suffering like a hat" (*CP1*, 131). Eman in his ordeal is in fact willing only when unwitting, and then, when witting, is unwilling. Paradoxically, his "strong breed" charisma and will power are most in evidence during the initial substitution, when he does not know what is to happen to him. After his subsequent enlightenment and flight from the beating disrupt the ceremony and so doom him, he becomes more like an ordinary human carrier, though with the important difference that he too now is a coerced victim; his sacrifice transmits no more moral, redemptive energy to the community than Ifada's. (The latter would have been made "willing" only through the application of sense-dulling drugs.) Perhaps because Soyinka takes too much time creating tension in the first part of the play, the symbolism of the closing flashbacks is overcompressed; the final one, in which Eman and his dead father converge upon the river with their respective burdens, seems to invite the conclusion that the son has been drawn to embrace his father's fate and dies in a knowing act of filial fidelity. In reality, however, Eman's martyrdom has little in common either with the average carrier's protracted psychosomatic atrophy,[4] or with the special survival capacity of his father and all the "strong breed." The primary symbolic point of the final meeting by the river is simply that Eman is about to join his father in the world of the dead. And yet there is a sense in which Eman keeps faith with his father by reinfusing into the debased rite some of the communally oriented morality of the original. His flight in midstream is not a choice of death but a decision to interrupt and halt the ritual process, because its supervision by corrupt authorities and the neophyte's unwillingness deprive it of its moral efficacy and so render it valueless. Eman's attempted curtailment of the ceremony is, in keeping with his ritual heredity, the ultimate altruism, springing as it does from his conviction that, in its present form, it can be of no benefit to his fellow men.

Eman fails, of course, and his death is of doubtful benefit. But in end-of-year ceremonies the sense of failure that periodicity builds into all ritual and the temporary character of something that has always to be done, cyclically, again are complemented by the New Year's traditional mood of reassessment. Thus the play's ending looks both ways, suggesting simultaneously a shortsighted repetition and a long-term revaluation of the past. On the one hand, the radical effect of the crucified Eman on the villagers and their desertion of their leaders imply that, in the local context, an established order has been shaken; it is possible that the village has cleansed itself, in a final exorcism, of its own cleansing rite as it exists in its present form. Thus Eman's death in the extreme perversion of a tradition meant to rescind the time of a single year may have wound back the clock on decades of corrupt malpractice and may portend their effective annulment as it simultaneously effaces his own 12-year apostasy. On the other hand, when the Old Man, in the flashback, looks into the future, it is only to foresee a repetition of the past in Eman's predestined resumption of the family role and in his wife's death in childbirth. (The strong breed are born out of a death, as the New Year they herald is born from the death of the old.) Jaguna's unmoved response to Eman's death indicates that a grim formality has taken its mechanical course, drained of any moral potency. The self-subverting rite seems to be locked into a vicious and futile cycle of repetition, meaninglessly expiating evil by an act that amasses more: the last purgation of the old year is also the first blood-guilt of the new one. *The Strong Breed* is an open-ended, noncommittal play in which a Brechtian antitragic stance and "complex seeing" of progressive alternatives[5] seem to exist alongside opposing cyclic currents of repeated cruelties, of old punishments triggering off new crimes—the hallmarks of classical tragedies of nemesis and fate.

The carrier reappears in Soyinka's adaptation of *The Bacchae of Euripides: A Communion Rite* (1973), in which his cleansing ceremonies have been perverted, almost beyond recognition, into "unspeakable rites": the metaphoric "killing" of the old year is brutally literalized in the annual flogging to death of an aged slave. The outrage can be ended and expiated only by the equally unwilling sacrifice of its deviser, King Pentheus, who, in one of his many ritual and mythological identities in the play, himself becomes the carrier's dismembered effigy in the rite's crowning perversion and exorcism. In the opening scene the priest Tiresias forlornly hopes that, by taking upon his own shoulders the detritus of the dying year and receiving himself the effigy's merely "symbolic flogging," he will be in a position not only to contain therapeutically the impending rebellion that the abuses have long provoked, but also to personally "taste the ecstasy of rejuvenation long after organizing its ritual" (*CP1*, 243). In this way he hopes to restore to the rite something of the moral logic that restricts its effective power of purgation to ordeals voluntarily undertaken. But as in *The Strong Breed*, the ceremony has for many years been an expression of and an excuse for the evil it is intended to expel: habituated to violence under Pentheus's brutal, disciplinarian regime, the overseers of the rite can no longer "tell the difference between ritual and reality," and the old prophet is, in Dionysos's words, almost "flogged to pieces at the end, like an effigy" (*CP1*, 241, 243). At the death of Pentheus, Tiresias ruefully observes that the perversions had been pushed too far for the merely token violence and symbolic blood of the original rite to have any remaining cleansing power in Thebes: "Perhaps our life-sustaining earth / Demands . . . a little more . . . something, a more / Than token offering for her own needful renewal" (*CP1*, 306).

Soyinka wrote in his introduction to the Methuen playscript that Euripides' drama "belongs to that sparse body of plays which evoke awareness of a particular moment in a people's history, yet imbue that moment with a hovering, eternal presence."[6] Hence, in his figurative treatment of the carrier rite the Old Year is made to mark, epochally, the whole of Pentheus's evil reign, the now moribund military despotism that needs "to embrace a new vitality." The dictator's violation of the rite by striking the old slave-carrier, correspondent here with "the body of the Old Year Dying," is a symbolic summation of his regime's collected desecrations and outrages, about to receive an equally violent purgation (*CP1*, 252, 264). This historical treatment is given a spectacular, apocalyptic orientation, however, by being linked with the vegetation myths of the earth's death and resurrection underlying Western tragedy. "Someone must cleanse the new year of the rot of the old or the world will die," says the Herdsman, and the Old Slave later speaks of nature's impending death, which is assured unless someone is chosen to "bear the burden of decay" (*CP1*, 237, 300). From here it is but a short step to Dionysos's likening of the mesmerized king to "those gods, who yearly must be rent to spring anew," and to Pentheus's admission, rended limb from limb, into an esoteric fraternity of dismembered deities—Dionysos himself, Prometheus, Zagreus, Osiris—and most particularly into Ogun's familiar realm of fruitful disintegration, the numinous hinterland of transition, where he experiences what Tiresias calls "the universal energy of renewal" (*CP1*, 243). Soyinka's Dionysos is in fact another incarnation of Ogun, the creative-destructive, suffering-vindictive deity who perversely turns on his own kin, as Agave is made to do. Connections between the two gods are established through wine, harvest, and the Ogunian hunting liturgy sung to Dionysos by the slaves.

In the play's apocalyptic finale wine spurts from Pentheus's severed head in a miraculous reverse-transubstantiation and floods the fields into a new fertility, turning Euripides' tyrant from an object of divine nemesis—or the pure, motiveless Dionysian joy in destruction—into an offering to the future, his sacrificial blood the revolutionary energy of the new age. In the light of the king's necessary but unwilling entrapment by the god, this transformation appears as forced and wished symbolism, but Soyinka has in this instance forsaken the moral logic of ritual for the political logic of revolution. Out of the delirium of wine came the shedding of blood, which is now converted back to wine and may in turn become blood again. The idea of endlessly repeated, alternating cycles of joy and horror, though suited to the makeshift character of annual purification, is inconsistent with the messianic notion of a final, lasting transformation. The newly militant, postinternment Soyinka was not interested in merely ritualized rebellion—in the containment of revolutionary energies by ritual, as sought by the politically astute Tiresias—but in revolution itself; his introduction argues that Euripides' play is "far too rounded a rite of the communal psyche" to allow the idea of a "next instalment" (*Bacchae*, xi). Soyinka halts, optimistically, at the wine and the rebirth and omits the threnody, thus implying a finality that takes the event out of the fatalistic cycle of alternation and gives it the permanence of a change to end changes. Attempting to close the gap entirely between ritual and reality, his adaptation asks whether societies benefit from any kind of substitutive individual sacrifice other than that in which the ritual form is strategically directed at the actual source of infection—the centers of power and privilege from which the evils emanate.

Soyinka was not entirely satisfied with his *Bacchae*, either in its published or produced form (*ADO*, 65–77), and it is not difficult to see why. Ritual and politics, mysticism and materialism, make strange bedfellows. Psychic liberation from a repressive rationality through religious ecstasy is not the same as revolution, and whatever the historical justification for Soyinka's concept of Dionysos as a liberative force for the oppressed masses, it is as priest of hallucinated, anarchic excitement, not as political insurrectionary, that he impresses in this adaptation. More broadly, Soyinka's Dionysos is a symbolic embodiment of the totality of human and natural experience: he is cosmic and chthonic man, in touch with the earthly powers, or in Soyinka's words, "the effective principle of the mass of people merged together with the forces of the earth" (Gibbs 1987, 71–72). In "The Fourth Stage" Soyinka, referring to "the Dionysian-Apollonian-Promethean essence of Ogun" (*MLAW*, 157), conceives the last as a balanced complex of the other gods' contradictory qualities, and similarly, in *The Bacchae*, Dionysos's "mesh of elements reconciles a warring universe" (*CP1*, 251), acting as a rather bland mediator between the human personality's contradictions, which we deny at our peril. Thus Soyinka's *Bacchae* is not Euripides'. Here the god is all balance, moderation, accommodation, the human Pentheus all narrow limits and unnatural repression. This Dionysos is conceived, Yoruba-fashion, as the primal creative energy source, of which the military megalomaniac's purely political power drive taps only a fraction. In his Ogunian incarnation the deity represents a harmonizing balance of extreme opposites, whereas in Euripides' original he is himself one of those opposites and is in fact a reductive force that acquires disproportionate, murderous power; a force that demands absolute submission once it has been excluded or suppressed. Hence, it is less easy, in this adaptation, to imagine the puritanical Pentheus as himself a potential Dionysiac, secretly craving the indulgences he condemns, and Soyinka's more polarized, dualistic vision is at times dangerously reducible to the dictum "Dionysos good, Pentheus bad." Though he retains the Greek original's closing outrage at Dionysos's heartless, unnatural justice, Soyinka's overriding, determining vision of his play as "a communal feast, a tumultuous celebration of life" (*Bacchae*, xii) precludes any condemnation of Dionysos; the play ends with only a disquieting acceptance, as undiscriminating as the god himself, of his joy and horror, ecstasy and pain, gentleness and ferocity. Even the savage animalism of the god's revenge may be construed, in hopeful political terms, as having healing and regenerative purposes that are not merely part of an endless cycle of atrocities. Soyinka's *Bacchae*, perhaps to offset the bleak view of political violence expressed in his other postinternment writings, is a largely unqualified celebration of Dionysos; Euripides' more skeptical and ambivalent work at least includes a warning that can be used as a weapon against him.

Though *The Bacchae* is generously supplied with festive music and dance, possessed movement and mime, the frenzied lyricism of its language places it closer to poetry than to drama. The earlier *Kongi's Harvest* (1967), though less decisive about the business of getting rid of dictators, is in fact a much more complex and exciting piece of festival drama. At one point in the play Kongi's Organizing Secretary protests that his pageant for the New Yam Festival is being turned into "a Farmer's Cabaret," and it is perhaps useful to think of the play itself in terms of a ceremonial cabaret or ritualized revue. *Kongi's Harvest* is richly composite theater, dispersed panoramically over seven different settings (unusual in Soyinka) and mixing the raucous political satire of part-Brechtian, part-illusionist sketches and songs with the visionary poetics and ritual choreography of the festival. In its festival form drama progresses less through narrative development than through patterns of contrasts and parallels, often substituting stylized tableaus for action, and it is common for plot, never of more than secondary importance, to be swamped in sheer spectacle. Certainly, the plot of *Kongi's Harvest* is no model of clarity, and there has been much critical confusion about what actually happens in the play (notably concerning Kongi's standing at the end). Kongi, the demented modern dictator of the imaginary African state of Isma, has imprisoned and robbed of his political power the traditional paramount chief, Oba Danlola. To legitimize his seizure of power Kongi lays claim to the Oba's spiritual authority through his ritual consecration of the crops of the annual New Yam Festival. (Kongi, in fact, seeks not to replace the Oba, who presents the first fruit, but, with more shocking blasphemy, to assume the role of the supernatural being, the Spirit of the Harvest, to whom the new yam is presented.) Danlola, a wily and engagingly mischievous old rogue, obstinately refuses to surrender his sacred functions and spends a great deal of his imprisonment play-acting and posturing so as to keep Kongi deceived and confused about whether he will attend the ceremony at which power is to be transferred.

The real challenge to Kongi's despotism appears to come not from Danlola, however, but from his nephew and heir, Daodu, the head of a successful farming commune, and from Segi, the strange nightclub hostess and ex-mistress of Kongi with whom Daodu is both sexually involved and in vague political league. In the first part of the play Soyinka's adroit cinematic cross-cutting has the Organizing Secretary scuttling to and fro between two simultaneous settings: Kongi's austere mountain retreat, where a brain trust of intellectual dunces called the Reformed Aweri Fraternity manufacture the leader's image and ideology and ghostwrite his books, and Segi's convivial, voluptuous nightclub, where a mysterious plot against Kongi appears to be afoot. The result of the Organizing Secretary's liaison work is that Danlola is persuaded by his nephew to agree to attend the ceremony in return for a promise from Kongi to pardon five men condemned to death for their part in a recent bomb plot. But the new plot, the aim of which is never clear either to Daodu or to us, evidently misfires when one of the condemned men, Segi's father, escapes and makes an unsuccessful attempt on the dictator's life, thereby losing his own. Because of this apparently unexpected turn of events, the conspirators have to improvise; after Daodu, substituting for his uncle at the festival, has delivered an ironic denunciation of the dictator, to whom he prepares to offer up the new yam, the play's main action ends with a startling coup de theatre: in the ceremony's climactic dance Segi presents to Kongi, aghast with terror, a copper salver containing not the customary yam but, in its place, the decapitated head of her dead father. In the brief epilogue (entitled "Hangover") both the Oba and Kongi's Organizing Secretary are discovered making a dash for the border. It transpires that the ceremony has broken up in confusion and plans are in motion to bundle Daodu and Segi safely out of the country. The Oba, characteristically, has the last word: he has refused to hand over the yam or his priestly functions. Though powerless, he has survived, whereas there is some doubt about how long Kongi will last. In the meantime, the dictator's repressive regime has tightened its grip, and the epilogue, like the prologue scene of the Oba's imprisonment, ends with the jail grating clanging down, only with the difference that the scene is now the public marketplace: now the whole nation is in captivity.

The pervasive presence in *Kongi* of the New Yam ceremonials, which are the focal point of the community's religious life, has the effect of polarizing the play's oppositions in favor of tradition. The still virile, lineaged Oba, who at least makes an altruistic show of identification with the community, seems better fitted to safeguard its continuity and to renew its human and natural fertility, by neutralizing the poison in the yam's root, than the warped and ascetic Kongi, who merely desires to incorporate the rite into his paternalist personality cult and who himself personifies the poison in the new body politic. Deviously self-seeking though he may be, Oba Danlola represents a broad-humored, humanist native tradition that Kongi has cast aside for rootless, made-up ideologies, the invented "isms" of his new Isma. Without the tempering continuity of tradition, there is only the power-crazed egomania of the modern dictator who grotesquely supposes everything to originate from himself and to exist only by his permission: "How dead? I don't remember condemning any of them to death" (*CP2*, 90). Danlola's earthy, bawdy hedonism at least keeps him realistically in touch with events, cognizant of the traditional need for a periodic change of rulers,[7] and free from the megalomaniacal delusion of immortality that names institutions and dates calendars from current regimes. The Oba is also, both culturally and linguistically, a more splendid creature than Kongi; richly laced with proverbs and riddling allusions, his verse-speech is supple and endlessly resourceful. Kongi's academic hacks speak in the shrill, sterile jargon of the political scientist, and the dictator himself is a notorious verbicide, a harvester of hate and death in words as well as in men: in the name of "positive scientificism" his African newspeak euphemizes hanging into "an exercise in scientific exorcism," and the ruthless extermination of opponents into "Harmony" (CP2, 78).[8]

Kongi, however, reveals qualifying continuities that, accentuated by the cross-cutting between scenes, make impossible any facile oppositions, whether of modernism to tradition (Kongi and Danlola) or of reactionary power to revolutionary challenge (Kongi and Daodu).[9] Danlola's outmoded autocracy may have restrained its rapacity—"They say we took too much silk. . . . We never ate the silkworm" (CP2, 66)—but it was still an absolutist, exploitative order that ruled the people by spiritual and magical power, through the obscurantism of custom and taboo rather than brute military force. Kongi terrorizes with jails and gallows, Danlola with the more ancient but no less awesome power of the royal curse; both men are dissuaded from using their respective weapons only by circles of professional flatterers who, to varying extents, insulate them from reality. Danlola is more concerned with the effect of Kongi's depredations upon his own comforts than upon his people and is no less prone than Kongi to the vice of identifying his personality with the nation, the only difference being that his personality is vivacious and hedonistic while the other man's is joyless and ascetic. Kongi and Danlola are in reality not opposites but mirror images. Both are in love with public adoration and the exercise of power on a super-human level; both are preoccupied with protocol, ceremony, and image-building; and both are vain and pompous poseurs who, as Daodu observes, love to act roles and strike attitudes, whether in visual poses for photographers (Kongi) or in verbal ones for sycophantic courtiers (Danlola). The Oba's petty irascibility and peevish tantrums over meager ceremonial provisions (none the less real for being acted) are the natural counterparts of Kongi's hysterical epileptic rages. Kongi and Danlola are products of the same continuous king-making process in African tradition: the dictator's official doctrine of "Enlightened Ritualism" is but an outgrowth from the traditional ruler's priestly mystique, his vainglory is an offshoot of the Oba's decadence, and the high-sounding nonsense of the new Reformed Aweri Fraternity is only a revamped version of the oracular "senile pronouncements" of the old Ogbo Aweri. As with the uncle, so with the nephew. In a 1970 interview Soyinka spoke of "a kind of doctrinal opposition" between Daodu's farming commune and Kongi's regimented "Carpenters' Brigade,"[10] but these largely symbolic and theoretical oppositions (plenitude and nourishment on one side, starvation tactics on the other) have no real practical issue. Though he takes refuge in sensual indulgence from the rival misrules of the two discredited leaders, becoming a sort of modern Prince Hal of the nightclubs, Daodu, as prince and modern agriculturalist, has a foot in the worlds of both men and is not absolutely opposed to either. He out-Kongis Kongi in the coining of slogans and is himself tainted with Kongi's messianism by festival celebrants who cast him as savior at his second coming. Indeed, it is his own expensive fertilizers that coax the prizewinning "monster yam," symbolic of Kongi's abnormal regime, from the soil of Isma. (Daodu refers to Kongi at one point as a *"farmer* of terror.") Significantly Daodu's most decisive act in the play is a Kongi-like piece of iconoclasm: impatient with his uncle's nostalgic ceremonial pranks, he tears his drum to indicate that firm action against the foe is not to be found in dreams of the past but in the dictator's own methods.

Kongi is subtle and searching theater, powerful in performance, and its main strengths are its verbal wit, its satire on dictatorship, and its striking theatrical devices. It remains, however, a politically vague and ritually indecisive play. Soyinka said in a 1966 interview that it was about "Power, Pomp and Ecstasy."[11] Though Kongi's power and Danlola's pomp are well caught, the ecstasy component, in the form of the more numinous Daodu-Segi entente, never quite materializes. The nightclub's weird cocktail of gentlemen-farmers, rehabilitated prostitutes, layabouts, and thugs makes it an unusual base for subversion, and Daodu himself is a shadowy figure, of undefined political aims and affiliations, and an ineffective challenger who offers no viable leadership alternative. The stage directions for the festival request "plenty of bustle and activity as if a great preparation were in progress" (*CP2*, 101), but exactly what it is, in political terms, that is being prepared is left unclear; the climactic event is itself eclipsed by the prolonged atmospherics of excited preparation. In plot terms, the climax of the festival merely provides an apt occasion for the assassination of the tyrant when, in supreme, taboo-breaking hubris, he is about to bite into the new yam and take on the ironic and, in this case, deathly role of Spirit of the Harvest. But the transposition of this final confrontation into a dance form overloaded with ceremonial motifs obscures the meaning of what ought to be the most dramatically exciting episode in the play. We do not recognize the stage head that is substituted for the yam because Segi's father never appears on stage, and it remains to ask what is the meaning of this puzzling melodramatic gesture. A demonstration to Kongi of the monstrous nature of his own appetites by ironically inviting him to or accusing him of literal or figurative cannibalism? Or a perverted fertility rite and reaping of sexual revenge by a violent ex-mistress who is herself described, by the Oba, as "a right cannibal of the female species"? No matter how operatic or chorically Brechtian the acting style,[12] the commune farmer and hostess are unequal to their mythological roles, as Spirit of the Harvest and Earth Mother, in the Yoruba masque. In the stylized tableaus of the nightclub scene they have to step, antithetically, out of character to assume their allegoric guises; the normally benevolent Daodu preaches a program of hatred, and the destructive Segi, functioning as Feminine Principle, counsels universal love. The dialogue's stilted, ritualized sexuality subsumes seasonal and revolutionary reawakenings into human passion in a way that sounds odd in its seamily realistic setting and alongside the language of realpolitik (Daodu: "I am swollen like prize yam under earth"; Segi: "I am soil from the final rains" [CP2, 98].)

According to the stage directions, the climactic orgiastic feast "permits no spectators, only celebrants" (CP2, 130). The play's own audience, however, is more rather than less distanced than is usual at Soyinka's ritual dramas, partly because in Kongi the satire is weighted as heavily against the barren ritualism of tradition as against Kongi's empty "progressive" modernism. The Oba's oriki praise-chants are put to ironic use both by and against him, thus exposing the petty pomp and vanity that often attach themselves to ceremonial displays; similarly sardonic barbs are aimed at the original Ogbo Aweri as well as at the "Reformed" version. Though there is a dim sense of loss in Kongi, the traditional past is not idealized or looked to as a specific source of value, and the partly satiric treatment that denies ritual any ultimate worth in the play problematizes its seeming reauthentification in the finale. Soyinka is also, dramaturgically, skeptical and uncertain of his ritual contexts in this work. Though he is not entirely prepared to contain and resolve its ritualism within a naturalistic and rational-critical idiom, as in the other plays discussed in this chapter, neither is he ready, as in the plays discussed in the next chapter, to explode that idiom and allow the ritualistic elements to control and refashion the drama according to their own interior, autonomous design.

Interrupted ritual and substitution are again the subjects in Death and the King's Horseman (1975), only here the drama is based upon an actual historical incident. In January 1945, a month after the death of the Oyo king, or Alafin, his horseman, called Elesin, was to join his royal master by committing suicide but was prevented from fulfilling his ritual duty by the British district officer, Capt. J. A. MacKenzie, whereupon Elesin's son Murana, a trader living in Ghana, returned home and took the unprecedented step of dying in his father's place. Partly to debate the different cultural values attached to sacrifice by the British and Yoruba, Soyinka moves the episode back into World War II and makes it coincide with a royal visit by the Prince of Wales, who is shown risking his life to make a gesture of solidarity with his imperial subjects. More innovatively, Soyinka turns Elesin's son, who in reality was still very much part of the local traditional world, into a Western-educated doctor. Olunde, as he is called in the play, was smuggled abroad for medical training at the instigation of the district officer and in the teeth of his father's opposition. Four years later, he has returned to complete his father's burial rites. The district officer and his wife, here called Simon and Jane Pilkings, are two well-meaning but misguided and myopic cultural chauvinists, given rather short shrift by Soyinka's slight characterization. They can make sense of self-sacrifice in secular and empirical contexts, where there is some practical, commonsense benefit or safeguard for the community (as in the case of a British captain who blows himself up with his ship to prevent lethal gases poisoning the coastal population), but not as an act performed to maintain some nebulous metaphysical continuum. Though capable of construing "murderous defeats" in the random slaughter of war as "strategic victories," they have no sense of the moral triumph of the controlled individual sacrifice, with its corollary principle that some must die so that others may live. Too obtuse to penetrate the paradoxes of Yoruba proverbs and crassly insensitive to native custom and belief, the Pilkingses' automatic inclination is, as Olunde tells Jane, to trivialize and desecrate what they do not understand; their irreverent tango in parodic egungun costume at the Resident's masked ball shocks even their most Westernized native staff.

Soyinka's most crucial alteration, however, is the addition of a wedding to Elesin's funeral ceremony. On his last night on earth the king's horseman succumbs to a sudden desire for a beautiful young girl who is betrothed to the son of the market-mother Iyaloja. Though shocked and full of foreboding, Iyaloja accedes to his request and offers up the virgin bride to his peremptory lust. The Elesin argues, disingenuously, that the unburdening of his physical desire will leave him lighter for his journey into the spiritual world and that the rare fruit of this union, "neither of this world nor the next," will be a liminal child of passage: the impregnation of the virgin, by the dying, with the unborn represents in miniature the whole Yoruba metaphysical triangle, the seamless human-spirit continuum that is to be kept intact by Elesin's transitional crossing. In reality, however, physical passion has no place in the metaphysical task of transition, which calls rather for abstinence, not the sensual indulgence that confounds the will. Because Elesin's mind is not on the other world, the "weight of longing" on his "earth-held limbs" ties him more strongly to this one. The rite is delayed, then aborted, and he who was about to join the ancestors ends by flouting their traditions and unnaturally reversing the normal cycle of existence. Properly, "the parent shoot withers to give sap to the younger" (SP, 207, 212), but here it seeks to renew the being it should relinquish. In the Yoruba worldview, which links everything in human experience, this refusal to go forward, sacrificially, into another existence breaks the bonds by which the old existence is regenerated, thus endangering the lives of the unripe (Olunde) and the unborn: "Who are you to open a new life," Iyaloja upbraids Elesin, "when you dared not open the door to a new existence?" (SP, 210). As in The Strong Breed, the initial breaking of precedent triggers a chain reaction that multiplies the ritual perversions, culminating here in Olunde's surrogate suicide. In the last scene Iyaloja hurls back at the horseman his earlier proverbs of strength and daring and presents to him in the white man's prison the body of his son, whereupon Elesin, unable to bear his shame and look upon the bitter fruit of his indecision, strangles himself with his chains. His suicide, however, is a futile, involuntary surrender to despair, not a purposive ritual act; it has therefore no sacrificial or restitutive value, and it comes in any case too late, after his son has charted the transitional passage for him. Before this vibrant drama is done, the whole cast has been drawn into the Alafin's funeral dance (even the Pilkingses become part of what they travesty); it ends with the young bride, under Iyaloja's guidance, sealing the eyes of her husband of a single night and turning to face what little is left of the future now that "strangers [have] tilted the world from its course" (SP, 218).

Mainly to discourage facile readings of his play as a mere clash of cultures, Soyinka stresses, in his author's note to the text, the merely catalytic role of the white official and the largely metaphysical nature of the confrontation. Certainly, on the surface, metaphysics is well to the fore, and history marginalized, in this play. Elesin's immediate task is to ease the passage of the late king's spirit toward his ancestors and ensure that it is not left aimlessly wandering in the pathway between worlds, cursing the living. His more momentous undertaking, of which this is a part and on which depends the continuation of his community and the renewal of the whole Yoruba world, is intercession with the ancestors and negotiation of a passage between them and the living. The closeness of the historical and numinous worlds is indicated in the play, however, by a set and script full of passages and pathfinding images and by the expression of otherworldly glory in the material form of rich clothes and sweetmeats, later reduced at the scene of Elesin's dishonor to rags of shame, dung droppings, and "left-overs." Such is the total interdependence of these two worlds, in fact, that Elesin's failure to die, and so keep faith with his ancestors, spells the death of the ancestral past and the betrayal of the entire community of humans and spirits existing over the whole of time. Consequently, the metaphysics acquires epochal dimensions, and the ritualized transition between phenomenological worlds— this world and the next—becomes entangled with the decisive historical transition from the indigenous to the colonial world. The inversion of a family transition signals the historical end of that tradition: Olunde dies young and heirless, so there will be no more Elesins, and the last Elesin is himself a mere "left-over" from an order of undiluted Yoruba values. Once its complex metaphysical worldview has been stripped away, this order is left "floundering in a blind future" and "tumbling in the void of strangers" (*SP*, 218). In Iyaloja's climactic denunciation of the hapless horseman, Yoruba religion is holed to rags, its cultural sweetmeats gnawed to bones, and its final historical home, it seems, is to be the spiritual rag-and-bone shop of the colonial culture, the theological vacuum represented by the Pilkingses. Elesin becomes, in the market-daughters' phrase for the racially emasculated colonial policeman Amusa, an "eater of white left-overs" (*SP*, 179), one who abandons what is left *to* him by his own dead for what is merely left *over* or left *behind* by a colonial culture that no longer has any use for it ("I have no father, eater of left-overs," Olunde rebuts him). He also becomes, significantly, a speaker of white prose. After the curtailment of the rite Elesin's extravagantly proverbial, ceremonial verse disappears with the worldview that it expresses and is replaced by a flat lusterless prose full of philosophical rationalizations and excuses, including the ultimate blasphemy that colonialism might be divinely ordained, that "there might be the hand of the gods in a stranger's intervention" (*SP*, 212).

Criticism of *Horseman* has ranged from metaphysical interpretations of varying degrees of orthodoxy—some along Soyinka's own guidelines and some with added historical incidentals[13]—to dissenting "leftocratic" political readings. The latter have construed the work as essentially historical drama in which Soyinka privileges a static, totalitarian feudal culture over more mobile and egalitarian alternatives and uses a distracting metaphysics to suppress social and ideological differences and claim a false cultural unanimity for Oyo society.[14] This conception is not entirely just. Unashamedly hierarchic though the play is in its interlarding of social and royal destinies, it does contain an implied critique of feudal leadership elites and ideologies, and the fact that the Western-educated Olunde, the play's agent of change, has to take charge of the ritual practice argues the need for its modification and redefinition in a changing world. Elesin is no paragon of Oyo courage and integrity but a pretender and prevaricator who mistakes honor for cheap worldly pleasures—he "thought it [honor] was palm wine and drained its contents to the final drop," runs one ambiguous praise-song (SP, 154)—and whose speech is so much self-deceiving bombast, full of swaggering, hubristic recitals of other men's indecisions and death anxieties. Furthermore, that Oyo society in the play is not all harmony and inner cohesion is evident from the suggestions of class friction in the dialogue between Elesin and the market women, who blame, warn, and suspect as well as adulate. Yet the ease with which these tensions are subsumed under the common religious beliefs and preoccupations that unite the society then begs the question of how homogeneous, historically, Oyo attitudes really were in religious matters such as ritual sacrifice. Soyinka's critical response to "leftocratic" readings of his play has been elusive and ambivalent, sometimes calling upon historical verisimilitude and sometimes sacrificing it for the sake of larger imaginative truths. In his defense of the market women's language he pleads historical authenticity, claiming that their language is adequate to its own self-apprehended time and place—that is, to a world presented as it saw itself, rather than in terms of alien cultural and social values taken from a later period in Nigerian history (ADO, 126). On other occasions, as in his refusal "to make Olunde reject suicide because of 'overseas' enlightenment" (ADO, 128), he urges polemical necessity. As numerous commentators have observed, the failure of a horseman to accompany a dead Alafin had ceased to have grave religious implications long before World War II, and a Westernized intellectual of the 1940s would have been much more likely to dissociate himself from the business of ritual suicide.[15] Clearly, Olunde's act is important to Soyinka as a symbolic demonstration—by one who has experienced at source both the native and colonial cultures—of native culture's superior ability to handle its crises through autochthonous resources, and so the act is morally and imaginatively true. It is an expression of faith in the essence of a culture, and specifically in an ethic of sacrifice, that has tenaciously survived the influences of Western education.

These poetic-historical ambivalences are also present in the play. Recent African philosophers have taken their continent's intellectuals to task for promoting nostalgic myths of primitive cultural unanimity and for opposing false unitary, totalitarian concepts of African society to the West's pluralisms.[16] Soyinka's own mythical distillations from history seem to do scant justice to the heterogeneity inherent in African, as in most other, value systems. Oyo society in *Horseman* is very much a world apart, impregnable and untiltable, "never wrenched from its true course" (*SP*, 149); the impression is of a pristine, indivisible, perfectly intact order, not yet hybridized by change. Indeed, at the start of the play there is a sense of two quite separate and exclusive worlds that are remarkably unsynchronized for a colonial situation, bridged only by the ridiculous native policeman, and about to be jolted out of their mutual ignorance and brought abruptly into collision. On the one side, the Yoruba world is oddly impervious to changes resulting from the colonial invasion. In the first scene the Praise-Singer's potted version of Oyo history mentions wars and slavery but omits white colonialism (Oyo society, Elesin boasts, has withstood "the termites of time"), and there is no evidence that the action is taking place in a colonial context. On the other side, the Europeans are reciprocally unaware of native customs still performed under their noses and learn too late to act upon them. And yet this static polarization of worlds is interrogated and belied by patent evidence of long-standing interactions (for example, the market-girls' masterly mimicry of the stereotypes of colonial parochialism in their mocking of Amusa), which prevents the options from being so epochally clear-cut. Plainly, the ritual priorities of Elesin's traditional world have already been deeply affected by colonial materialism, so that his failure is not a sudden isolated episode but the culmination of a gradual historical process. The most important testimony to historical change is, of course, Olunde. Since his own views on sacrifice are defined exclusively in opposition to white ones, it is tempting to see Olunde's choice of suicide—which, being forced upon him by heredity, is in reality no choice at all—as a deliberate rejection of Europe and an assertion of cultural freedom. Nevertheless, despite the moral imperative to maintain a sense of his own society's differentness from Europe, Olunde is yet a force for radical change in that society. Though he has respect for the past, he knows that history, stubbornly resisted by his father in the form of Western education, does not stand still: he expects to resume his overseas medical training after burying his father, for in the completion of this rite the old order that the father embodies is also buried to make way for the new. Soyinka's changing of Olunde into a been-to is not a mere matter of cultural polemics but has to do with the paradoxical nature of the ritual process and its highlighting of one of the author's favorite motifs. In the first chapter of this study I observed that the Yoruba world has traditionally distrusted any excessive stability or stasis and that ritual is one of the key instruments for incorporating modernizing currents of change from one generation to the next, an idea that is given a special clarity by Olunde's expatriation. The crucial paradoxes of *Horseman* are, firstly, that Elesin must cross into the other world to renew this one; and secondly, that when he fails to do this, the son must *die* in the place and manner of his father partly to indicate that he did not intend to *live* like him. The business of the rite of transition is to keep in flux the currents of change from father to son, to bury the past so as to prevent it from becoming permanent, and to maintain a volatile balance of continuity and transition that resists stagnation.

The tragedy in *Horseman* and in each of the plays dealt with here is that the violent alteration of the ceremonial pattern by substitution—Olunde for his father, Eman for Ifada, perhaps even Segi's father for the harvest offering—has the ironic effect of impoverishing the future to which the rite admits passage by wastefully consuming, as the sacrificial offering to that future, one of its most important dimensions. In *The Strong Breed* this dimension is the healing figure himself, whose free mind belongs to a progressive hereafter; in *Kongi*, some rather vaguely embodied humanitarian political ideals; and in *Horseman*, in the person of Olunde, the intermediary between Africa and the West, tradition and colonialism, and the figure personally involved in historical change and best fitted to ease the national rite of passage from colonialism to independence. In each play what should be the end is used up as fuel for the means and the future arrives empty. Nevertheless, the plays appear to valorize these substitutive sacrifices by altruistic outsiders, usually a visionary healer or artist-teacher for whom distance is necessary to focus the disturbing elements of society and bear the burden of its conscience, and whose power to heal society's sicknesses seems to be paradoxically dependent upon his differentness and estrangement from it. Thus in *The Strong Breed* Soyinka unashamedly allocates a ritual form that on his own account emphasizes the common ordinary identity of carrier and community to a hereditary spiritual elite of exceptional beings, a superior aristocracy of suffering far removed from its Eyo prototype.[17] Though *The Bacchae* makes concessions to collective revolutionary fervor, the main tendency in these works is to place communal redemption with the solitary sacrificial heroism of special individuals rather than with shared energies or acts of the corporate will and to link that redemption with a process of personal self-discovery (a pattern repeated in Soyinka's work in both the Ogun myth and the Orphic quest). Eman, who tells Sunma that he can "find consummation . . . only in total loneliness" and when he has "spent [him]self for a total stranger" (*CPI*, 125), finds that his lone quest and 12-year dereliction of his ancestral duty lead him circularly back to the task of removing the pollutions of 12 months: the self's pursuit of meaning is telescoped into communal service, and private expiations are subsumed into public ones. The broad pattern is repeated by Olunde's circular journey of exile and return. The lonely sufferings of these figures in the world outside nurture the disinterested compassion necessary for a renewed, strengthened commitment to their heritage and the recovery and redefinition of its traditions. Linked with the privileging of this charismatic stranger-carrier figure is Soyinka's controversial employment of myth and ritual to express an epochal and apocalyptic view of history. Pulling against the complex currents of interaction between old and new in these works is a more simplistic view of historical change as a series of abrupt leaps forward in the wake of world-shattering, time-annulling individual acts. In the prologue to *Kongi* the elders sing a dirge for the rapid demise of Danlola's effete traditionalism at the hands of Kongi's iconoclastic modernism. In *The Strong Breed* and *The Bacchae* the stock-taking spirit of the New Year and the millenarian and utopian associations with which the expulsion of dying years has habitually invested the carrier motif result in the respective reassessments of the ritual form itself and of the value of the civilization that practices it, metaphorically washing away whole eras and their regimes. In *Horseman* there are strong intimations that a rooted ethnic culture has been pushed from its historical moorings and nudged closer to the sprawling anomie of the modern nation-state by a single, epochal dereliction of duty. Soyinka has, albeit with great power and vision, mythologized history in these dramas, and the continuity-in-transition present in his dramatization of ritual forms is not extended to the historical worldview they are made to serve.

A final word on the rituality of these plays. Their dominant mode is still naturalism, and though ritual is the subject, it is not the structural pivot and formal determinant of the drama. Each work enacts some form of transition, but none of them takes place in the chaotic, scrambled time limbo of the transition rite. In *The Strong Breed*, for example, the time shifts are part of a rational framework of well-signposted, chronologically sequenced flashbacks from a clearly defined present. This conventional discursive structure conveys no loss of temporal bearings, no confusion of reenactment and present occurrence, and the time disturbances do not seem to be intrinsic to the nature of the ritual experience but are there to express a metaphysical point about the protagonist's destiny. The inclusion, in *Horseman*, of scenes presenting Western characters and viewpoints inevitably distances the ritual action and resists any collective catharsis of actors and audience, an effect apparently intended by Soyinka's oddly divisive staging in his 1976 Ife production.[18] Moreover, events that fail to happen, like Elesin's suicide, or that happen offstage and unknown to the audience, like Olunde's, are not the stuff of properly ritual drama. Nothing in the mannered incantation and elegiac dance of *Horseman* matches the terror of the masked dance in *The Road* or the maniacal chanting of *Madmen and Specialists*, and though laughter, in the proper ritual matrix of these two latter plays, is built into the very fabric of catastrophe, in *Horseman* it is cordoned off in the scenes involving Amusa. (Elesin's stagy, ebullient gaiety elicits little real mirth.) *Horseman* talks endlessly of transition, (and in the process the protagonist talks himself out of it), but no more than the other plays dealt with here, the play does not enter performatively into the realm of transition and confront its malign chthonic forces. For such confrontation we must turn to the more intense rituality of Soyinka's esoteric drama.

Chapter 5
Ritual Theater:
Esoteric Soyinka

The Bacchae is subtitled *A communion rite,* and the earlier *Camwood on the Leaves, A Rite of Childhood Passage.* In practice, however, most of Soyinka's early plays use ritual with great economy, dramatizing ceremonies or patterning the action with undercurrents of ritual meaning in what are still, essentially, conventional European theatrical forms. The next group of plays to be discussed are, by contrast, experiments in "total theater": complex choreographies of song and drumming, mimetic and acrobatic dance, stage image and speech, that are meant to be absorbed experientially (in Soyinka's words, "through the pores of the skin"[1]), to be undergone rather than fully understood. There are still echoes of Western drama in these works—of Shakespeare, Brecht, and Jean Giraudoux in *A Dance of the Forests,* Beckett in *The Road,* Arden and the Theater of the Absurd in *Madmen and Specialists*—but their oracular, unresolved climaxes and confusion of esoteric masque and cabaret often appear incoherent according to the expectations of the European stage, with its text-tied dialogue and sequential, illusionist action. Some of this confusion, though not all, has its source in ritual.

If the previous group of plays are "ritual-inclusive" in that rites are a critical plot element in them, then these are more properly described as "ritual-intensive," insofar as they approximate much more closely to the condition of rites per se. In Soyinka's two most esoteric plays, *A Dance of the Forests* and *The Road,* the simulated rites do not so much take place in the plays as the plays take place during the rites, or more precisely, during the interrupted phases of rites—the *agemo* (dissolution) phase of the egungun in the Drivers' Festival of *The Road,* and at the threshold of a tribal gathering ceremony that, in the poetic scheme of *Dance,* corresponds with an epic suspension of history. These plays, in a more immediate sense, *are* the interrupted ritual sequences that *The Strong Breed* and *Horseman* are merely about, and their actions cannot end, and order be restored, until the broken sequence is resumed and completed and the disturbance caused by the interruption repaired: that is, not until the propitiatory death of Professor, which substitutes for the omitted sacrifice in *The Road,* and not until the return in *Dance* of the symbolic Half-Child to its mother and of its restless, revenant father, whose "incompletion denies him rest" (*CP1,* 63), to history. The child's "half-birth" from an arrested 800-year-old pregnancy has been held over from the historical past, as Murano's half-death in the Ogun festival is held over from the recent past. Both processes have to be ritually reactivated so that the performers can be released from their suspended, indeterminate existences between states—into death, in Murano's case, and into birth (if this is what happens) in the Half-Child's—enabling them to complete their unfulfilled destinies.

A *Dance of the Forests* (1960) was produced to coincide with Nigeria's independence celebrations, though, not surprisingly, it was rejected as unsuitable by the official independence committee. Its ceremonial "Gathering of the Tribes" distantly alludes to the euphoric occasion of the founding of a new nation. The councillors of the unnamed town where the tribes are to gather have asked the local deity, Forest Head, to send them illustrious ancestors to mark the occasion, but the deity, by way of a sharp recall to reality, sends not the nostalgic, negritudinous abstractions they desire but the forebears they deserve: two victims of behavior most continuous with their own present crimes and corruptions. Dead Man is the Warrior, who refused to fight in the unjust war of a fictitious twelfth-century emperor, Mata Kharibou, and was castrated and sold into slavery at the behest of Kharibou's demonic queen, Madame Tortoise (whose abduction was the cause of the war, though the "Greeks" in this version did not consider her worth fighting over). Dead Woman is his pregnant wife who subsequently committed suicide and still carries, in limbo, their unborn child. These inglorious dead are chosen because, in the words of the spirit being Aroni in the prologue, they are "linked in violence and blood with four of the living generation" who appear in the opening narrative action: Rola, a vicious whore with a trail of dead lovers and, in her earlier incarnation, Madame Tortoise; the charlatan priest Agboreko, in his previous life the royal Soothsayer who assured Kharibou that the "thought cancer" of independent minds like the Warrior's had no future; the corrupt councillor Adenebi, formerly Historian to Kharibou's court and specious defender of his wars, and the cause of many human deaths by his licensing, in his respective existences, of unseaworthy slave ships and overcrowded passenger lorries; and the carver of the celebration totem, Demoke, who in his former existence as

Court Poet allowed his novice to sustain a broken arm retrieving Madame Tortoise's canary from a rooftop, and who in his present life has committed a much greater crime. Demoke has, in a fit of envious rage, pulled down from the totem pole his apprentice Oremole, who had a better head for heights than himself, and hurled him to his death. Posing as a humble records clerk, Forest Head proceeds to probe and unmask the criminal lusts and hypocrisies of the human four and leads them on a spiritual journey deep into the forest where, at the masque of the court of Mata Kharibou, they witness the misdeeds of their past selves and are given the opportunity to make the atonements that are necessary if new beginnings, at both the personal and national levels, are to be possible. By the end of their night in the forest the guilt-ridden Demoke, the first to confess his crime, has made expiation by carrying a sacrificial basket to the top of his totem, and even Rola is "chastened," touched by "the same lightning that seared us through the head" (*CP1,* 73–74). Only the contemptible Adenebi, who has crept quietly away, refuses to admit anything and remains beyond redemption.

If this were the sole or even a seminal narrative thread of *Dance,* the play would be a very straightforward affair. But in this most uncentered of works, there is no discernible main character or plot line, and critics have been at a loss to say what kind of play it is, or if it is a play at all and not a pageant, carnival, or festival. In addition to the random single appearances of a superabundance of anonymous functionaries, villagers, and courtiers, the human action is punctuated by the exchanges and interventions of Yoruba gods, tutelary forest spirits, and other supernatural or allegorical beings; Demoke's story is complicated by the rivalry between two of these figures. The totem carver is naturally a patron of the iron god Ogun, but he has incurred the enmity of another god, Eshuoro, by cutting down, first, the top of the god's sacred silk-cotton tree, and then Eshuoro's devotee Oremole when the latter attempted to decorate the tree as an alternative to decapitating it. The result of this sacrilege is that both gods pursue Demoke through the forest, one to protect and the other to destroy him. But this is not all. No sooner has the curtain fallen on the splendidly theatrical masque of Mata Kharibou when the drama is largely given over to dance, and the dialogue to music and mime. A protracted and tumultuous climax, or series of climaxes, follows, and balletic masquerades, divination, children's games, and all manner of animistic spirits and offended earthly and cosmic powers crowd confusingly onto the stage. Through the three ritually entranced and possessed humans, a pantomime chorus of animals, insects, plants, and elements sings the whole of earth's ruined history. The Ants, representing the anonymous, toiling mass of humanity in the slow march of time, are confronted by three blood-gorged monster Triplets, who present facile political justifications for their exploitation: Posterity, the Greater Cause, and the End that Justifies the Means. Dead Woman is finally delivered of her burden, which now appears on stage as the symbolic Half-Child, apparently signifying the abortive new nation or the entire future of mankind, and performs a grim dance of death with the Triplets. The whole amazing farrago, impossible to summarize, culminates in a frantic tug-of-war for the child between Ogun and a bewilderingly disguised Eshuoro, and in Demoke's returning of the child, in an act that has caused much critical puzzlement, to its mother. After Demoke has made his penitential climb, fallen, and been caught by Ogun, the masque is dissolved and the play ends quietly with the reunification of the forest sojourners and the townspeople who have been searching the forest for them.

No critic, Western or Yoruba, has been able to find a safe and reliable path through Soyinka's bush of ghosts and say what all of this means; the author has confessed to an eccentric use of mythology and "of religious rites . . . to interpret a theme which is quite completely remote from the source of its particular idiom" (Duerden and Pieterse, 170). Much of the play's confusion arises from its setting in the space between worlds, where different orders of reality meet and many different levels of significance intersect. This is recognizable, of course, as that chthonic storehouse of generative and destructive essences, the transitional gulf, in which are found all the uncreated energies and incomplete, ambiguous half-beings who belong, elusively, neither to one world nor the other but are simultaneously of both: thus, the half-human, bibulous tree spirit Murete, and the one-legged intermediary Aroni, with his other invisible foot in the spirit world. The forest, be it Arden or the abode of a thousand demons,[2] is in many folklores ready-made transitional territory, an otherworldly place where miraculous repentances, supernaturally aided recuperations, and the shedding of old selves to discover new ones, as in African initiation rites, are commonplace events. Soyinka's forest, however, is altogether a more comprehensively and exhaustively transitional domain. The eerie, moisture-dripping set, when it is not oozing ripe fertile decay to suggest the chthonic realm's "inchoate matrix of death and becoming" (*MLAW*, 142), is in a constant fury of transformation. Woodland clearing is whisked into primeval glade, and royal court into phantasmagoric forest masque, as the scene metamorphoses from celebration to trial, debate to spectacle, and the characters change from humans into revenant spirits and from disguised into unmasked deities. Language, too, is in transition in its polyphonic shifts from an elevated Shakespearean English, for the timeless mythologized world of the forest, to earthy, vernacular invective for Murete and Rola, and to gnomic incantation in the final numinous masque. The sustaining principle of the zone of transition is a complementarity whereby all things partake in some way of their opposites, signified by the Triplets' and the Half-Child's game of Ampe, which is competitive and yet involves the taking up of imitative mirror positions.[3] Thus, in the masque of Kharibou, the intransigent moral absolutism of the Warrior finds its political counterpart in the despotism of the tyrant he opposes, and the visionary carver-poet, like his barbaric emperor, brooks no rival or critic and murders the minion who refuses to obey. What distinguishes Demoke from the Warrior, however, is a saving ambivalence that enables him to live with the duality of human nature and understand that destruction is a part of creation. Demoke murders to create. Only after killing his apprentice is he able to summon the frenzied demiurge to produce a work of genius, and it is significant that the original inspiration for his totem was the legendary Madame Tortoise: by giving ecstatic expression to her violent, bestial lusts, his totem becomes at once both exorcism and testament. This Ogunian artist is, in his crime and expiation, the model of the ritual protagonist who in the transitional gulf is "stripped of excrescences" (*MLAW*, 149), or in Forest Head's words, is shown "the mirror of original nakedness" (*CP1*, 71) and then, purged by its cleansing violence and suffering, reemerges with some beneficial redemptive wisdom. "It is the kind of action that redeems mankind," says Forest Head of the totem, and in his shielding of the Half-Child in the closing masque Demoke becomes, by way of atonement, the protector of the unfulfilled promise of the future that he has either injured or destroyed in his previous incarnations.

In its passage through the forest's twilit transition zone *Dance* acquires a distinctively ritual temporality. It characters move fluidly in time and sometimes out of it, into the timeless realm of mythology and the suspended, deferred time of the ritual hiatus. The Crier's annunciation that Demoke's crime has closed the link in a chain and, atavistically, completed a cycle has the effect of placing the collected revenants at the end of one era and the beginning of another; this image suggests that the play is loosely structured around a New Year festival, in which ends and beginnings are confused, the participants look both backward and forward, and everything is of the double nature of transition. (The play even includes a comic version of an annual purification rite and a fatuous fumigation of the forest to expel the unwanted dead.) A New Year festival is, in fact, but one strand of a three-pronged motif of the returning dead—the egungun welcoming ceremony and reincarnation are the other two elements—that erodes the distinctions between living humans and ancestors, present and past, and employs ritual masks and disguises to superimpose the human identities of one era upon those of another. Thus even the foothold in a historical present that is given to the audience at the beginning of *Dance* (and denied the audience for *The Road*) turns out to be a slippery one, for Demoke and his companions do not reenact the past from a vantage point in the present but, like Murano in *The Road*, ritually return to it and witness in their personal purifications what are strictly neither historical prototypes nor previous incarnations but innate ancestral selves, heightened by caricature and existing alongside their present personalities. Therefore the remarks of Demoke and Forest Head do not distinguish between Rola's present scandalous life and Madame Tortoise's legendary notoriety, and the dead couple appear not as ghosts but as they were when last alive—filthy and bloated with pregnancy. The past is made physically present, and Dead Woman, who carries both the unborn future and the shameful burden of the past into the limbo between life and death, is a further concrete representation on Soyinka's stage of the coterminous planes of existence in his tripartite Yoruba metaphysic, straddling in her predicament the ancestral, contemporary, and transitional time dimensions that are linked by ritual. In this play it is not a rite that is held over from the past and left hanging (as in *The Road*) but history; yet it is upon the reactivating power of the ritual process that history, in the symbolic form of the Half-Child, depends for its renewed gestation and deliverance.

There is a limit, however, to what can be artistically justified in the name of transitional indeterminacy, and a point at which confusion can become a virtue. By any criteria there are loose ends in this sprawling work. The haphazard frequency of reincarnation is never explained (we hear nothing of the Warrior's other two incarnations); the amount of Murete's stage time is disproportionate to his importance; and the presence of a multitude of peripheral characters is hard to defend. Furthermore, the proverb-foaming "Elder of Sealed Lips," Agboreko, has, unlike the other three humans, committed no specific crime and so seems not quite to belong to the quartet of guilt; he is essentially a satiric character and has not been worked satisfactorily into the pattern of penance. More seriously, the play's transitional metaphysics is puzzling. *Dance* relays little sense of that animist interfusion of all matter and consciousness, and of nature and supernature, that is described in Soyinka's metaphysical essays. Of course, the degree of sheer physical contrivance in the stage representations of the phantasmal, numinous beings of the climactic masque tends automatically to allegorize them into beings of another order, but even within these strict dramaturgical limits, the transitional realm haunted by spirits and essences touches only very slightly the contemporary-historical one peopled by humans. Theoretically—that is, according to Soyinka's reading of Yoruba mythology in *Myth, Literature, and the African World*—the historical cycle of human horrors is tied to a cosmic cycle of violence and reparation (represented, for example, by the Ogun-Obatala complementarity); in the play the gods Ogun and Eshuoro attempt to elevate Demoke's murder of Oremole to the level of this kind of mythic, archetypal struggle between their rival powers. Forest Head resists this attempt, however, and his own stagy confrontation of the present with the past for the purposes of self-knowledge and communal purification is never dramatically integrated with the tedious Ogun-Eshuoro rivalry that constantly disrupts it. In fact, the divine agencies, or essences, lead a life strangely apart from the human action. Ogun and Eshuoro converse only with the tree spirit Murete, and their paths of pursuit keep missing those of the humans, who seem to be oblivious of and unaffected by their presence; the impression is of two quite separate, parallel actions, yoked artificially together by the device of the closing masque. Forest Head is a curiously remote and external Christianized divinity, and his feuding deities are not the complex anthropomorphic emanations of Yoruba belief but uncomplicated Greek-style deities, reductive extrapolations of single, isolated human impulses, whose chief concern is to protect their mortal protégés. The idiosyncratic Eshuoro is more Oro than Eshu, but not much of either; though he demonstrates certain theoretical common ground between these apparent opposites, he is not really an ambivalent deity at all but, on the contrary, represents quite singular forces (notably a blind vindictiveness, perversely wrecking his own trees to punish his foes) at work in human affairs. Finally, it is to be wondered why such an elaborate apparatus is necessary for the apparently simple purposes of thwarting Forest Head's redemptive plans for mankind and further diminishing his capacity for intervention, which has already been shown to be severely limited. Despite his futile knowledge that "nothing is ever altered," that mankind, left to the mercy of his own contradictions, is "a

doomed thing," Forest Head continues the struggle to "torture awareness" from human minds. Soyinka seems to be torn between similar
conflicting impulses: between, on the one hand, a deterministic pessimism that views man as perennially trapped within an infernal cycle of
cruelties and follies and, on the other, a messianic hope that the creative
will of individuals, particularly artists, can break the cycle in
consciousness-raising acts that have a redemptive value for more than
themselves alone.[4] In the symbol of the Half-Child this indeterminacy,
or indecisiveness, has opened up a Pandora's box of possible meanings.

The child is only "half-born," with the spirit-being Aroni as midwife,
and he speaks of his birth as something that is still to happen: "I'll be
born dead." Consequently, critics have been undecided as to whether this
creature is an epically sustained embryo doomed never to be born; a fully
gestated child who is stillborn; or an abiku spirit-child who is born but,
being still half-spirit, is not yet assured of its human existence and may
be doomed to die in infancy and be reborn to die again to the same
mother. (The child's circling of "branded" and "yawning wombs" supports this latter option.) The child may thus be an innocent whose birth
is desirable, or a thing of supernatural evil and demonic will, representing a historical cycle of violence and premature death, whose birth would
be best prevented. Demoke's returning of the child to its mother can be
interpreted, with equal validity, as putting an evil history back where it
belongs; as tampering with the past to reverse the cycle of destiny; or, by
removing the child from transition to the historical past of the slave
trade—where it did not in fact get born—as reactivating history and
keeping it to its former repetitive course. (Certainly, this latter interpretation is the one that the gleeful Eshuoro, who wants to destroy the child,
gives to the placing of the unborn future back into human hands.)[5] The
abiku's ambiguous two-way crossing between unborn and living and
between living and dead may suggest the new nation's passage into
either life or death—or, as in Soyinka's more recent thought, the choice
between artistic creativity and political oppression.[6]

The business of the Half-Child is tantalizingly elliptical, operating on
too many and too tenuously abstract levels, at which the different
possibilities and permutations—historical, mythological, metaphysical—
tend to cancel one another out and dissolve meaning, as if there were some
basic, insurmountable ambivalence or ultimate aporia at the core of the
symbolism. At transitional stages, whether in the personal or national
context, human decisions are bound to be hedged around with qualifications
and dilemmas; no "correct" choice is ever possible. The problem here,

however, is a dramaturgical rather than a moral one. It is simply not clear from the dramatic symbolism what the alternative choices to Demoke's would be and what they would signify (for example, granting custody of the child to Forest Head or to the war god Ogun), or whether there is really any choice at all: "Child, there is no choice but one of suffering," says Forest Head (*CP1*, 61). *Dramatic* is perhaps the wrong word because the abandonment of dialogue at the climax of the final masque is a sign that the play has been plunged into the purest essence, the very quick of transition, at which the action passes from words into music. (Music, says Soyinka, is "the intensive language of transition" [*MLAW*, 36.]) In the audacious, spectacular fantasia of ballet, acrobatics, and mime that follows, the represented action is too intellectually complex to be performed to music alone; the result is a theatrical effect rather than a meaning. There is no denying the dramatic power of these non-narrative elements, and one of Soyinka's talents as a producer of his own plays has been the creation of exciting scenic effects that communicate before (or instead of) being properly understood, acting upon the nerves, senses, and raw intuitions and bypassing the intellect's complex grappling with the paraphernalia of mythology.[7] Yet *Dance* is also a densely, intricately verbal play that makes considerable intellectual claims upon an audience in its poetic allusions and moral debate. Hence expectations are raised that its dilemmas will be resolved in language; these expectations are not fulfilled. In the absence of verbal exposition, the multiple interactions of past, present, and future betokened by the mime of the Half-Child are portended rather than fully apprehended, so that fusion becomes confusion. It is arguable, of course, that the confusion is the point and is meaningful as a complex emanation from a confused and indeterminate situation, namely that of the new state in its chaotic passage from colonialism to independence.[8] Though a formalist would answer that a play about confusion is not the same as a confused or confusing play, *Dance*, in this last view, gives expression to historical confusion by being itself confused and can no more anatomize its dilemmas than Dr. Bero, in *Madmen and Specialists*, can comprehend intellectually the meaning of "As"—because he himself *is* that thing, and it is not expressible in any form other than itself. *Dance* is reflexive and symptomatic of transition (as D. H. Lawrence's *Women in Love* [1920] is of war and social upheaval), not diagnostic of its ills.

In *Dance* Soyinka gives immediacy to epochal change by distilling its essence into the ritual of transition, a remarkable effect achieved only at a great price. Not surprisingly in a work cannibalized from diverse unpublished earlier works, it is bafflingly multidimensional drama, without any focal narrative or character strong enough to hold together its several actions or keep its dense forest of symbols afloat. The play exists in many versions, each with different endings, and takes on many themes: war, art, the environment, history's unlearned lessons. The actors play many roles, and the multiple disguises within the roles involve further duplications of identity.[9] It has been estimated that there are at least four and as many as nine different levels of being on stage, and even an identification parade, itemizing the multiple disguises in an opening tableau to Aroni's prologue, would probably place too great a strain on an audience's memory.[10] *Dance* is a magnificent, impossible theatrical hybrid, a young dramatist's own experimental Half-Child, and is best seen as a huge theatrical laboratory from which less ambitious and more concentrated and discriminating works would soon come. It was, and remains, coterie drama in the tradition of the court masque and religious pageant, having some broad appeal at the level of spectacle but at times rarefied to the point of indigestibility. (The stagy moral debate at Kharibou's court between high-minded moral idealism and unprincipled power recalls a more famous masque, Milton's *Comus* [1637].) It is an occasional work, written for a special ceremonial event, and since its 1960 debut it has not been performed, except in extract, outside of academic circles.

The Road (1965), which, sadly, is also seldom performed, is a work of more concentrated power, and though the decisive events have all taken place before the play begins and are revealed elliptically in its action, the plot is easier of access. The passenger-lorry driver Kotonu, much to the chagrin of his tout Samson, has given up driving after a traumatic accident in which he knocked down the masked egungun celebrant, Murano, at the very moment of his possession by the god Ogun in the Drivers' Festival, an ordeal he survived only by hiding the victim in the back of his lorry and donning the mask himself. In a bewildered state Kotonu transported the body to the local "Aksident Store," where it was stolen by the store's proprietor, the part-visionary, part-mad Professor, a disgraced lay preacher who now earns an exploitative living as a wrecker and a forger of driving licenses. It becomes apparent that Professor, who sleeps in the graveyard to which the road's daily dead are taken, has used necromantic powers to nurse Murano back to partial life and to restore him to his former occupation as a palm-wine tapper—all of this un-known to Kotonu, who did not see Murano's face and does not know that the tapper and the slain celebrant are one and the same. The truth, however, is that Murano is really dead, struck down while in transition between worlds, and his dying has been held over, in a state of mute, suspended animation, from the past, where the incompleted rite is still going on. Thus he cannot speak, his legs are of uneven length to indicate that he has one foot in the spirit world, and he can be seen only in the transitional twilight hours, for to look upon an egungun is to die. This is almost the fate of the would-be driver Salubi at the end of the first act, when Murano mistakes a church funeral requiem for Professor's evensong communion and returns early from his wine tapping, and something much like it is the fate of Professor at the end of the play. The purpose of Professor's strange behavior is to "hold a god captive" and, by means of the wraith-celebrant, to penetrate vicariously the ultimate mystery or esoteric "essence" of death that he calls "the Word." This latter "may be found companion not to life, but Death," and Professor's aim is to know death without actually dying and so "cheat fear by foreknowledge" (*CP1*, 159, 227). Thus he rushes ghoulishly to the scene of accidents not merely to scavenge spare parts for his store but to pluck from the dying the secret of death-in-life. Meanwhile, Kotonu, who harbors suspicions of Professor even while taking over his trade in death at the store, has retained the Ogun mask from the festival accident. At one point this mask, which maintains its inherent energy and power to possess and repossess while the ritual process is still in motion, tumbles from the tailboard of the lorry and reenters the action, catapulting Kotonu and Samson back in time to the accident. In the play's terrifying climax Professor attempts to stage his own private egungun ceremony in place of the usual evening communion. As organ music swells eerily from the nearby church where he once worked, he presents Murano, wearing again the ritual mask and therefore repossessed by the god, to his horrified followers. In the scuffle that follows this sacrilege Professor is knifed to death by one of the thugs, Say Tokyo Kid, and as Murano is released into his death in this world and the god into the spirit one, the dancing figure vanishes, leaving behind a spinning mask. Ogun—if it is his doing—has apparently chosen to revenge himself not upon the driver who killed his celebrant and who has steadfastly refused to run down a dog in offering to him, but upon the perverse quester after forbidden knowledge who has tried to trap a spirit in transition between life and death.

The mountains of exegesis heaped upon this most profound and perplexing of Soyinka's plays have ranged from the astutely sociopolitical to the abstrusely metaphysical, but in fact its diverse subject-matter is remarkably cohesive.[11] Once again, though in a more controlled and deliberate way than in *Dance,* the keynote is transitional indeterminacy,[12] the quality of being peculiar to the liminal phase of the rite of passage in which the celebrant is neither wholly one thing nor the other. Thus once again in a Soyinka play a plurality of identities and multidimensionality reigns. Murano is at once the god Ogun, the Alagemo spirit of flesh dissolution in the prefatory poem, the masquerader knocked down by Kotonu's lorry, killed in the body but still posthumously alive in the spirit—and in his "resurrected" form, the tapper of Ogun's favorite palm wine, which he brings each evening to Professor's communion. Similarly, the murderous Nigerian highway on which he is launched into his limbolike condition is, simultaneously, the existential route of life between rival oblivions, the transitional territory between life and death skirted daily by the drivers, and the pathway of Professor's pseudo-Ogunian quest. At a broader symbolic level, Murano is an image of the new nation-state, suspended between worlds and uncertain of its survival of the historical accident of independence, and the road is the historical track upon which it careers aimlessly forward in its passage between a lost past and an ill-prepared, uncertain future. In this strange and haunting play, in which the religious and numinous touch upon the practical world of automobile parts and forged licenses, the road is at the same time a province and aspect of Ogun—its "Aksident Stores" and drinking shacks are his shrines and tabernacles—and a man-made evil, the product of the corrupt bureaucracies and "fatalistic driving habits" that Soyinka inveighed against in his capacity as a road safety marshal (Gibbs 1983, 29). In social terms the demented Professor is a parasite and predator: in addition to running a profiteering trade in death, he actually engineers road deaths by uprooting signs and forging licenses that put more unqualified, incompetent drivers on the roads; then, with the aid of a venal officer of the law, he falsifies police reports. Yet this exorbitant living is but a material base for vicarious research into the experience of dying, to which end Professor, operating as a kind of spiritual voyeur, attaches himself to daily purveyors of death on the roads. Thus he exploits his drivers and touts on both physical and metaphysical levels ("You neglect my needs and you neglect the Quest," he tells Kotonu). His exploitation is reflected in a multilayered rhetoric that is full of obtuse shifts from the mundane to the esoteric—he regards football pools as cabalistic signs and road crashes as "showers of crystal flying on broken souls"—and that constantly overinterprets and fails to connect with the utterances of more literal-minded interlocutors. Indeed, the play, in its self-conscious reinterpretation of egungun ritual, Ogun mythology, and Christian doctrine in the light of contemporary urban experience, is partly about its own transitionality and exists, like its abducted god, in an interpretative limbo between historical and metaphysical meanings.

The close interpenetration of rival orders of experience is largely the dramaturgical doing of the artist, however, and the historical transitions within the play, from a ritual to a secular order and from a traditional to a technological culture, are in reality anything but smooth. Soyinka wrote in a 1988 essay that "traditional religion is inextricably bound with the technological awareness and development of the society of that religion" and cited the example of the Ogun-worshiping drivers and touts of *The Road* (*ADO, 308*). In fact, the play's Ogun dues-payers feature mainly in Kotonu's roll call of dead drivers, and Samson's solitary sacrifices to Ogun are superstitious insurance payments rather than acts of worship, all of which seems to argue for the god's somewhat obsolete status and to deny him any ultimate value in the skeptical mind of the play. *The Road* is, revealingly, a drama of explosive transitions—of abrupt interruptions and resumptions of the ritual process that involves sudden violent deaths (both Murano's and Professor's); in one of these transitions a too rapidly moving technology, in the form of a hurtling juggernaut, literally collides with a traditional religious practice that clearly has not kept pace with it. In this brutal acceleration of the flow from the old to the new, in which the egungun is left stranded in an ensuing hiatus, the present does not fruitfully interact with the past but simply interrupts it. No collaborative continuity exists here, only chaos and confusion.

Materially, the road symbolizes a very doubtful kind of progress in a new nation reeling from postcolonial culture shock and alienation. It brings automobile technology but not the proper expertise to handle it; education and literacy, but unevenly distributed and leading therefore to the exploitation of the illiterate by the semiliterate; and urbanization, but without the industrialization needed to provide work for the lumpenproletariat of the new shantytowns, thus spawning webs of crime and official corruption. (Professor's store is patronized by a bizarre assortment of touts, thugs, layabouts, local factional chiefs, and corrupt policemen.)[13] The play's roadside community wavers, culturally, between outmoded orthodoxies and experimental novelties—hence its indecisive response to Professor's sacrileges—and, linguistically, between a rich confusion of registers, shifting from debased biblical rhetoric to a racy contemporary pidgin and from Yoruba to American gangster slang. The references to commerce in goods and sex seem to have no place in the drivers' dignified Yoruba dirges, nor Say Tokyo Kid's Hollywood idioms alongside his superstitious awe of timber spirits. This radical divorce from religious tradition is most marked in Professor. Misled by a too hastily and ill-digested Victorianized Christianity that he has never fully renounced, and specifically by its emphasis on the verbal incarnation of divine revelation, Professor is unable to understand the essentials of indigenous religious practice: for example, the nonverbal medium of egungun ritual, and the mysterious, indeterminate power of the Yoruba Ashe (unwritten Word), which, because of its dynamic, priestly power for annunciation and imprecation, has the effective status of a deed and is not to be found in the debris of abandoned print where Professor searches for it. Most important, he is hampered by an obsessive Christian typology and divisive eschatology that have caused him to lose touch with the complex interflow of life and death in the Yoruba worldview. "The Word," he insists, is to be found "where ascent is broken and a winged secret plummets back to earth" (*CP1*, 187): that is, where the elevation of Murano as celebrant to spirit status, through possession, is interrupted and he is left suspended in a half-human, half-divine state. But the scene of this fracture is, paradoxically, also the area of supreme connectedness, for the road is Ogun's terrain of transition, the ritualized space where boundaries disappear and all the traffic of existence holistically converges. The purpose of the egungun is to socialize death by putting ancestral spirits in communion with the living, but the egocentric Professor seeks to appropriate, compartmentally, a part of the life-death continuum (the death phase) for his own private revelation in life. In his communion service he subsequently confuses the functions of Christian and Ogun priests and the Alashe (priest of the agemo) and, unqualified to be any of these, blasphemously parodies all three. In the place of the Christian palm symbol he offers palm wine to Ogun, a double blasphemy because he is making a thanks offering to the god for his unintended gift of his celebrant. As "companion to death," the word made flesh is now associated with its decomposition and the priest-messiah, reversing the sacrificial pattern, arranges for others to die so that he may live to savor, vicariously, the knowledge of death. Finally, as mock-Alashe, he keeps personal custody of a deity who is customarily shared; attempting the power of a god by holding one captive, he turns his market (the agemo priest is also an Oloja, or lord of the market) into a roadside shack full of scavenged loot.[14] Whether these violently sundered elements can be brought back into relationship with the resumption of the ritual sequence violated by Professor—whether, for example, the sensitive and life-revering Kotonu will be able to reconcile the road's senseless slaughter with traditional beliefs—is left an open question.

The violence of transition in the play is perhaps most acutely felt in its treatment of time. *The Road* covers a single day, with time lapses curtailed even to the extent of performing without an interval, but this outward adherence to the classical unities is deceptive. The second part of the play, though its duration is only a single twilight hour, takes longer to perform because so much time is spent reproducing the accidents of the past week. These are piled up so thick and fast—the Drivers' Festival, the rotten bridge, Sergeant Burma's death, the morning's crash at the uprooted sign—that it is difficult, in the various retrospections, to tell them apart or to say what happened when. Meanwhile, the first part, which is about the same length, spans the better part of a day, though its single continuous action conveys no impression of abridgment. The audience's temporal bearings are deliberately destabilized at the outset. The clock's striking three times—rushing through an hour in a minute—at Murano's dawn departure bespeaks nothing so simple as a malfunctioning clock or crazily condensed stage time but indicates that we have already entered the fluid, liminal time element in which the dumb god-apparent exists. A sense of ritual enclosure, and of a suspension of normal activities that intensifies or reorders time consciousness, is crucial to an understanding of the way time works in this play. There are no "flashbacks" from a clearly defined present but a concurrence or synchrony of past and present moments. The past suddenly elides or erupts, without warning, into the present, charging the instant with its special energy when it is satirically represented (Sergeant Burma) or intensely recalled (the accident at the bridge), or when one of its ritual properties, such as the Ogun mask from the Drivers' Festival, rolls onto the stage to reactivate the dormant but ongoing ritual process.

In fact, even these three modes of interaction with the past—imitation, remembrance, and the ritual recurrence that is often inaccurately called reenactment by Western critics—are not kept entirely distinct. For example, Samson's impersonations of Professor and Sergeant Burma are closer to the ritually possessive than to the parodic, and therefore closer to the cultic than to the satiric part of the egungun, for one of these men died a week before and the other will be dead before the end of the day. Thus, by assuming Burma's garb and voice, Samson, as he realizes to his horror, is dangerously close to calling up spirits: imitation of the living slips into invocation of the dead. In the agemo phase of "flesh dissolution" into which Kotonu and Samson have been physically drawn, the difference between occurrence and reenactment is itself dissolved; they do not relive the past but literally return to it. They slip erratically through doorways between worlds, through holes in time that lead into the other time dimension of the ritual process, the hinterland of transition where recent events are not finished but, because they were violently interrupted in midflow, are held over into the present and are still happening. The transitional phase of the festival rite is, technically, still in progress, and the innate power of the mask, and of the god to repossess it, continue to be operative. By getting under Murano's bloodstained mask at the scene of the accident (for which he is made momentarily blind and Murano dumb, so that neither can tell of the transition), Kotonu enables the rite to go forward in both the material and metaphysical senses: the masqueraders' suspicions are averted and the unhoused god is given temporary residence. But Murano has passed on to the traumatized Kotonu only his transition agonies and his condition of listless limbo, not his ritual powers, and Professor's ritual antics are the fabrications of an intruder. It remains for the true celebrant, in the climactic dance, to reassume the mask and reinvoke the god in order to carry the impeded transition through to completion. In one of the theatrical sleights-of-hand for which egungun dancers and designers are famous, mask and costume collapse to reveal that there is nothing inside them: the divinity is released from the dissolving flesh of the human celebrant and, as the latter passes into nothingness, becomes invisible again. Whether this action closes the play in the evening of the "present" day or in the rite of a week before, when Murano was originally reduced to a human nothing, does not strictly matter because in the transitional time dimension the past is alive in the present. Moreover, because the ceremony in which the accident occurred is not expressible in any terms other than itself, it cannot be rehearsed or summarized but can only "happen" dramatically, with the theatrical immediacy of the ritual event: the masked dancers swarm onto the stage in what is not reenactment but original performance.

As with the rite, so with the death that Professor uses the rite to acquire knowledge of. To know what Murano knows, he must be where Murano is: to truly live his quest, instead of having it by proxy, he must in fact die. Death is not actable, knowable, or statable: it is a unique event that has its own inimitable embodiment, and paraphrase and analogy can do no more than liken things distantly to it. In this endeavor language, as is to be expected in the hands of a forger, is a fraud. Led astray by literacy and the Logos, Professor's deranged rant about the "the Word" is so much noisy, meaningless verbiage, beside which Murano's profound silence is pregnant with revelation, though what his silence communicates is the very inexpressibility of knowledge gained from proximity to death; it confirms Professor's fear that "death's revelation must be total, or not at all" (*CP1*, 226). Subsequently, this knowledge proves to be a featureless blank, like the faces on the fatal lorry to which Professor, at the moment of revelation, refers back. While the audience's attention is held by the vanishing trick of the spinning mask, his dying peroration adds nothing to what has already been said but merely restates the enigmatic quest of the road in a simile that sounds like a recipe for survival—"Be even *like* the road itself"—and then turns, in its shift into metaphor, into a suicidal imperative to kill or be killed: "*Be* the road" (*CP1*, 228). Professor's closing exhortation can in fact be seen as the final shift in the play's passage from imitation to identification, and from simile to a mode of ritual meaning that partakes viscerally of its own reality. Appropriate to a quest in which knowledge of the conclusion is not available, no attempt is made to resolve, intellectually, the puzzle of Professor's own death, which may be seen as either nemesis or accident: as a ritual sacrifice in payment for the violation of a rite; as retribution upon a Faustian overreacher for his hubristic spying on the gods; or as a casualty in a squalid brawl. Because of its strong sense of ritual completion, *The Road* will not easily sustain a wholly secular interpretation, yet the vindictive nature of the egungun at the end seems to argue only for the narrowest of theological readings.[15] Ogun seems to be present here only in his deathly, not in his regenerative-sacrificial, element, and the prevailing imagery is of abortive waste and decay: the purposeless deaths of the road are imaged as menstrual refuse, the doomed lorries "pregnant with stillborns" (*CP1*, 196–97), and the play exudes a rich mixture of smells, from Salubi's stinking mouth to the odors of police corruption and the wormy stench of stockfish and the corpses they resemble. *The Road* is brilliantly bleak drama, wrenching a great deal of humor (in the conversational crossfire of the touts and thugs) but only the slenderest of redeeming visions from its anomic squalor and decay. At the practical level, life on the highways will be marginally safer after Professor's death. Beyond that there is little light at the end of the road, and Soyinka's next dramatic excursion into the esoteric was to be even darker still.

"Unborn generations," prophesied the Warrior in *A Dance of the Forests*, will "eat up one another" (*CP1*, 49), and in *Madmen and Specialists* (1971), the bitter fruit of Soyinka's internment during a civil war that fulfilled his worst fears for independence, they do exactly that. Unbalanced by the suffering he has witnessed in the recent war, Dr. Bero's father (called Old Man) has served up an Atrean feast of human flesh to his son and fellow officers to bring home to them, by an act that is the ultimate expression of power over one's fellow humans, the true enormity of war. He pursues to insane extremes a conservationist moral logic by which the remedying of one of war's catastrophic products (famine) by another (corpses) is viewed as a natural extension of the inhumanity that already exists. To avert the wrath of the military authorities, Dr. Bero, whom the war has transformed from a doctor into a sadistic intelligence specialist, has his father certified insane and smuggles him away into the basement surgery of the family home. Here the Old Man is guarded, and Bero's innocent sister Si Bero spied upon, by a surrealistic quartet of deformed Mendicants whose lives have been shattered by the war (two of them are given the names 'Cripple' and 'Blindman') and who are discovered at the start of the play gambling away their limbs in a symbolic representation of its hazards. The loyalties of this raucous, scurrilous chorus appear, however, to be divided. Though they are in the pay of the sinister specialist-son, it was the madman-father who, in a wartime rehabilitation center for the mutilated and disabled, taught them to think critically about and rail against their situation (placing, in the son's words, "a working mind in a mangled body"), and who indoctrinated them with his subversive cult of "As," the meaning of which his son tries unsuccessfully to torture from him. In fact, the Mendicants' entire behavior in the play consists of unannounced satiric sketches taught them by Old Man, in which they parody features of the evil military regime served by his son: interrogation with torture, summary trial and execution, the populist and propagandist antics of power-hungry dictators. In the course of the play this freak show threatens to get out of hand, and the parodies, increasingly hard to distinguish from reality, culminate in an explosive climactic performance in which Old Man dons his son's surgical garb and seems really about to "practice" upon one of his Mendicant-disciples, the Cripple, on the operating table when the son shoots him down. The distraction caused by the father's death allows Si Bero's mysterious companions, the Earth Mothers Iya Agba and Iya Mate, to set fire to the house and so prevent Bero from getting his unworthy hands upon their collection of traditional herbal medicines. In the final unresolved, ambiguous tableau, Old Man slumps dead onto the table in the place of the Cripple, the two old women walk calmly away from the holocaust, and the Mendicants break off, in midword, their hideous ritual incantation of As.

"You want to borrow my magic key," Old Man tells his son. "Yours open only one door at a time" (*CP2*, 263). The play's title implies deceptively categoric divisions much along these lines. On the one hand is the narrow, fanatical "specialism" of the icy technocrat Dr. Bero, whose "mind has run further than the truth"; on the other, the broader, visionary "madness" of Old Man's traditional humanism and the "magical" irrationalism of the two Iyas' elemental powers, over which Bero has no control. In the vertical, three-story set, the elevated sanctum of the Iyas' hut, the ground-level movements of Si Bero and the Mendicants, and Bero's cellar suggest, respectively, a supernatural moral order, human duality, and subhuman bestiality What this grim play really depicts, however, is the single, indivisible mental family of man, in which father, brother, and sister, loosely correspondent with conscience, ego, and spiritual superconscious, all exist in a horrible symbiosis. "You don't learn good things unless you learn evil," says one Iya in response to the other's observation that curative and poisonous herbs grow, like Si Bero and her monstrous brother, from the same parental root (*CP2*, 225). In the liminal chaos that is the grotesque Mendicants' natural element, there is no clear line between health and sickness, surgery and torture, therapy and murder, or reason and insanity. (In the insane context of war one is declared mad for teaching men to think.) This confusion is especially acute, in a play full of "performances," in the border territory between parody and the thing parodied, role-playing and reality, and it is in this twilight zone that the worlds of madmen and specialists converge.

Old Man's modest proposal that the army save on meat by eating its dead was not Soyinka's first exercise in Swiftian irony, and his earlier use of the satiric persona in a newspaper item, in which he pretended to approve the flogging of women offenders for "insulting behavior" to political opponents, must have alerted him to its dangers.[16] In a world so crazed and desensitized by war and terror as to be rendered impervious to irony, parody, instead of subtly sharpening perception and awakening indignation and self-disgust, has a tendency to miss its mark and to have its hyperbole taken for literal truth, causing it to backfire and to end up promoting what it set out to pillory. By using cannibalism as a symbolic test, moral yardstick, or analogue, Old Man's banquet actually dares it into existence, whereupon it quickly takes possession of its testees. After their initial revulsion the officers develop an appetite for human flesh, and the breaking of the ultimate taboo liberates Bero, personally, from all civilized inhibitions, carrying him into an amoral terrain beyond

good and evil where everything is permissible. Furthermore, meaningless though Old Man's mad doctrine of As is in the absence of any statable
philosophical rationale, it promises to provide an ideology for the
barbaric reality of which the son is himself the perfect embodiment and
personification. Dr. Bero, for all his shocking boasts and insinuations and
his stagy posturing as a Grand Guignol caricature of evil, is actually a
curiously insecure character who appears not to have fully confronted the
horrors brought home to him by his more knowledgeable father; he
needs to have them identified, labeled, and dogmatized in intellectual
terms that will not require him to face up to their visceral realities. "The
fool is still looking for labels," says Iya Agba; the truth is that Dr. Bero
cannot know or name As but can only *be* it.

The basic pattern of the cannibal feast is repeated in the play's
climactic parody, in which the earlier motifs of surgical torture and the
carving up of human meat come, appropriately, together. Old Man's
figurative dissection of the Cripple, intended initially to demonstrate the
futility of the latter's dream of a miracle-cure operation and the power-
lessness of surgery over diseased souls, rapidly develops into a parody of
his son's surgical "practicings" upon his patients and, specifically, into a
mock excision of the human questioning capacity, in which the Cripple
plays the part of the father, and the father that of the son. The madman
thus takes on the role of the specialist to show the specialist that he is
really a madman. But more than this, the father seems to be ritually
exorcizing from his own being the spirit of the son whom he has created
and is responsible for, a spirit who must be summoned in order to be
driven out and who must first be imitated to be conjured up. The ritual
model here is the egungun celebrant in his passage from the satiric to the
cultic phase of the rite, and from parodic imitation to the point of actual
possession, at which he becomes what he has hitherto merely represented
(an impression borne out by the Mendicants' hieratic chanting and by
Old Man's trancelike frenzy and symmetrical collapse, in the Cripple's
place, onto the altar of sacrifice). In this figurative egungun rite the
father is "possessed" by his spiritually dead son, a maker of corpses who
promptly dispatches his summoner to the world of the dead; for, as Old
Man has warned Bero, the father can be rid of his son, and the son of the
father, only by the father's death, an event the son devoutly wishes but
has to be forced to execute. Thus, Old Man has directed the Cripple in a
performance of his own prophesied death at the hands of his son,
stepping into the victim's role himself when parody passes into "possession" and the acting becomes real. In this grotesque new twist to the filial

relationship, exorcist and exorcised reverse positions and the parent is cast out by the son: by shooting the mad, humane man who fathered him, Bero severs his last link with humanity, expelling its remaining vestiges in himself. And yet, though it is primarily the madman's truth-telling capacity that is being put to rest here, it is surely no accident that the murder is performed at the precise moment when he is himself behaving inhumanly, and most like the specialist, as if he were calling forth from himself something of his son's quintessential evil. Old Man is, after all, partly responsible for the style of the regime, for which he furnishes a mock ideology, and his sanity-saving nihilism, though it has its source in outraged humanitarian impulses, is finally as despairingly all-permissive as his son's swaggering amorality. The madman's paranoid brinkmanship logic is as deliberately and callously utilitarian, as blindly disregarding of moral and human issues, as the rival fanaticisms of the specialist. Their respective moral and military terrorisms are driven by the same compulsive consistency and hideous totalitarian logic: bestial irrationality and rationality run mad yield the same results.

Little seems to be left over from the ashes at the end of this dark and forbidding play except for the destructive legacy of "the cycle of As," As being the collective names man gives to the mind-enslaving systems and ideologies that sanctify slaughter, and by which he absolves himself from responsibility for his own pervasive, indestructible evil. As is "the end that justifies the meanness," and its promotion from adverb to noun portends transitions from an ongoing, presumably unending process with which man chooses to comply—"As Is, Now, As Ever Shall Be, World Without"—to an unchallengeable, godlike being: "As chooses, Man accepts" (*CP2*, 244, 272). Subsequently, the sacrificial hope that something good may grow out of the consuming, purgative fires of war is severely subdued in this play, and the Iyas' holistic wisdom, which sees good and bad as conditions for one another in an inescapable cycle—"you can cure with poison . . . what is used for evil is also put to use" (*CP2*, 225, 274)—only becomes ground for a more insidious form of fatalism. Old Man's self-sacrifice, by ensuring the destruction of the herb-store, limits Bero's capacity for evil by placing the secret potencies of traditional medicine beyond his reach but, throwing out the infant with the bathwater, also deprives the world of the latter's potential for good. Moreover, Old Man dies not to redeem humanity but to allow his irredeemable son to sever all bonds with it. He knows that his last attempt to acquaint Bero with the full horror of himself is as doomed to failure as his earlier one: his dying deed is really a desperate revelation of the futility of individual sacrifice in a world inured to carnage. Though it is possible to see the play as a personal and political exorcism that had to be experienced if renewal was to take place, the triple failure in health and succor at its climax—the healer turning killer, the mock murder by surgical operation, the Earth powers' withdrawal of their gifts—suggests that the Obatalan wholeness after the Ogunian rendings of pain and horror was becoming harder to find.

Madmen and Specialists is Soyinka's most bitter and anguished play—not surprising, given its prison genesis and its treatment of the madness or war—and it is also deeply subversive of audience expectations, both in its use of role-playing techniques and in its language. Since the Mendicants are not differentiated by individual psychologies or histories, we come to regard them as stylized marionettes who merely mouth Old Man's intellectual ravings and who are always, in some measure, "performing." They exaggerate and control their disabilities and present themselves, by turns, as victims and persecutors, alternatively mocking and indulgently identifying with official sadism. Thus even their most realistic-sounding quarrels have a histrionic edge. Their prevailing god As is, appropriately, a theatrogenic deity who "wears a hundred masks and a thousand outward forms," and the point of Old Man's plan to take his circus grotesques off on a world tour seems to be that audiences can become accustomed to and applaud even the shocking and the terrible if they are presented unseriously, at the required level of unreality proper to the stage entertainment. It is then, at the point where a degree of the audience's acceptance of "playing" has been established, that Soyinka, in a subversive switching of frames that also shifts all the conventional touchstones and guidelines, suddenly turns the shock power of his material back upon the audience by actualizing the horrors, indicating that the insanity is really "out there," not something merely acted on a stage. The play's radical language experiments are equally unsettling. The Mendicants, who are themselves human remnants, tell their stories in fragments and through broken bits of words whose associations veer crazily from plants to plastic surgery, peeled roots to severed limbs and vocal cords (stifling dissent), and elections to electrodes (thus, democracy to political torture). The implication of this linguistic anarchy, and of Blindman's burlesque of imperialist apologetics, is that in our time political inhumanity has so brutalized and debased language, allowing it to swallow whole what it should choke on (madness, cannibalism, genocide), that all that is left to the writer is to anatomize it, to take it apart and see what it is made of. In Old Man's closing tirades the play, imitating his "dissection" of the Cripple, performs a surgical operation on its own language in a vain attempt to root out the rot and drain the poison from its marrow. The result is a frenetic series of semantic implosions, a truncation of words into their interior syllabic components that, by a technique of scatological reduction, exposes the internal contradictions and inadequacies inherent in all idea systems, all verbal and ideological constructs: "the dog in dogma . . . the mock of democracy, the ham in Mohammed . . . an ass in the mass . . . the pee of priesthood" (*CP2,* 275). The visceral theatrical power of gibberish should not be underestimated (witness Artaud, Jarry, and Lucky's tirade in *Waiting for Godot),* but without seeing a production of *Madmen and Specialists* one is finally unsure whether this agonized hammering at the gates of language, unhinging words from their rational semantic and syntactical frames, is intellectually meaningful in performance or whether it comes across as so much virtuoso, pit-pandering paronomasia. The deliberately undefined As, like the symbolism of the Half-Child in *Dance,* represents something basically ineffable, something hostile to discursive meaning, at the heart of the play: it invites literary-critical "specialists" to bend the work's opacity to their own interpretative will, as the play's military specialist bends people and nature to his—to remake reality *as* you like it. *Madmen and Specialists* is the ultimate in esoteric Soyinka and dramatized ritual chaos, a figurative exorcism of the demons of war in which the esoteric style, pushed to its limits, finds its own simultaneous apotheosis and exorcism. As theater per se, this play was a dead end. It did, however, in the grisly cabaret of the Mendicants, bring to center stage for the first time a feature of Soyinka's work hitherto glimpsed only intermittently: the free-wheeling, satiric, agitprop revue style of theater that would preoccupy his writing for the stage from *Horseman* onward.

Chapter 6
Shot-Gun Satires:
The Revue Plays

Soyinka did not coin the term "shot-gun writing"—"you discharge and disappear"—until the 1970s (Gibbs 1987, 63). He had, however, produced occasional subversive satiric sketches throughout the previous decade ("The New Republican," produced in 1964; *Before the Blackout* [1971]), and his unpublished one-act entertainment "The Invention," performed at the Royal Court Theatre in London in 1959, had been written in the broad satiric tradition of the revue. This well-conceived but unevenly executed piece is set in a futuristic South Africa in which a nuclear accident has caused a loss of color pigmentation. A team of pseudoscientists, backed by international finance and racial fervor in roughly equal measures, toils away at a contraption for the infallible testing of racial identity, with a view to restoring the "natural" and proper order of race hatred, discrimination, and segregation. No one in this caustic tour de force is spared: South Africa's high priests of apartheid, the American South's lynchers, British landladies, manufacturers and researchers with vested interests in racial division, and bigots of every kind are drawn into the radius of the grim and often quite grisly satire.

In the early 1960s Soyinka turned his attention to matters closer and more urgently at hand. During the deepening crisis of the first republic, as political murders became more frequent and blatant intimidation by power-addicted local chiefs escalated daily, he opted for the direct thrust and immediate corrective impact of the revue sketch performed hot on the heels of the event. In *Before the Blackout* the targets are various acts of public cowardice and sycophancy performed by citizens and officials before both the new time-serving, opportunistic politicians and Nigeria's traditional rulers, portrayed here as so many obnoxious, lecherous rogues who have betrayed their people throughout history. The sketches "Death before Discourtesy," "Symbolic Peace, Symbolic Gifts," and "Go North, Old Man" satirize the lengths to which the new Westernized professional elites are prepared to go to accommodate and ingratiate themselves with the local chiefs: namely, offering up their homes and daughters; patronizing decrepit octogenarians still living in the days of the empire; and accepting 15-year-old girls from northern feudal chiefs in return for censoring the news. Other sketches have a broader, continental scope. "Babuzu Lion Heart" burlesques the murderous paranoia of an African dictator who even feigns death to find out who is loyal to him, and in another sketch a modern political pope offers state pardons in the place of former indulgences and terrorizes his "heretics" not with excommunication but with preventive detention.

The splendidly deadpan dialogue and barbed wit of these sketches give just cause for regret that more of them have not been published, but Soyinka acknowledges in his preface (1971) the familiar paradox of the satirist: the acute topicality of the material made it libelous in print and dangerously open to political reprisal, but once its targets were dead or dethroned and it ceased to be a threat, it also ceased to be topical. Thus, those sketches have worn least well in which Soyinka, working on the assumption that wrongs are only correctable if identifiable, attacks the individual villain rather than the villainy and takes little trouble to camouflage his identify. Possible afterthoughts on the short life of close-range satire prompted him, in his prefatory comments, to leave loopholes for updating and contemporary adaptation, and it is significant that the two most enduring and enjoyable sketches make no specific contemporary references. These are "Obstacle Race," a timeless satire on state inaction over road safety presented from the viewpoint of a hilariously downbeat taxi driver, and the perennially popular *Childe Internationale*, in which a traditional Yoruba father takes in hand his affected been-to wife and his obnoxious daughter, outrageously Americanized by one of the new international schools.[1]

Though there is much serious and urgent matter in *Before the Blackout*, there is also a great deal of lighthearted and diversionary satire that is more intent on ridiculing folly and affectation than exposing vice and crime. But with *Jero's Metamorphosis* (1972), written in exile and out of despair over the debacle of General Gowon's postwar military government, the bitter-satiric element of Soyinka's drama becomes more dominant. The first play about the beach prophet ends with Brother Jero's parodic identification with a minor member of an elected parliament. The sequel ends with *General* Jeroboam taking down the statutory photograph of the bemedaled Head of State from the comfortable whitewashed office of his newly formed Church of the Apostolic Salvation

Army and substituting his own. The military bearings are not accidental. The 12 intervening years had seen the war prophesied at the end of *Trials*, the installation of Gowon's victorious federal regime, and a postwar wave of violent crime that the regime had tried to stem by the usual soldierlike solutions: notably, the public execution of armed robbers by firing squad at the Bar Beach near Lagos. In mid-1972 a member of the military junta was appointed to the task of clearing the Bar Beach of prophets and separatist sects so that the general public attending the executions could enjoy the spectacle without evangelical molestation. Giving historical reality but the slightest fantastical twist, Soyinka has the regime promoting the tourist trade by building the National Execution Amphitheatre—"the sole amphitheatre of death in the entire nation"—and planning to empower the local Salvation Army with sole prerogative over prayers, last rites, and musical entertainment. (The Bar Beach executions were, in fact, performed with all the cheerleading media hype of the carnival and amusement park, complete with sideshows, television cameras, and ice cream vendors.) The wily Jero responds by using his still hapless ex-servant Chume, now a Salvation Army trumpeter, to infiltrate the former colonial organization and proceeds to unite the beach prophets—a ragged band of thieves, cutthroats, and sexual offenders, themselves suitable firing-squad fodder—under the umbrella of his own rival, pseudoindigenized "Apostolic" version. With the aid of a confidential file purloined for him by a former tourist board secretary (now his infatuated convert Sister Rebecca), he then uses information about shady contract deals to blackmail the board's Chief Executive Officer into giving his own outfit "spiritual monopoly" over executions and sole trusteeship of the beach. At the end of the play Jero's religious mafia controls the beach, the den of his one remaining rival is about to be razed, and his new brethren are set to embark upon a ghoulish, commercial predation upon the dying that makes the mild extortions from the living in the first play look relatively innocent.

Jero's metamorphosis has been a drastic affair, and the comic dramatist's lightness of touch has vanished with the civilian governments of the past. The Chief Executive Officer remarks, in tones of virtuous moral protest, that the prophets stand in the way of progress and decency, and then goes on: "They are holding up a big tourist business . . . the land value has doubled since we started public executions on this beach" (*CP2*, 185). In these new times it is the executions themselves that, in Jero's words, are designed "for the moral edification and spiritual upliftment of the people" (*CP2*, 202). There are a few moments of pure farcical fun in the manner of the first play, such as Chume's bewilderment of a pompous Salvation Army major by his gastronomical transcription of music, but the fun quickly evaporates as Jero unveils his ghastly scheme and makes quite clear where he has turned for his model and "required image." "Let the actuality of power see itself reflected in that image, reflected and complemented . . . such an image as will make our outward colours one with theirs. . . . We shall manifest our united spiritual essence in the very form and shape of the rulers of the land" (*CP2*, 203–4). As in the first play, we are invited to see the beach world of the prophets as a mirror and microcosm of the political world; there is even a ghostly echo of the 1960s parliaments in Shadrach's ineffectual "walkout" from Jero's meeting. But now the prophets and their congregations are not merely creatures of greed and ambition but uniformed thugs and criminals, the rotten apples of society thinly veneered with an odor of sanctity, and the implication is, of course, that the ruling junta, which is attracted to their militarized evangelism and protocol, is not very different. The new prophets feed the dreams of soldiers as the old ones fed those of clerks and traders, promising their regimes long and even eternal life. They use a similar mixture of bribes, threat, and brute force to keep themselves in power (one jailbird-prophet is an ex-wrestler), and their symbol, like the regime's, is blood. Jero has become the spiritual arm of military power. *Jero's Metamorphosis* is bitter, brittle satire and a deeply subversive piece of comic nihilism in which the horror is uncomfortably close to the humor. Behind the prophet's mimicry of the antics of power is loathing and disgust at the squalid brutalities of military misgovernment and at the moral and intellectual bankruptcy betokened by the superstitious recourse of power regimes to fortune-tellers. Though less savage than his other postimprisonment play *Madmen and Specialists* (1970), it is a fierce indictment of early 1970s Nigerian society. The new reality of the Bar Beach is a freakish circus of anomie, rapine, and death, with its ringmaster distinguished from his rabble of prophets only by his superior ingenuity and resource. Its 1960 counterpart now looks quaint and idyllic; there could never be such innocence again. In the decade between had come the collapse of the republic into massacre and civil war and, for Soyinka, the embitterment of prison and exile.

The year 1975, when *Death and the King's Horseman* was published and Soyinka returned to Nigeria, is something of a watershed in the writer's dramatic career. After this date Soyinka, whether in response to the exigencies of the worsening political situation or to the pressures of criticism leveled at his work by the Nigerian left, chose to strip from his drama its complex ritual and mythological idiom and informing Yoruba worldview in favor of the subversive, agitprop satiric revue, written for performance rather than publication. He adopted this more popular form for the purpose of urgent political communication with a mass audience, and the works he wrote in it, usually published some years after production and in some cases not at all, are theatrical amphibians with one foot in the textual world of Western drama and the other in the improvisational, more openly experimental comic folk theater, or Alawada. This largely unscripted, hit-and-run kind of street theater, best suited to the raw atmosphere of marketplace and parking lot,[2] targeted specific political enormities and was mounted with minimal publicity, usually vanishing before the players could be rounded up by the police of the latest repressive regime. Over the next decade the links between Soyinka's theatrical and political involvements were to be particularly close, and the "shot-gun" satires, running a constant, caustic calypso on public affairs, were a frontline force in the responses to Nigeria's succession of political and economic crises and subsequent scandals and outrages: shrinking oil revenues, plunging foreign exchange, the chronic shortage of books and information, and multiplying ministerial embezzlements and political murders. Sometimes pointedly Nigerian in reference ("Before the Blow-out," "Priority Projects") and sometimes concerned with evils on the African continent at large (*Opera Wonyosi*), the revue satires have in their favor the urgent relevance of their political comment and the spontaneity of the theatrical "happening," with its capacity for surprise, shock, and audience involvement. In their published form, however, they inevitably suffer from a limiting topicality and ephemerality. Performance here has priority, and when their virtuoso satiric techniques are allowed to interfere with the dramatic integrity of fully crafted stage plays, the results are apt to be disappointing: a satiric meanness of characterization, instanced in the mechanical lining up and wheeling on of slight and insubstantial targets (*Requiem for a Futurologist* [1985]), and a linguistic flatness and general thinness of texture (*A Play of Giants* [1984]), the more noticeable after the verbal richness and somber grandeur of *Horseman*.

Opera Wonyosi, a ballad opera first performed in 1977 but not published until 1981, is the most substantial and sustained of these satires. With the aid of an eclectic medley of English ballads, Kurt Weill songs, jazz and blues, and the tunes of the 1950s Ibo folksinger Israel Ijemanze, Soyinka transposes the eighteenth-century London of John

Gay's *The Beggar's Opera* (1728) and the Victorian Soho of Brecht's *The Threepenny Opera* (1928) to a bidonville of Bangui, capital of the former Central African Republic, on the eve of the imperial coronation of Jean-Bedel Bokassa (who was to be overthrown two years later when his involvement in the murder of schoolchildren became widely known). The obscenely decadent extravaganza of Bokassa's coronation, in one of Africa's poorest countries, took place in the same week as Soyinka's Ife production and substitutes for the royal jubilee that forms the background to the action in the Gay and Brecht originals. The Emperor's amnesty provides Macheath with his royal reprieve at the climax. (Significantly, in Soyinka's African version the royal pardon that liberates vicious criminals is not extended to political detainees.) The Emperor Boky, or "Folksy Boksy," a crazy caricature of feudal barbarism mixed with servile, sentimental Francophilia, makes one unforgettable appearance in the play, during which he drills and clubs senseless his goon squad before stomping off to "pulp the brains" of the children who have refused to wear his uniforms. The motley collection of rogues and thugs who make up the cast of *Opera Wonyosi*, however, are Nigerian expatriates: the "beggarly" racketeers of Chief Anikura (the Peachum of the original); the venal police chief and security expert "Tiger" Brown, on loan to the Emperor; the psychopathic Colonel Moses, military adviser to the same; and the thieves, arsonists, drug peddlers, and murderers gathered around the highway robber Macheath. But lest the audience jump to the conclusion that the Nigerian military regime has exported all of its undesirable elements, it is made clear at the outset that the expatriate cliques of the Nigerian quarter are meant to serve as a satiric microcosm of the home country during the oil boom of the 1970s. In a program note Soyinka insisted that "the genius of race portrayed in this opera is entirely, indisputably and vibrantly Nigerian."[3] Preferring Gay's ebullient indictment of specific historical vices and corruptions to Brecht's portrayal of universal human depravity, Soyinka uses the wisecracking cynicism of the expatriate scoundrels to draw up a ghastly inventory of Nigerian outrages in the years of the oil dollar, or *petro-naira*: government-sponsored extortion and assassination; arson and atrocities by a power-drunk soldiery; the public flogging of traffic offenders and execution of felons; murderously punitive industrial conditions and levels of state responsibility so low that month-old corpses were left to decompose on public highways; and a general craze for wealth that was epitomized by the wearing of the gaudy *wonyosi*, the absurdly ragged-looking but fantastically expensive lace that was the rage of the Nigerian nouveau riche in the 1970s.

Anikura's beggars are, of course, more than what they seem, and their feigned physical deformities are more than distant symbolic allusions to the moral deformation of their country. Among the ragged band are lawyers, professors, doctors, and clergymen whose begging is used by Soyinka as a precise metaphor for the shameless sycophancy to "khaki and brass," the groveling in military gutters, by which the professional classes won preferment and promotion during the years of "nairomania" ("Khaki is a man's best friend," runs the refrain of one song). Sycophancy, backed up by coercion, is the way to a slice of the national cake. In the words of the garrulous Dee-Jay, who replaces Gay's beggarly poet and Brecht's Moritatensänger, "That's what the whole nation is doing— begging for a slice of the action. . . . Here the beggars say, 'Give me a slice of action, or—give me a slice off your throat'" (SP, 303). But Soyinka literalizes—and labors somewhat—his metaphors by having his mendicant professionals turn professional mendicant. Professor Bamgbapo, who has "bagged" the chairmanships of a number of industrial corporations as well as his university chair by "sucking up to the army boys," has come to Anikura for "a refresher course" in the form of fieldwork with full-time beggars! Thus the street beggars become synonymous with fawning bureaucrats, and the small crooks actually turn into the big ones before our eyes. Anikura, the brain behind the beggars' protection racket, is "chairman of highly successful groups of companies," and his daughter Polly plays the stock market and amalgamates "Macheath enterprises" with a multinational corporation: "Let's go legitimate like the bigger crooks" (SP, 358, 377). The links between legal business practice and crime, and between capitalism and gangsterism, are certainly present, but Soyinka's play is not the assault on capitalism that Brecht meant his to be but is essentially a satire on power. The culprit was the oil-produced wealth that promoted power, and Soyinka's target is the criminal lengths to which people were prepared to go to get the money that would buy them power.

Opera Wonyosi is devastating, merciless satire, and the government's prompt intervention to prevent a Lagos production was proof that it had struck powerfully home. Sometimes the tone is brash, swaggering cynicism in the Brechtian mode, as in Anikura's remark that fraud by one's fellow countrymen is an infallible alibi for destitution since everyone knows "that any Nigerian will rob his starving grandmother and push her in the swamp" (SP, 307, 368), and in his threat to have an army of real

beggars march on coronation day, not to embarrass tyranny with poverty
but to blackmail it into arresting his personal enemy Macheath. At other
times the satire is pure vitriolic rage, as in the Bangui equivalent of the
Bar Beach show at Macheath's execution; schoolchildren are given a
holiday to watch the spectacle on television, and a deathbed patient from
the hospital falls over his wheelchair in righteous blood lust for a ringside
seat and promptly bursts into a gruesome parody of Donald Swann's hit
record The Hippopotamus Song: "Blood, blood, glorious blood . . ."
(*SP*, 398). Reality here seems always one step ahead of satiric invention,
and the unspeakable needs little enhancement from the writer to provoke
a sense of outrage. The terrorization of civilian populations by megalomaniacal military buffoons and the squalid compliance of the professional classes, cowed by a mendicant mentality, were the painful
Nigerian and African realities of the 1970s, and satire targeted at them
walks the fine edge between the real and the surreal. Soyinka stated in the
playbill to the 1977 Ife production that "the characters in this opera are
either strangers or fictitious, for Nigeria is stranger than fiction, and any
resemblance to any Nigerian, living or dead, is purely accidental, unin-
tentional and instructive" (Lindfors 1981, 31). In performance the
preposterous reality broke through to dissolve the conventional safe
divisions between the stage and the "real" worlds in a number of surprise effects: Soyinka had the notorious "Attack Trade" women who
stripped corpses in the civil war descend into the audience at the interval
to sell their grisly wares, and a coffin, ostensibly containing the real
corpse scooped from the roadside the previous day by a real-life reform
campaigner Tai Solarin, was carried by pallbearers into the auditorium,
thus implicating everyone in willful blindness to the daily public ob-
scenity. In one performance the shock tactics of the "theater of the real"
were even turned against his own actors: on Soyinka's secret instructions,
the orchestra halted the opening number so that Professor Bamgbapo
(played by a real-life academic) could be dragged from the chorus and, in
front of a university audience, thrashed by a figure looking very much
like a real-life Nigerian army officer (Ogunbiyi, 13). Time has inevitably
taken the sting from the satire in these topical allusions but Soyinka has
been equal to the task of constantly updating them. One year after
Bokassa's coronation he reassembled his beggarly crew on Nigerian soil
to satirize political opportunism at the lifting of the ban on political
activities and a contemporaneous national wave of car thefts. In the two
sketches of "Before the Blow-out" Chief Onikura (formerly Anikura)
returns home to pursue the career of a popular philanthropic politician

and smuggles in new and stolen cars to sell at inflated prices or use in his electoral campaign.[4] In a 1983 revival of *Opera Wonyosi* Soyinka dispensed with Colonel Moses altogether and replaced him with a subtle and slippery academic adviser more suited to the civilian government of the second republic.

The published text of such works can give little indication of their effectiveness in performance, but few critics would single out *Opera Wonyosi* as Soyinka's best work. Even within the loose and highly stylized form of the Brechtian play-with-songs, the plot creaks with some rather obvious devices. Chief among these is Macheath's invalidation of Anikura's charge against him by having the begging fraternity declared a secret society of the kind banned by the Nigerian military regime: the point is simply to set up the satiric tour de force of the beggar-lawyer Alatako, who succeeds in proving that the government is itself a conspiratorial secret society, a cartel created for mass exploitation and terrorization, implemented always by "unknown soldiers." The extreme length of *Wonyosi* draws attention to its episodic, patchwork structure—neither a full-length play nor a series of revue sketches—and tying the action back to the Gay and Brecht originals proves irksome and mechanical at times. Mackie's sexual intrigues and betrayals are poorly integrated into the anti-Nigerian satire; in accordance with the original models and the conventional happy ending of light opera, he turns out to be a lovable rogue whom we feel, in some way, deserves to cheat his fate—an impression quite at odds with the one conveyed by the local satire that he is a vicious and evil force rotting society from top to bottom. Macheath, in all three versions, is a rather artificial villain and something of a satiric dead end, and Soyinka's use of the character has a free rein only when he departs from his originals or takes such liberties with them as to make them say something entirely new.

Soyinka has replied to his critics on the Nigerian left[5] that the satirist's business is not exposition but exposure—in this case, of the "decadent, rotted underbelly of a society that has lost its direction"—and that programs of reform and revolutionary alternatives are the province of the social analyst and ideologist, to whose roles the writer's own distinctive vocation is merely complementary (*SP*, 297–98). Yet depths and densities of exposure may vary; if there is in *Wonyosi* surprisingly little penetration, for such a long play, of the forces underlying the crimes and corruptions passingly referred to, then the fault is not that exposure is unaccompanied by analysis but that too much is being exposed for anything to be focused very clearly. In the last third of the play the topical references to guilty parties crowd too thick and fast into the text—some speeches are mere lists of suppressed riots, arson, and lootings—and the result is satiric overkill. The opera takes on too many issues, is too thinly all-embracing, and its satiric intensity is diffused as a result.

Soyinka has always been more of a crusader than a revolutionary; he has campaigned for selected causes rather than the total transformation of society. In the late 1970s he advanced some of these causes by chairing the Oyo State Road Safety Corps and by bombarding the press with letters on police harassment, censorship, and political corruption. In 1980 he affiliated himself with the short-lived People's Redemption party. Nevertheless, Soyinka's use of his University of Ife Guerrilla Theater Unit to mobilize opinion against the Shagari government and his attempts during the years of the second republic (1979–83) to reach a wider audience by experimenting with the more popular mediums of street theater, phonograph records, and film, have all the makings of confrontational and revolutionary art. The 1981 production of "Rice Unlimited," in which the actors piled sacks marked "rice" in front of the police-guarded House of Assembly, attacked the government racketeering in the sale and resale of imported rice, a practice that had made staple foodstuffs unavailable or unaffordable for most of the population. "Priority Projects," provocatively performed in 1983 under the nose of Shagari's personal security guards during a presidential visit to the University of Ife, targeted abortive agricultural and building schemes designed to enrich a ruling party in open connivance with business tycoons, police commissioners, and traditional chiefs. In these sketches the nation that the civil war was fought to keep one is seen as two countries: "Mr. Country Hide and his brother Seek." The big political brother hides millions of naira, pouring them down bottomless pits of extravagance and corruption, while his brother on the street searches in vain for some visible return from the reckless spending. Some of the songs from "Priority Projects" appear on Soyinka's hit record, *Unlimited Liability Company* (1983). The scandals of the anarchic Shagari administration—illegal currency exportation, private jets for government officials, criminals appointed to company directorships, arson and massacre, municipal breakdowns resulting in part-time electricity and mountains of uncollected refuse—are mercilessly exposed in sharp, instantly graspable pidgin lyrics: "You tief one kobo, dey put you in prison / You tief ten million, na patriotism."[6] The writer's last word on the Shagari government was the film *Blues for a Prodigal* (1984), about the political recruitment of scientists as demolition experts to blow up the opposition. Filming commenced in the dying days of the now thoroughly rotten republic, but the film still had to be shot secretly, using the guerrilla tactics of minimal scripting and several switches of location to evade the authorities, and had to be processed abroad. Ironically, the Lagos print of the film was immediately impounded by the security forces of the new military regime, which thus implicated itself in the repressive policies of its civilian predecessor.

Soyinka published only two full-length dramatic works in the 1980s, and both were, predictably, in the "shot-gun" mold. Returning in *Requiem for a Futurologist* (1985) to the theme of religious charlatanism, Soyinka pokes fun at the astrologists and parapsychologists who came to exercise considerable influence over public and political life during the Shagari years. (The main target was one of Shagari's toadies, the powerful Dr. Godspower Oyewole.)[7] The play is built around the classic comedy motif of the master rogue outmaneuvered by his equally rascally but cleverer protégé, but the more specific model, fully acknowledged by Soyinka in the introductory material, is Swift's satiric prediction and later announcement, in *The Bickerstaff Letters* (1708), of the death of the astrologer John Partridge, who then had great difficulty convincing people that he was still alive. The trap has been sprung, and the master caught in it, some months before the start of the action when Eleazor Hosannah, the apprentice, departs from the rehearsed script of predictions during a television program and, with a view to superseding him, predicts the death of his master, the Rev. Dr. Godspeak Igbehodan. As Eleazor has the Godspeak pedigree, everyone instantly believes the prophecy—such is the fate of successful prophets—and the only way out for Godspeak (though even this is to no avail) is to confess that all their "futurology" has been a fraud. When Eleazor publishes Godspeak's obituary, an impatient mob of the faithful lays siege to the master's house, determined to pay their last respects, and no amount of live appearances can change their mind. Meanwhile, Eleazor, the arch-manipulator and master of disguise, has tricked his way back into Godspeak's employment under the semblance of a new servant, Alaba, and using his access to the house, he appears to Godspeak in yet another guise, that of one Dr. Semuwe. In the riddling philosophical cross-examination that ensues, Eleazor-Semuwe, who is more metaphysician than physician, causes the hapless Godspeak to doubt the reality of his own existence and to entertain the possibility that he may, after all, be dead. In this cause Eleazor even bribes the local egungun to feign recognition of a fellow spirit in Godspeak's figure at the window. (No religion is sacred in this play.) At the close, as the furious mob prepares to storm the house, the bewildered master reluctantly agrees to play dead, and Semuwe, becoming Eleazor again, proclaims himself the reincarnated Nostradamus, a figure who is the source of much comic disquisition in the course of the play.

The limited amount of political satire in *Requiem* takes the form of parallels between religious and political opportunism. Regimes, like the prophets they refer to and rely upon, promise what they fail to deliver and cling to power long after their authority has outrun its legitimacy. It was no accident that in the 1985 published version Godspeak's demise is predicted for New Year's Eve 1983, the date of Shagari's downfall, and when Soyinka took the play on a tour of the university campuses he made a point of opening each performance with a procession of political parties and different religious faiths. There are also a few sideswipes at favorite local abominations, such as "the highly original driving habits" that provide a roaring trade for the play's undertaker, and some satire at the expense of the death industry itself, notably the Ghanaian "Master Carpenter" who allows his clients' vulgar fantasies of wealth and status to carry over into the grave in the form of designer coffins shaped like their Cadillacs and television sets. But the bulk of the satire is reserved for the human gullibility that invests superstitious faith in the pseudoscience of charlatans. Because of their automatic and absolute belief in astrological predictions, the prophet's followers are unable to accept the idea that Eleazor has merely pretended that Godspeak is dead: they therefore believe that the master is really dead and pretending to be alive. Thus is Godspeak boxed, farcically, into a corner from which every protest that he is alive is taken to be one more proof that he is dead. A great deal of visual and verbal humor ensues, as when Godspeak's plate throwing is put down to poltergeists and an Indian parapsychologist hunts for mystical explanations for what to common sense is obvious. The prophet's followers, who know a walking corpse when they see one, cry "There he is, large as death!" when they spy Godspeak at the window, and in the play's crowning comic inversion, they rush in in a fury to kill a man for refusing to accept that he is dead and to agree to be buried. Underlying the humor, and the fantastically credulous newspaper cuttings cited in the introductory paraphernalia, is the disturbing picture of a society caught in a spiritual malaise and thirsting after illusion. The play, with its multiple disguises and costume changes, is itself a kind of conjuring trick, depicting a world where all is trickery, where appearance is everything, and no one is what he seems to be. Yet, whatever its darker implications, *Requiem* is essentially lighthearted and acutely local satiric comedy, though it is disappointingly slight as a stage play and the elaborate joke on the life-death inversion carries on perhaps a little too long. If *Requiem* is really, as Soyinka has bemusingly claimed, part of a "trilogy of transition," following *The Road* and *Death and the King's Horseman*, then it relates to these two towering achievements as the satyr play related to the tragedy in the Greek festival: as satiric postscript and light counterweight.

A *Play of Giants* (1984), in which the playwright turns his attention to the most monstrous manifestations of power ever spawned by the African continent, is more substantial fare and represents the author's political satire at its most ferocious. Soyinka gathers under the roof of the Bugaran (meaning Ugandan) embassy in New York, and under the transparent anagrams Kamini, Kasco, Gunema, and Tuboum, a gruesome quartet of real-life African dictators: Idi Amin, Jean-Bedel Bokassa, Teodoro Obiang Nguema Mbasogo of Equatorial Guinea, and Joseph Mobutu of Zaire. In the first part of the play, while ostensibly sitting for a sculpture for Madame Tussaud's Exhibition, these strutting, gibbering psychopaths explain with sadistic relish how their power-hungers are satisfied, their people terrorized, and their barbaric despotisms maintained: by voodoo (Gunema), cannibalism (Tuboum), and an imperium of "pure power" (Kasco). Kamini, who has no talent for analysis, does not have to speak of power: he *is* power, in its most fearsome and ridiculous embodiment, and never ceases to exercise it. The play is a succession of Kamini's psychopathic explosions, which, like those of the real Amin, arise from willful misconceptions, the paranoid twisting of trivial offenses, and pure, groundless delusions, such as his bizarre notion that the Tussaud statuettes are really life-size statues intended for the United Nations building across the road from the embassy. When the chairman of the Bugara Bank delivers himself of the sentiment that the national currency is worth toilet paper, Kamini has his head flushed repeatedly in the toilet bowl, and when the British sculptor, revealing the true destination of his work, utters the unguarded aside that its subject properly belongs in the Chamber of Horrors, Kamini has him beaten up and maimed. The sculptor represents symbolically the obsolete, lame Western view of Amin—that he was not a dangerous threat but a circus freak whose savagery could be contained like a waxworks horror in a museum—and it is ironically apt that when the sculptor next appears *he* is the museum piece, gagged and "mummified" in bandages from head to foot. Kamini's anxiety complexes are not entirely gratuitous, however: defections of Bugaran diplomats are constantly reported, and the mounting crises culminate in the news of a coup in his absence. Instantly assuming that the coup has been engineered by the superpowers, Kamini reacts by taking hostage a group of visiting Soviet and American delegates and threatening to unleash rockets and grenades from his embassy arsenal upon the United Nations building unless an international force is sent to Bugara to crush the uprising. In the fantastic, apocalyptic finale the rockets go off and the last light fades on the sculptor, quietly working away at what is now a living Chamber of Horrors. Kamini, who in Soyinka's prefatory words, "would rather preside over a necropolis than not preside at all,"[8] turns his embassy into a fortress and then into a tomb, a pyramidal monument to his own barbaric excesses and the sycophantic self-interest of the West.

Soyinka has often seen the artist as the human seismograph or barometer of his times. "As a writer I have a special responsibility," he once said, "because I can smell the reactionary sperm years before the rape of a nation takes place."[9] Certainly, he was one of the first to see though Amin's populist antics and buffoonish claims to African revolutionary leadership, and from 1975 onward he waged a determined campaign against the dictator in the African press, exposing the facts of his reign of terror and mercilessly lambasting Western and African governments and intellectuals who either actively supported Amin or cultivated a convenient deafness to the horror stories that were emerging from Uganda. In the play the latter forces are represented by the Scandinavian journalist Gudrun, mindlessly devoted to the dictator out of some romantically twisted concept of racial purity, and by the black American academic Professor Batey, who, out of misplaced loyalty to notions of black brotherhood and pan-Africanism, holds up to the black peoples of the world a mass murderer as a model for emulation. Both play and preface make clear that Kamini and his cronies, like their historical counterparts, are originally the postcolonial products of the Western superpowers. Kasco is a Gaullist, Gunema a Franco-worshiper, and Tuboum a Belgian puppet given to fake Africanization schemes. Kamini is placed in power by the British, financed by the Americans, armed by the Soviets, and finally deserted by all of them when support for insane African dictators is no longer in their interest. *A Play of Giants* is a surreal fantasia of international poetic justice in which Western support systems catastrophically backfire and the monster runs out of his makers' control: the Soviet-supplied weapons are now trained on their own delegations, and the horror comes home to roost in the American sponsor's own backyard.

"I'd rather kill them, but I acknowledge my impotence," Soyinka has said of his power-grotesques. "All I can do is make fun of them."[10] It is, inevitably, a horrific kind of fun, and these characters are the more terrifying precisely because their historical originals were once thought to be merely ridiculous comic figures. Soyinka commented in the same 1984 interview that the work was not intended to be "a realistic play," that his "giants" are artificial, composite constructs, endowed with more intelligence, introspection, and eloquence than their originals could muster (Borreca, 36–37). Nevertheless, many of their mouthings are reportage material based on original speeches and press statements, and the fantastic virtuoso satirization of Amin, enough to burst the bounds of any "well-made" play, infuses the historical figure's own devilish, manic hysteria into the mood of the play. Soyinka claimed in the interview that all those in the rogues' gallery of A Play of Giants are "excellent theatrical personalities." History plus burlesque does not quite equal drama, however, and if, as Soyinka remarked, Amin was "the supreme actor," he was a rather obvious, unsubtle one, best suited to broad farce and the 1970s television sketches that made him the constant butt of their satire. If dramatic effigies of Hitler and Mussolini were put up on stage and their mouths stuffed with their speeches and press releases, they would not be much more interesting or authentic as dramatic creations than Soyinka's gruesome foursome. At odd quirky moments one of them springs to life, as in Gunema's chilling, shocking anecdote about his attempt to "taste" the distilled elixir of power by sleeping with the wife of a condemned man and then having them both garotted. For the rest, they are vaudeville freaks and puppets, burbling nonsense and twitching at the behest of every passing sadistic whim and crack of the satiric whip, and the fact that their real-life models were much the same does not make them theatrically viable. Though having just enough distance from contemporary history to work as convincing satiric creations, they are too close to it to succeed as autonomous dramatic ones. The result is that A Play of Giants, like so much politically engaged art, is dramatically unengaging. It is also curiously unpenetrating. Soyinka expressed the hope that the play would "raise certain intellectual and philosophical questions about power" (Borreca, 36), and the text tosses a few ideas about. It is suggested that power calls to power, that "vicarious power responds obsequiously to the real thing," and that the "conspiratorial craving for the phenomenon of 'success' . . . cuts across all human occupations," which would explain the professor's admiration of the idiot-tyrant (*Giants*, vi–vii). There is also a hint that the African dictator's power mania is the pathological product of colonialism's suppression of traditional male authority and the continued taunting of African manhood in the postcolonial world.[11] But these suggestions appear in the preface more than in the play, which is concerned with deriding and debunking, not analyzing, and which does not add much to the knowledge of the nature of dictatorship already gleaned from *Kongi's Harvest* and *Opera Wonyosi*. Its claustrophobic set and nervous constricted laughter are a far cry from the expansive metaphysical universe of the dramatist's middle period; for the first time a Soyinka play includes no music, dance, mime, or any hint of the spectacle of festival theater. As his bitter-satiric tone has deepened and come to constitute his characteristic response to Africa's worsening political crisis, the rich texture of Soyinka's stage work has thinned out. It is perhaps unreasonable at the present time to hope for a return to subjects that have a greater dramatic viability.

Chapter 7
Ritual and Reality: The Novels

Soyinka's two novels are a poet's novels, given to dense metaphoric overloading and massive rhetorical redundancies. At its best, his image-burdened, impressionistic prose style culminates in moments of great power and beauty and flashes of exuberant verbal wit. (A traffic police-man turning a blind eye to vigilante justice in the first novel is "Pontius Pilate" continuing "to wash his hands in the stream of traffic.")[1] At its worst, it is responsible for some of the most inept features of Soyinka's writing: an opaque, hermetic word-mongering (*scapeclan, drink lobes, earth-bull*); a thought-fogging abstractness of diction; and a convoluted, clotted hypotaxis that delights in piling predicates at a disabling distance from their activating verbs. Even in compulsively readable stretches of narrative and satire there are determined obscurities of expression, either in naturalistic scenes charged with gratuitously poetic resonances (the airport scene in *Season of Anomy*) or arising from the confusion of real and metaphoric identities, as in the interpreters' several pursuit of their mythical essences in the Yoruba pantheon of Kola, the artist in *The Interpreters*. In both novels character is conceived, as in Kola's painting of the godhead and in the cosmic dome of his engineer colleague Sekoni, as a plurality of manifestations that are nevertheless facets of a single being, subtly interconnected even when most isolated. Instead of rounded individual characters, we are given unevenly developed and erratically focused composite personalities, which seem to embody in action different aspects of the awareness or temperament of the author, who uses the device of the pantheon in the first novel and the archaic morality tradition of externalized alter egos in the second. Equally, both novels are preoccupied with the dilemma of the artist and the question of the proper function of art during seasons of corruption and catastrophe.

Soyinka has said that his first novel "was an attempt to capture a particular moment in the life of a generation which was trying to find its feet after independence" (*SP*, xiv). *The Interpreters* (1965) focuses upon this independence generation through the disillusioned impressions of five recently returned university graduates, cutting backward and forward across their lives in a series of interlocking time shifts: Sagoe, a journalist; Sekoni, an engineer; Ebgo, a foreign office functionary and "apostate" heir to the remote ancestral fiefdom of Osa; Kola, an artist and academic; and Bandele, a university lecturer. This corporately alienated group is in revolt against the evils of brazen government corruption and abuse of power, press dishonesty, and academic hypocrisy. In theory, the "interpreters" are well placed to tackle those evils and transform their society: through investigative journalism attacking poverty and corruption (Sagoe); control of technology (Sekoni); the opportunity to modernize a hereditary chieftaincy (Egbo); and teaching (Kola and Bandele). In practice, however, they are excluded from real power, and their reformist zeal is blocked by time-serving editors, vested monopoly interests, the rival piracies and chicaneries of traditional rulers in the creeks of the Niger delta (only marginally less disreputable than their urban counterparts), and a preposterously anglicized academic establishment. In its frustration, the group turns it abrasive honesty and satiric eye for the phony and disingenuous upon this latter elite of "new black oyinbos," on its social pretensions, vulgar philistinism, and hypocrisy. Among them are Dr. Lumoye, who performs abortions only for patients who grant him sexual favors, and the despicable Professor Oguazor, who fulminates against the "meral turpitude" of pregnant students while hiding abroad his own illegitimate daughter. Thwarted by a corrupt public system, and unwilling to besmirch themselves by participation in it, the five friends become "apostates" from their true purposes; in effect, they abandon the attempt to translate their desire for change into practical action and retreat into private, self-gratifying quests and preoccupations: Egbo into an esoteric religious mysticism, Kola into art, and Sagoe into the cynical scatological raptures of "Voidancy," through which he seeks to exorcize revulsion at the moral filth of public corruption by raising excrement to the level of a philosophy.

The only one of the returning interpreters who does not take refuge from the national malaise in private fulfillment and satiric egoism, and who remains idealistically dedicated to the service of his society, is the engineer Sekoni. Sekoni alone rises to the challenge of outgoing, active struggle, though his myopic daydream of the magical powers of technology causes him to take on single-handed the whole corrupt edifice of state industry, foreign advisers, and local chiefs and to be mentally broken by the burdens of its injustice and fraudulent wastage of talent.

Already an outcast from his family and Islamic religion because of his marriage to a Christian girl, and from social intercourse because of a terrible stutter, Sekoni is banished, professionally, to the wilderness of Ijioha after expressing impatience with his bureaucratic sinecure in the capital. Here he devises an experimental power station for the people, but a local politician, who has a monopoly on the electricity supply, bribes an expatriate "expert" to condemn the work as unsafe. In the course of Sekoni's subsequent psychological derangement, the regenerative, innovative energies of the engineer that the corrupt authorities refuse to unleash upon a thirsting community pass into the artist's powers of cathartic release. In his sculpted figure "The Wrestler," which symbolizes his solitary struggle with social reality, the "balance of strangulation before release" catches faithfully the liberation of his stuttering, inarticulate energy, his impeded speech signifying an impeded life. Sekoni dies soon afterward in a car crash, a victim of the technological incompetence he had tried to remedy, and his death, during the cleansing period of flood rains, is presented unmistakably as a sacrificial offering. (The July deluge gushes like blood from the "slit arteries" of a slaughtered bull.) But Sekoni, because of his extreme naïveté, is too easy a victim-offering, and his own redemptive, purificatory release through art is not extended, through the medium of his death, to his society and fellow interpreters. As so often in Soyinka, a skeptical question mark is left hanging over society's capacity to avail itself of and benefit from a lone figure's transformative powers.

Sekoni's personal symbols are the bridge and dome, and, appropriately, he is the first of the many tenuous points of focus or connection that, in this sprawling and vertiginously uncentered novel, the interpreters' disparate thoughts revolve around at one time or another. But Sekoni's "dome of continuity" shatters at his death. Instead of bringing the members together in a cleansing solidarity of grief, his death only isolates them further in fragmented, locked-in egoisms, causing them to revert to their former characteristic postures: Kola to his painting, Sagoe to drunken Voidancy, Egbo to a frenzy of Ogun mysticism. Sekoni serves, in fact, as a negative catalyst who indexes the character of each member of the group as he betrays his inadequacies in response to Sekoni and his memory. In the second half of the book his mantle is posthumously assumed by two other stranger figures. The first of these is the mysterious albino Lazarus, to whom the five switch their collective attention after the fatal accident and who reveals their several shortcomings in their different reactions to his bizarre religious rituals. Bandele articulates their real, unconfessed motives for attending the ceremony by voicing the shared notion that Lazarus is, in some unspecified and remotely metaphoric way, a reincarnation of Sekoni; that the albino's own derangement and alleged resurrection, literally washed white of sin, somehow grows out of Sekoni's death. Sekoni returns from the mental death of madness, Lazarus from actual bodily death; both interpret their mystic crises to others, the one through a sculpted figure, the other by establishing a strange, islanded religious sect; and Soyinka uses the same deliberately inflated lyricism, mixing celebration with burlesque, in the accounts of both men. Sekoni's second spiritual successor is another outcast, Lazarus's convert and acolyte Noah, and it is in the episodes surrounding this nondescript figure that the interpreters are themselves interpreted, the critics most severely criticized.

Earlier in the novel Egbo tells the silent, motionless Sekoni that he, Sekoni, is sometimes "the most non-existent person in the world." Indeed, Sekoni's presence in the novel is felt mainly through the way he affects and is perceived by others, and the meaning of his life is gathered in death. As with Sekoni, so—only more devastatingly—with Noah. To Kola, Noah's face is "unrelieved vacuity, absolutely nothing," and Egbo calls him "a blank white sheet for accidental scribbles" (*TI*, 227, 231). In fact, Noah is exactly what he is—a poor, futureless African youth driven to theft and an eternally running fugitive—but in the manipulative minds of the artists and intellectuals this reality is annihilated by "interpretation." Noah's neutral blank is maneuvered by them into whatever shapes their egotistical whims dictate, even though none of the scriptural identities attributed to him in rapid succession by Kola are borne out by his fate.[2] Each of the interpreters, Bandele informs them, is bent on "getting something out" of Noah and exploiting him for his own ends. Kola takes him back to his Ibadan studio to pose as the rainbow god Esumare in his pantheon, a composite portrait of the Yoruba godhead, and Sagoe pursues him as an exciting news feature. Egbo, meanwhile, uses Noah to feed his religious obsessions, eccentrically linking his own psychic rebirth by the River Ogun with the new identities offered to the socially alienated by the resurrected Lazarus, and, with equal perversity, connecting the "rainbow of planed grey steel" over the river with the Noah-Esumare motif in Kola's painting. Egbo, the most obtuse member of the group, is especially prone to subsuming people under private mythological identities: the courtesan Simi is "Queen Bee" and "Mammy Watta," the *apala* dancer "the exultation of the Black Imma-nent," and the student he seduces (and whose name he does not trouble to discover) "the new woman of my generation" (*TI*, 235). But each of the interpreters is tainted with this vice to a greater or lesser extent. They take no interest in Noah's common humanity, having no desire to help him, only to "interpret" him, and once each has appropriated the youth in his own peculiar way during the Ibadan visit, they simply forget him. He is subsequently left at the mercy of the neurotic American quadroon Joe Golder, whose attraction to blackness is more sexual than racial and whose inevitable homosexual advances result in the boy's death. Noah is sacrificed, pointlessly and perversely, to art, publicity, religious mania, and inverted sex, each separate abuse indexing the callous indifference of the individual interpreter, and his scapegoat's death at the altar of their monstrous egoisms is linked with the slaughtered goat at Sekoni's posthumous exhibition. The perpetrators, however, are quite oblivious of their corporate blame for the death and squander the sacrifice, returning to a cheap satire that fails to penetrate the surrounding social malaise. Only Bandele, who disinterestedly seeks "knowledge of the new generation of interpreters," rises morally to the occasion, pronouncing judgment and confronting Egbo with his part of the collective guilt, and it is the passive but vigilant Bandele who, toward the end of the book, takes over Sekoni's role as conscience and moral touchstone of the group. Moreover, Bandele, who sees worth in everyone and constantly amazes his friends by his tolerance of the academic buffoons they find unbearable, is the novel's great mediator and reconciler. In his pragmatic concern with social harmony, his insistence on connecting people with one another, he is a more concrete version of Sekoni's symbolic bridging powers.

Soyinka's ambitious first novel is difficult, demanding, and not without its flaws. It is, like Kola's pantheon, an undisciplined and overcrowded canvas, containing enough material for four or five novels and more characters than can be treated satisfactorily, with the result that it loses in economy and evenness of design what it gains in abundance and variety. Sagoe's Voidancy is overindulged, and disproportionate space is given to Lazarus. Noah never really comes alive, existing only as a mental projection of others, and it is not until the last quarter of the novel that Joe Golder acquires definite features as a character and that Bandele emerges from the shadows to become a binding force in the group. The novel's multiple time shifts, which reveal events as they have meaning to the characters themselves in erratically sparked reminiscences, make it difficult to place incidents in relation to one another or to graph them by reference to anything that can be identified as the book's "present."

Additionally, the novel's sharply divided picture of postindependence Nigerian society, of corrupt public servants and servile academic hacks on one side and their interpreter-critics on the other, obscures the fact that the latter are of the same professional middle-class elite as the former. In historical terms the interpreters are the most highly articulate members of this class—its ultrasophisticates and intelligentsia—but they have been outmaneuvered by its powerful if incompetent bureaucracy and now seek refuge from and revenge upon its vulgar philistinism in an elitist cult of sensibility and taste. Caricature makes a few concessions to complexity in their satiric tirades. The venal judge Sir Derinola and the politician Chief Winsala are seen as wretched and pitiful as well as disgusting, and the hapless, status-seeking radiographer Faseyi, who must have done something to earn Bandele's friendship and the love of his independent-minded British wife, keeps challenging the fiercely angled satiric vision. But the habitués of the Oguazor-Lumoye circle are so many crass sitting ducks, set up to be righteously and hilariously shot down, without much attempt at understanding the nature and origins of their muddled elitism. In attacking them the interpreters, rather like the Lagos mob in pursuit of a scapegoat in Noah, are unleashing their negative satiric energies not on the sources but on the symptoms of the disease, a disease that, moreover, includes themselves: Sagoe acquiesces in the suppression of truth to keep his job, and Egbo has no right to spit in Lumoye's eye in righteous indignation at Oguazor's party since he, not Lumoye, was the first to seduce the student.

More problematically, Soyinka's extraordinary Menippean mélange of mystic-satiric and realistic-fantastic styles produces some jarring modal switches, notably from satiric vignette to mythological speculation, and creates uncertainty about the exact register or dimension in which some of the characters are to be regarded. The lyric intensity of the writing leaves it unclear, for example, whether Egbo is part of a collective indictment of human limitations or a partly celebratory self-portrait by the author. Like Soyinka, he associates himself with Ogun, but the ritualistic trappings and numinous rhetorical effusions with which he surrounds his mystical trances by the river Ogun are ambiguous: they denote, realistically, a precious and confused adolescent sensibility and at the same time appear to carry some ultimate religious or mythological value. In Egbo's sexual initiation by Simi the inflated rhetoric presents penetration, quite impenetrably, in terms of cosmic communion—"a lone pod strode the baobab on the tapering thigh, leaf-shorn, and high mists swirl him, haze-splitting storms" (*TI*, 60)—and Egbo later sees

himself as offering up the girl student's virginity to the river as in a
religious sacrifice, spilling her blood upon the god's toes. The hard facts
insist, however, that the sacrifice is to his own fantastic, egotistical
impulses, and that his creed is a pseudoreligion of self-worship. Lazarus's
bizarre religious prophetism is also, like Egbo's Ogun mysticism (and, to
a lesser extent, Sagoe's Voidancy), given more attention and made more
portentous than is warranted by the amount of illumination it provides.
If, as one critic has suggested,[3] Lazarus is to be seen merely as one of the
interpreters, using his cult as another piece of private mythotherapy, it is
hard to explain why Kola gives him the central position in the pantheon,
as link figure or "ladder between heaven and earth," or why so much
fascinated descriptive detail is lavished upon his weird religious antics
and the ritual ordeal he inflicts upon Noah. In theory, the albino, his
thief-turned-acolyte, and the hermaphroditic mulatto Joe Golder are
transitional half-creatures, able to transcend their own doubleness and
overcome contradiction to forge creative connections between worlds,
and Soyinka's interview remarks on albinos are consistent with this idea
(Morell, 118). At the level of practical reality, however, they have no such
transitional bridging powers but are merely freaks, frauds, and neurotics
who remain repressively locked into their own inner oppositions: Noah is
only half a convert; Golder cannot accept that he is both male and female,
black and white; and Lazarus's extraordinary tale of rising from the dead
as a "white" man may finally be no more than a psychological strategy for
coping with his albino status. Appropriately, these three characters
expose the divisions and disunities of the group, through its reactions to
themselves, and the only connecting power that they have in the novel
exists at the artificial, figmentary level of Kola's painting.

The main difficulty, however, is in the determination of the status of
Kola's pantheon, a problem not aided by the fact that neither the
painting nor its creator are seen very clearly or provided with histories. In
the second part of the novel human life is conceived as the locus of cosmic
rather than social forces, and the interpreters are seen in terms of a
metaphysical reality much larger than themselves. Yet Kola's traditional
religious-humanist attempt to represent the divine through the human
does not appear to be informed by any theological dynamic. The young
men are not priestly intermediaries, for the pantheon interprets men
through the gods, not the gods to men, and Kola himself is a godless
artist, completely lacking any numinous apprehension of his deities.[4]
The only godlike power glimpsed in his painting lies in his release of the
creative impulse by his combination of opposing forces (though Kola, in

fact, lacks this power of combination), and this creative power in turn reflects the godlike power within men to explode contradictions into creation and so escape from a destructive one-sidedness (a power lacked by Joe Golder).[5] It is never completely clear whether the pantheon is to be seen as defining the characters or the characters the pantheon: Kola's friends act as models for, but also model themselves on, the divine figures. Nevertheless, though he is clearly searching for levels of correspondence beyond mere surface resemblances, Kola does not discover to his friends their "true" natures in the form of the "god" in each of them—that is, as a dormant, inherent mythical identity or religious essence waiting to be given expression. Rather, he translates his friends into the gods, and his dependence on their physical reality is given special force when a piece of Golder's peeled, frizzled skin actually comes away and gets pinned into the paint, literally earthing the divine in human flesh. There are, as a result, no absolute or exact one-for-one correspondences between the human models and their pantheon prototypes; the painting is not so much a carefully worked-out allegory as a crazy patchwork quilt in which consistent patterns evaporate, the reference points shift, and identities become interchangeable. Something of Ogun, for example, appears to exist in each of the interpreters: his dangerous violence in Egbo; his revolutionary outrage in Sagoe; his exploring, experimenting will and risk-taking energy in Sekoni; his artistry in Kola; and his protective powers, restorative justice, and guardianship of sacred oaths in Bandele.[6] Meanwhile, Sekoni seems to contain aspects of all the deities within himself: the lightning power of Sango in his work as an electrical engineer; the wise passiveness and patient harmonizing power of Obatala (shared by Bandele); Ogun's personal disintegration and restitution, together with his refusal to believe in any absolute oppositions in the continuum of existence; and in his figurative posthumous dispersal among the other characters, the original godhead, or "universal dome," Orisa-nla.

The interpreters are meant to be seen, I think, not as discovering their natural and proper essences but as consciously manipulating and negotiating mythic personae, trying on each one in turn in their attempts to understand themselves. If the novel itself fails to find a clear identity it is because at the end its characters are still searching for one. The adopted archetypes are often wishful self-projections (Golder as a wholly black deity, Egbo as the "primal artisan" Ogun), and although the festive convergence of sculpture exhibition, concert, and completed painting suggests an impersonal, harmonizing resolution in an ordained framework of meaning, each member in fact interprets the exhibition and his

place in the pantheon in his own highly idiosyncratic manner. Egbo, for
example, links the slaughtered ram, in his mind, with the "sacrificed"
virgin by the river; Bandele connects it, more naturally, with the dead
Sekoni. Kola, who sees more comprehensively if not more correctly than
either of them, occasionally strikes a more objective note, as when he
paints Golder as the multicolored Erinle, and when he affronts Egbo by
identifying him not with Ogun the artist but with the "bestial, gore-
blinded thug" (*TI*, 233). Egbo's association with Ogun throughout the
novel has been visceral and rapacious, and (with ironic appropriateness)
his anger at Kola's carelessly destructive Ogun image leads him to
another act of careless destruction, the fatal abandonment of Noah to Joe
Golder. As he bears down upon Lumoye at the end of the novel, his "eyes
outheld on black cuspids, embers on the end of a blacksmith's tong," he
is the very epitome of the warmongering Ogun (*TI*, 249). Kola has
captured on canvas something in Egbo's character that is already visibly
there: Ogunism at its most fruitlessly introverted and egocentric. Elsewhere, however, Kola's assignation of prototypical identities to individuals is quite capricious; they appear to be no more reliable than the ones
the characters have given themselves. He first, mysteriously, paints
Noah as Christ, then as Esumare the rainbow spirit, and finally, without
explanation, he substitutes the master for the acolyte and gives Lazarus
the central linking role. At this point the pantheon becomes a whimsical
creation, its fanciful "correspondences" as shifting and unstable as the
novel's styles and time schemes, and it becomes difficult to say at what
level and in whose mind Noah and Lazarus are projected as unifiers, or
wherein, if anywhere, the meaning and value of the pantheon is constituted. The prose in these climactic episodes is cluttered by a superfluity
of meanings, of rarefied symbolic connections and crossed identities. It
seems finally that the novel has itself retreated into the esoteric aesthetic
mystique of Kola's painting, as if the latter offered the novel's diverse
elements more than a precious artistic coherence and contained an
ultimate revelation about reality instead of being one more subjective
interpretation of the contemporary scene. Art, because of its plethora of
theorists and practitioners, occupies a prominent place in *The Interpreters*,
but its role is problematic. It is, except for the book's one true artist
Sekoni (and even he withdraws from social commitment into sculpture),
an escapist opiate, merely sublimatory and consolatory; nevertheless,
that quality is seen by the artists themselves as a supreme fulfillment. At
its worst art is a dangerously desensitizing and distracting influence: the
completion of Kola's painting leads indirectly, through the self-

absorption of its subjects, to a death. At its best it is a harmless harmonizing of anguish for purposes of private purification or an expression of frustration with a public ugliness and corruption that the artist has long given up trying to change. Unable to alter their society, Kola and his confederates merely "interpret" it.

In the second novel's more testing context of political catastrophe, art ventures out into the public domain, first in a prostitutive and then in a subversive role. *Season of Anomy* (1973), a more openly allegoric work that lacks the metaphysical intricacies of the first novel, is a free adaptation and surrealistic transposition to fiction of the military crises and massacres of the summer of 1966 that led to the Biafran secession and civil war. The musician and promotions executive Ofeyi begins, in his advertising campaigns, to undermine both the giant Cocoa Corporation for which he works and the ruthless military-industrial ruling "Cartel" of which it is a part by disseminating the communalist political ideas of a village utopia called Aiyero. Further to this, he borrows some of Aiyero's revolutionary cadres to spread its ideals through the Cartel state in the hope that they will bear fruit beyond the rural boundaries of the commune. The Cartel's response is to arouse local tribal hatreds against the Aiyero men who are working in the region of Cross-Rivers (thus implying that the federal regime directed hatred at all Ibos, from whom many progressives and activists came). In the wave of terror and massacre that is unleashed, most of Ofeyi's musical troupe is wiped out and their dancer, Iriyese, is abducted. The ensuing quest for Iriyese takes Ofeyi on a nightmare trip through a relentlessly horrifying and graphically described landscape of genocidal slaughter and mutilation, a journey that is underlaid by the seasonal myth of Orpheus's search for Eurydice in the underworld. This mystical underpinning links together Ofeyi's personal pursuit of his stolen love, the nationwide revolutionary violence emanating from Aiyero, and nature's seasonal cycle of renewal observed by ritual, a continuum that is reflected in the chapter titles—"Seminal," "Buds," "Tentacles," "Harvest," "Spores"—and in Ofeyi's earlier advice to Pa Ahime, the head of the commune, that Aiyero's "grain must find new seminal grounds or it will atrophy and die."[7] Ofeyi's Aiyero-inspired humanistic initiative and individual quest are counterpointed by the ruthless assassin and revolutionary Demakin, better known as "the Dentist" because of his "unassailable logic of extraction before infection" (*SOA*, 88). After much agonizing by Ofeyi over the rival options of Aiyero's utopian idealism and the Dentist's dedicated selective violence, it comes as something of a shock to learn that Demakin has secretly been an agent of Aiyero from the start and that these two are not in opposition but are working in concert. It is, in fact, Demakin who carries Ofeyi through the last three "circles" of his infernal voyage—the circles of cripples, lepers, and lunatics in the bowels of Temoko prison—and who accomplishes the rescue of Iriyese. In Soyinka's version Eurydice is not lost to Hades but emerges in a coma, representing the sleep of reason and sanity in the nation around her but also recalling her earlier stage act in which she bursts, in triumphant fructification, from the sleeping seeds of a giant cocoa pod. Symbolically, in the novel's closing cliché, "in the forests life began to stir" (*SOA*, 320). Ofeyi's challenge to the Cartel has been crushed and the forces of Aiyero are in retreat, but their seeds have been sown and may, like Iriyese, stir into life.

Despite Pa Ahime's stray remark that Aiyero "grants Ogun pride of place," the god is a silent presence in this novel. His restless revolutionary energy is replaced, at the realistic level, by the Dentist's political praxis—in which violence now stops at itself and leaves the business of renewal to others—and at the mythical level, by the lone private quest of the Orphic artist figure. Ofeyi's journey is across rather than through chaos (it has in places a spectatorial dream quality, and Ofeyi seems to lead the charmed life of the protagonist of an adventure story), and the recovery of the somewhat dubious revolutionary figurehead Iriyese is a symbolic salvaging operation, not an armed insurrection, a relief action, not a revolutionary one. Indeed, it is one of the peculiarities and inconsistencies of the novel that, with the reappearance of Demakin as an Aiyero agent, the political action begins to dissipate into ritual and myth. After the Cartel's massacre of their kinsmen, the survivors ritualize their trek back to Aiyero as a "cleansing act" that will "purify our present polluted humanity" and cure them "of the dangers of self-pity" (*SOA*, 218), and the political campaign is abandoned for the symbolic rescue of Iriyese, whose superior value as ideological weapon and standard-bearer even the Dentist is made, rather unconvincingly, to agree upon. There follows a fantasy of abstract ideological concord that shelves but does not solve the moral and political debate, at the heart of the book, between the humane scruples of the liberal individualist and the drastic surgical measures of the hardheaded assassin. Doubtless, rural utopians, revolutionary assassins, and liberals all have something to contribute to the struggle against tyranny, and the Dentist's violent eliminations and Ofeyi's visionary programs of reconstruction are conceivable as separate phases of a single process. Nevertheless, they are in themselves radically unlike and opposed in spirit—the vision, for Demakin, must come after the action, not inform or interfere with it. In the hard terms of realpolitik the ritual quest is an obscure diversion that draws attention away from active opposition to the Cartel.

Early in the book the cocoa seed's cycle of germination is made to prefigure both a personal and collective rite of passage—"the parallel progress of the new idea, the birth of the new man from the same germ as the cocoa seed"—and even the revolutionary violence emanating from Aiyero is earthed in the seasonal cycle: "The sowing of an idea these days can no longer take place without accepting the need to protect the young seedling, even by violent means" (*SOA*, 19, 23). The Orphic seasonal archetype tends, however, to align the novel's sympathies with Ofeyi's lone sacrificial quietism and against Demakin's committed activism. This tendency not only has the effect of upholding the artist's merely intellectual assumption of the burden of suffering—in this case, knowledge of the futile genocidal sacrifice of ethnic groups at fake altars of national unity—but, more seriously, it tends to subsume the Cartel's massacres into the rhythm of natural cycles, camouflaging pogrom as purification. Watching the corpses float past the Shage Dam, Ofeyi battles with the consoling fictions that the slaughtered men of Aiyero are not only scapegoats for the nation's guilt but regenerative sacrificial offerings in a mass vegetation rite, that seasonal and political revolution, and nature's and men's deaths, are the same and the human destruction will "tear up earth and throw it back in stronger, fructifying forms." Ofeyi unearths "a feeling of great repose" from human carnage: "Perhaps it all seemed part of the churned up earth, part of the clay and humus matrix from which steel hands would later mould new living forms. I am lying to myself again he said, seeking barren consolation" (*SOA*, 173–74). The temptations, to which Ofeyi is alert in his more astute moments, are to see elements of constructively beneficial action or even revolutionary struggle as present in all sacrifice, which is therefore never construed as mere waste, and to dissolve anger into self-deluding fatalism or indolent justification. As in the lyric poetry and the description of Sekoni's death in *The Interpreters*, human suffering and death are absorbed into the neutral contexts of nonhuman nature and cosmic cycles, where their individual pain and horror no longer impinge. For all its graphic and horrifying realism, *Season* finally seeks a suspiciously facile refuge in the seasonal fatalism of myth, and though the horrors are at least equal to those treated in *Madmen and Specialists*, the Obatalan wholeness, after the rendings of pain and terror, is here restored with a puzzling ease. On the ritual front Ofeyi becomes a kind of reverse carrier who, instead of

conveying the infections from an otherwise healthy community, bears
the healthy seeds from the nerve center of an infected system, but the real
effect of this ordeal on the blasted, wasted society appears to be no more
redemptive or purificatory (unless too much is pinned on the conversion
of the gatekeeper Suberu) than that of Sekoni on the interpreters in the
first novel. *Season*, though stylistically and mythologically complex, is a
politically simplistic novel, not least in its rather crude, cartoonlike
polarization of wicked imbecilic potentates and impotent visionaries.
Political history is conceived conveniently in terms of cartelized, powerful individual personalities who are untouched by the ethnic currents
they manipulate and are removable en bloc by policies of selective
assassination, as are their victims by concerted rescue actions. Ofeyi never
questions the practical effectiveness of either of these solutions.

There are also problems of style and mode in Soyinka's second novel.
Though the book excels in moments of startling, horrifying wit, as in the
"spattering [of] schoolroom walls with brains hot from learning" (*SOA*,
110), the style is often gratuitously grotesque, as in the lurid, voluptuous
account of Ahime's slaughter of the white bulls in the early part of the
novel: "The . . . flutist blade was laid again and again to ivory
pipes . . . a last spriglet of blood blossomed briefly . . . [and] a final
shudder of love gave all to a passive earth" (*SOA*, 17). The hectic,
tongue-twisting rhetoric that some of the characters are given to speak
("Leave me to track my own spoors on the laterals, Tailla"), though in
some ways suited to lyrical fiction in which the lines do not have to be
spoken in public, contains in its cyclic-seasonal imagery allegoric tendencies that are more easily accommodated by stylized modes of drama.
In the more rounded flesh-and-blood world of fiction there tends to be a
divergence of what in the plays is able to converge: the conceptual and
immediate, mythological symbolism and naturalism, ritual and reality.
In *The Interpreters* these dual realities are often at odds, and "metaphysical" and "realistic" explanations of events, such as Egbo's mystical
trances and the whole Lazarus episode, are contradictory. In *Season*, the
chief casualties of these unresolved tensions are the merely functional
"morality" characters Tailla and the Dentist, who have no existence
except as Ofeyi's "good and bad angels," representing the alternatives of
mystical contemplative withdrawal and revolutionary activism. Another
casuality—one who suffers from the same expressionistic thinness—is
that impossible combination of "gin and tonic siren" and earth mother,
Iriyese, who has little real substance outside Ofeyi's male imagination
("Vision is eternally of man's own creating") and who, like the expatri-

ated Aiyero youths, remains miraculously untouched by the corrupting influences of the modern state. At the heart of the antinomy is Ofeyi himself, constantly trying to shrug off habits of metaphysical rationalization and mythologizing that obscure rather than sharpen understanding. For example, he frames the misshapen Cross-Rivers man Aliyu in a "metaphysic condition called evil," seeing him as determined by apolitical factors such as climate, geography, and innate "natural" forces, and as a mere instrument in one of history's cyclic seasons of anomy. But Aliyu, characterized as "another deformity like the effects of meningitis or the blood-poisoning of the tse-tse fly" (*SOA*, 276), turns out to be a good Cross-Rivers native who has outgrown infection by the regime's racist poison as he has outgrown his smallpox, and his subsequent courageous, altruistic deeds indicate that the tribal mob evil engineered and orchestrated by the Cartel is a political, not a metaphysical phenomenon, calling for a practical, not a ritual remedy.

The main movement in both of these books is an inward retreat from clearly defined public failure and catastrophe into an ambiguous and indeterminate private mythology, albeit one collectively subscribed to within the fictional frames—Kola's pantheon, Iriyese as torchbearer awaiting ritual deliverance from the underworld. *Season*'s "floating style" of reportage, though it catches eerily the unreality of horror and atrocity, also blurs their objectivity into the introspective consciousness of Ofeyi, whose spectator verbiage of "recognizing," "confronting," and "understanding" evil is not a great advance in real terms on the dreamy idealism of Sekoni. It remains to inquire what are the uses of Ofeyi's effort, through his search, to "immerse [himself] in the meaning of the event" and acquire "a new understanding of history" (*SOA*, 218) if his effort does nothing concretely to stem the tide of contemporary cataclysm, and what a "consciousness" of the need for armed resistance to tyranny practically amounts to if it does not lead to the thing itself. Ofeyi espouses violence only in the curiously externalized form of acknowledging the necessary role of the assassin; but he does not practice it himself, so we are left uninformed about any real changes in his inner nature resulting from this acknowledgment and, therefore, about the degree to which he is actually implicated. *Season* offers no blueprints for popular revolution but pinpoints the individual conscience of the liberal and humane artist, and though Ofeyi's mental harvest and ideological ripening are a stage on from the self-preoccupied, consolatory art of the interpreters, they achieve no greater results. The switch of focus from the first to the second novel is therefore not so much from private fulfillment to public commitment and collective action but from the intellectual elite's isolated individual sensibility to the trials of its tormented conscience. It is not Soyinka's wish to persuade us that years of isolated contemplation have made Aiyero's experimental ideologies ready for export into the larger society, or that they have the capacity to transform a militarized monopoly-capitalist despotism into a nation of decentralized communes.[8] Rather, Ofeyi's failure to extend Aiyero's values beyond its rural boundaries implies a critique of its parochial utopianism. But it is suggested, not very persuasively, that the paths leading deep into the recesses of the private consciousness finally, by some mysterious process analogous with Ahime's restorative pool, bring the lone visionary hero out into the public domain and into sociopolitical reality. The problem is partly that, in his temporary abandonment of Ogun, Soyinka has saddled himself with an excessively individualistic Western myth of the artist-hero that does not easily blend with the revolutionary political myth of Aiyero.

Chapter 8
History and Fiction:
The Autobiographies

The term "autobiography" is here given the widest possible interpretation to include fictionalized family memoirs and childhood remembrances alongside a civil war record garnered directly from jottings in improvised prison diaries.

The Man Died (1972), though it draws upon the dramatist's skilled observation and uses the novelistic devices of flashback, foreshadowing, and juxtaposition, was not conceived as imaginative literature. It is too painfully raw and immediate, too close to what it describes, and is not so much a work of art as an account of the artist's mental and bodily survival—in his own words, "not a textbook for survival but the private record of one survival" (*TMD*, 26). The book is a narrative of Soyinka's interrogation and imprisonment by the federal military government, interwoven with the crucial events of 18 months prior to his arrest. The writer had lobbied the United Nations for a ban on arms supplies to both sides in the coming conflict and, with Victor Banjo, had attempted to form the "Third Force," composed of bipartisan intellectuals, to prevent the war. His travels across the country had taken him in August 1967 to Enugu to meet the Biafran leader, Col. C. O. Ojukwu, and on his return home he was detained on the trumped-up accusation of having given active support to the enemy by assisting with the purchase of jet aircraft for the rebel leader. A forged confession of his guilt was produced, and though never formally charged and brought to trial, Soyinka was imprisoned from August 1967 to October 1969, including 15 months in solitary confinement at Kaduna Prison in the North (the original of Temoko in *Season of Anomy*). An attempt on his life before his removal to Kaduna was thwarted only by the forewarnings of informants and his own quick thinking. At Kaduna he was refused medical treatment, adequate clothing and blankets, and, most seriously for Soyinka, reading and writing material of any kind. Here he fasted, partly as a hunger strike in protest against privation and to demonstrate to his captors that he was still in charge of himself, and partly as a strategy of self-withdrawal, cutting off memories of the past and thoughts of family and, by teaching his body to require nothing, asserting his mental control over reality. One day, after a pen stolen from an official had given out, a kindly crow molted a strong-quilled feather through his roof grating and, using as ink the juice squeezed from berries in a tiny vegetable garden adjacent to his cell (he christened it "Soy-ink"), he scribbled on toilet paper, cigarette wrappers, and, later, in the margins of his own book *Idanre*, notes for what would become his quartet of civil war writings, including *The Man Died*. More than once the prisoner looked over into the abyss of madness as his lone mind meandered through a labyrinth of lofty outrage, apathy, and wild exhilaration and then, as reality was erased, became a hallucinating "cotton wool consciousness," mystically weightless as it shuttled back and forth in the vacant crypt of his cell.

The Man Died is a shocking and harrowing book that recreates frighteningly the special paranoid climate of terror prevailing in police states in crises of civil war. In one scene the prison inmates cheer the release of two bragging, Ibo-murdering soldiers (both "Very Important Prisoners") to express their loyalty to what Soyinka calls "a genocidal-consolidated dictatorship." Imprisoned innocents are routinely butchered or flogged for no other reason than their tribal membership, and mass denunciations, for any expression of Ibo sympathy, become commonplace. But the book is equally unsparing in its documentation of the protracted psychological torture tactics—the petty subterfuges, pointless harassments, ingenious cruelties, and perverse quirks of compassion—by which totalitarian regimes intimidate (and incriminate) their recalcitrants and wreak their mental and spiritual deaths. A mixture of bureaucratic bungling and calculated malevolence, in imponderable proportions, decrees that chains be placed on the eminent author's feet, removed, then replaced. The vegetable garden that humanizes the prisoner's life for a few precious weeks is wantonly destroyed by the guards. Paper, typewriter, radio, and new clothes are provided for his wife's visit and then whisked away the moment she is out of the prison. He is enticed with rumored prospects of a Christmas release and then, without explanation, left to rot another nine months by sadistic officials who like "to play Father Christmas with justice" (*TMD*, 221).

"Justice," Soyinka asserts, "is the first condition of humanity," and it is the larger, shared imperatives of justice and morality, seen as the ultimate authenticators of human identity, that prevent *The Man Died* from becoming an exclusively self-enclosed, narcissistic work. "Surely it cannot be a strictly personal experience," Soyinka muses atavistically as his feet are chained, and though his prison experience strikes him, increasingly, as "unique among the fifty million people of my country," he struggles to give his private suffering a public dimension by casting himself in a typifying role (*TMD*, 40, 13). Unwilling to let his burning sense of personal injustice fruitlessly feed upon and consume itself, he directs it outward to identify with the general injustice perpetrated everywhere in the name of authority and mass conformity. Significantly, it is his own letter deploring the miscarriage of justice by which the two self-confessed murderers were acquitted that seals his own fate and prolongs indefinitely the injustice done to himself, for it is the circulation of this letter, smuggled out to academic colleagues and betrayed to the military authorities, that causes the federal leader, General Gowon, to cancel the order for Soyinka's release. The very title of the book is taken from injustices done to others: they are the words of a cable announcing the death of a Nigerian journalist after being savagely beaten for an imagined personal slight to Gowon, and the reply of a warder when Soyinka asks why the untended invalid in the next cell has finally stopped groaning: "The man died, he said" (*TMD*, 200). The man, meaning the human being in each of us, "dies" when we keep silent in the presence of all such suffering. Moreover, some of the most moving and absorbing parts of the book are its statements of solidarity with fellow prisoners, notably the vignette of the Ibo woman in the Lagos jail who both gives and gathers strength in her brief encounter with the chained author, and the marvelous account of the brutalized Ibo prisoners who, from conditions of appalling squalor, sing in a defiant expression of comradeship and courage: "They wound their voices round our innermost guts and made each man partake of the brotherhood sacrament of blood and guilt and pain" (*TMD*, 111). Throughout his chronicle Soyinka insists upon his need for exchanges "within a community of minds," and it is, finally, not any single indignity inflicted upon himself but the ultimate public, communal outrage—the newly married Gowon's feudal evaluation of the fall of the Biafran capital as a belated wedding present—that draws his most vitriolic scorn. There are, moreover, even in those elevated passages where Soyinka gives his mystical inclinations free rein and the mind withdraws from the senses into irreducible extremes of introspection, moments of glorious self-transcendence: as when, for example, with a Thoreau-like blend of exact observation and private whimsy, he chronicles the insect and reptile life in the miniature world of his cell, or when, multiplying marvels from the monotony of prison life, he derives unguents from plants and fashions flutes from sunflower stalks.

Yet, for all this, *The Man Died* is—as to a large extent all records of solitary confinement must be—an essentially personal and highly subjective statement, and in the minds of some critics it is seriously marred by its egoism. Soyinka is much given to anticipating himself in his own writing, and in the remarkable twelfth chapter he finds himself once again in familiar territory: "I know that I have come to this point in the cycle more than once" (*TMD*, 88). He is now, in real life, in the position of the Warrior in *A Dance of the Forests*: interrogated as a traitor for opposing an unjust war. With a flourish of bitter self-congratulation, he finds his earlier prophecies and his view of history as a cycle of recurring evil borne out by events. In what follows Soyinka wrestles with the facile temptation to cast himself in the special roles of existentialist hero, tragic martyr, and fated sacrificial victim. Shrugging off the scapegoat mentality, he gives himself the pragmatic reminder that his death will not be morally or socially beneficial but futile because it will not challenge but only further the interests of a corrupt military regime. The "poetic snare of tragic loftiness" diverts constructive energies into martyred egoism and operates as a social safety valve, retrieving human unhappiness, subsuming it and "justifying it in the form of necessity, wisdom or purification. . . . History is too full of failed prometheans bathing their wounded spirits in the tragic stream" (*TMD*, 89, 90). "Suspect all conscious search for the self's authentic being," Soyinka warns. "This is favourite fodder for the enervating tragic Muse" (*TMD*, 88-89). Yet his posing of the dilemma "Do I or do I not recognize the trap?" still focuses, inevitably in the ego-centered prison narrative, on the self-dramatizing, introspective "I," which in the immediate straitened context can progress no further than recognition. There is, moreover, with an ambivalence characteristic of Soyinka's refusal of all simple, one-sided positions, a certain self-advertisement even in his self-mockery and parading of self-doubt, and a self-importance in his reluctant admission of common humanity with the ignorant masses: "Brainwashed, gullible fools, many-headed multitudes, why should your voices raised in ignorance affect my peace? But they do. I cannot deny it" (*TMD*, 90).[1] Though he is selected by circumstance to bear witness to the collective moral failure of the nation and illumine its general predicament, the fact that he *is* selected makes him, unhesitatingly, an exemplary figure and a model for lesser beings: "If *he* could break and break so abjectly then anyone can break . . . who are we to struggle?" (*TMD*, 80, 96). It must be said in mitigation, of course, that his "spiritual in-locked egoism" that he guards against in the soul-searching of chapter 12 is at other times a deliberate and necessary strategy, a way of holding on to an inalienable human core of reality to stay sane: "This creature is irrelevant, he is not real. I represent reality" (*TMD*, 100).

More seriously, Soyinka's conspiracy theory of profit-motivated pogroms and his attribution of absolute personal responsibility for genocide to political leaders, though acceptable when removed to the fictional zone of the Cartel in *Season of Anomy*, have been found rather thin and simplistic as political analysis, particularly the facile inculpation of colonialism and its original disposal of African "peoples" into artificial "nations": "What God (the white man) has put together, let no black man put asunder" (*TMD*, 181). In these passages Soyinka is engaging in indictment rather than analysis, and he is more the prophet than the political scientist and historian: "Militarist entrepreneurs and multiple dictatorships: this is bound to be the legacy of a war which is conducted on the present terms. . . . The war means a consolidation of crime, an acceptance of the scale of values that created the conflict, indeed an allegiance and enshrinement of that scale of values because it is now intimately bound to the sense of national identity" (*TMD*, 182). This is, in fact, an uncannily accurate prediction of Nigeria's anomic postwar future—the continuing criminal tyranny of the Gowon regime, the powerful "Kaduna Mafia" of the Shagari years and Soyinka was right, in the circumstances, to stress that "this book is *now*." (The beating incident that gave the book its title happened well after the war.) But conspiracy theories are notoriously difficult either to disprove or to substantiate, and whether the "alliance of a corrupt militarism and a rapacious Mafia" was in fact a cause or a product of the war is still a matter for speculation. For some commentators, the vague characterization of the Third Force as "a truly national, moral and revolutionary alternative" that "thinks in terms of a common denominator for the people" (*TMD*, 95, 178) is patently inadequate, providing no information about its political aims, policies, and methods. Moreover, Soyinka's identification with it appears to be dictated by an instinctive, emotional attraction to charismatic individuals, such as Banjo and Fajuyi, rather than by any ideological bond.[2] Others have been disturbed by elements of the book's rhetoric, namely, its therapeutic, self-sustaining vituperation, its vilification and bestialization of foes, and its venomously categoric judgments: "These men are not merely evil, I thought. They are the mindlessness of evil made flesh. . . . They are pus, bile, original putrescence of Death in living shapes" (*TMD*, 228). Of course, an innocent victim of calumny has a right to respond in kind, and Soyinka does initially acknowledge (anonymously, for their own safety) those individuals who helped him and showed him kindness in his northern prison. But it is clear from these disparate elements of the book that its personal introspections do not quite gel with its politics, and the attempt to juxtapose, in Soyinka's words, "the most transcendental phases of human subjectivity" with "squalor, sordidness, ugliness" (Agetua, 37) only deepens the divide, since the poetry is largely reserved for the personal passages and the scatological abuse—the "languages of sheer deliberate brutality"—for the political material. Whatever Soyinka's claims to the contrary,[3] the outstanding value of *The Man Died* is as a human and personal, not a political document. It is a brave and brilliant testament to the resilience of the human mind in extremity, thrown back entirely upon itself and its own inner resources in its bid to survive. It remains, however, one man's vision.

After the torrid egocentricity of the *The Man Died*, Soyinka's next volume of memoirs is a joyously dispassionate work. *Aké: The Years of Childhood* (1981) is remarkably free from the narcissistic self-indulgence of which Soyinka, as a critic, has long suspected autobiographical forms. This is no mean feat given that the book recounts the first ten years in the life of a child prodigy who takes himself off to school before his third birthday, speaks English to a white colonial officer at the age of four, enters the local grammar school at nine, and serves as a teacher and messenger in the Egba Women's Movement at ten. The saving factor here is the sharply tongue-in-cheek, delightfully self-mocking prose that Soyinka uses to evoke the child's sense of himself. The brooding, precocious genius muses, prepubertally, about prospective wives, falls into fits of distraction in which he wrecks his father's rosebed and fires off his shotgun, and transforms into comic human personae the mystifying abstractions "Change," "Temperature," and "Birthday": "Birthday proved to be all that was expected once it had got over the one disappointing limitation—Birthday did not just happen but needed to be reminded to happen" (*Aké*, 30). Of equal importance is the title's indication that Soyinka is writing about the place and time of his childhood and equating them with it. "In a sense there was never any real dichotomy, no will to separation, between me and the influences of Aké," Soyinka has said. "It was one seamless existence" (Gulledge, 514, 518). Of course, in every autobiography there is a necessary degree of estrangement between the egotistical narrative persona and his community—the memoir that achieves a perfect organic fusion of self and society has yet to be written—and Soyinka, in his interview statements, allows that the immediate emphasis falls on the child's "fragmented sensibility" but adds that his childhood self is motivated "even more by a desire or a need constantly to link one thing to another." His wider aim in writing the book was to "capture a period" that "began with my childhood consciousness, with my immediate family, and then opened into other things" (Gulledge, 518, 520). The father's parsonage and the mother's shop in the town of Abeokuta are focal points for the turbulent comings and goings of a community of friends, traders, and visiting dignitaries, not to mention a constant stream of "stray" relations and wards, and provide outlets into the life of a whole people. In the nostalgic chapter 10 the town market's glorious synaesthesia of sounds, sights, and smells, now coarsened and drowned out by car horns and Western pop, are "part of the invisible network of Aké's extended persona" (*Aké*, 149).

The narrative's progress, in pursuit of this extended self, is a series of outward expansions, beginning with the child's personal development and rebellion against "the irrational world of adults and their discipline," and ending with a nation's growth to political maturity and organized protest against both internal and external oppressors. At the personal level, the young Wole undergoes a succession of inductions into an ever-expanding outer world, from his initial breeching of the parsonage walls in pursuit of a police band to his initiation into grammar school discipline by his uncle Daodu, and into manhood and the traditional Yoruba world through scarification rites supervised by his grandfather in Isara. This crossing of boundaries, and the "mental shifts" entailed, are then reenacted at another level in the bourgeois professional wives' negotiation of lines of both class and gender (they admit women traders to their group meetings and undertake active protest) to challenge the patriarchal powers of the Alake, the local king, and the colonial administration. In the process a ladies' club's welfare task force designed to resolve the domestic and educational problems of newlyweds becomes entangled with the move to put an end to white rule and finally takes on global dimensions when its leader, Beere, harangues the white district officer on the racist implications of the dropping of the atom bombs on Japan. The broken boundaries are not merely social and political, however, but also linguistic, psychological, and ontological: the spoken language ranges across parsonage English, trader's Yoruba, poor relations' pidgin, and policeman's Hausa, while, ontologically, the worlds of living and dead are bound together by the abiku child and by the egungun, a connection that expresses the extended metaphysical being of elders and grandparents as the Egba Women's Movement expresses the wider social being of the women. And the boundaries are none the less real for being crossed, exacting a great price in pain or persecution for their transgression. The abiku Bukola, who breaches the boundaries of the spirit world, is a plague and torment to its parents, and the normal child who challenges the adult boundaries that regulate and socialize his existence meets with the severest discipline. When the local madwoman Sorowanke forfeits the spirituality normally accorded the mad by becoming pregnant and attempts a version of conventional domestic life, the local food-sellers, unable to accept this violation of accepted limits, close in to stone her and burn down her improvised dwelling. And when the local eccentric Paa Adatan challenges the imperialist African soldiers (the Bote), his self-transformation from colonial stooge to nationalist rebel carries him across the border between harmless paranoia and dangerous lunacy.

Except for the odd intrusions and backward projections of adult prejudice, such as the hostile view of the *ogboni* (priestly elders) and the mischievous chauvinism that attributes progress in the Egba Women's Movement to male initiatives, Soyinka meticulously sustains the miniaturized, self-apprehended worldview of the child throughout *Aké*. The opening impressions of the "sprawling, undulating terrain," the unspecified "loyalty to the parsonage" and the agentless "resentment" that God should view the landscape from a pagan mountain, all manage to contrive, without any Joycean rhetorical plunge into infantile babble, an impression of raw sensory experience transformed directly into language, and in the absence of any mature mediating consciousness. The strange dislocations that derive from the child's mixture of acute observation and partial comprehension are, of course, the stuff of all childhoods, and Soyinka turns these to rich comic effect, as in the child's supposition that the music issuing from the His Master's Voice gramophone is made by a "special singing dog locked in the machine," or in the juvenile paronomasia by which children customarily name and control their world: thus Canon Delumo is assumed to be so named because "his head was like a cannon ball," because "cannons looked immobile, indestructible, and so did he," and more inventively, Soyinka's father, called "S. A." from his initials, is transformed into "Essay" because of his elegance and fastidiousness and the methodical habits that turn eating into a "geometric exercise" (*Aké*, 13-15, 41). Keeping close to the words and ideas of the child's autonomous perspective and banishing anything extraneous to it, Soyinka supplies none of the obvious interpretative additions, as when, for example, the young Wole, in a rage at his rejection from his mother's bed, wrestles with pythons in his dreams and discharges his father's gun. In addition to the above, however, the peculiar displacements, silences, and evasions of Soyinka's narrative are the staple fare of the colonial childhood. The colonial writer, Soyinka also said in his 1987 seminar on *Aké* at Louisiana State University, lives two lives, the colonial experience and the emergence from it, and he speculated that it was at the point of transition between worlds that the need for autobiography, and its desire to focus a once unquestioned and now disappearing differentness, arise. Soyinka's childhood, like all colonial childhoods, was a hybridized, duality-ridden affair, rent by cracks and fissures that militate against the child's early illusion that all roofs and walls are connected with his own "in one continuous seam" or "overlapping, interleaved planes" (*Aké*, 2, 37).

The child's behavioral touchstone, for example, is a Western elitist individualism that prizes outstanding achievers like Daodu and is quite at odds with indigenous communalism: "I hated the communal mat. . . . I simply preferred to be on my own" (*Aké*, 83). Furthermore, his immediate reading of his African world is a Europeanized, Christian one. The very attempt to find an African identity for the Edenic apple takes as its points of reference a biblical fable that, like the Church and the English language, is a cultural transplant and is itself evidence of colonial cultural hegemony. Thus a feeling of fragility undercuts the child's complacency, a feeling of something that refuses to belong in spite of his creative transformations, and the matter is further complicated by the knowledge that the chosen tropical analogue for the apple, the pomegranate, is itself "foreign to the black man's soil," an agricultural—as its Edenic original was a theological—import. Yet what appears to be a straightforward division of superior and inferior cultures is really a much more egalitarian and mutually interactive phenomenon, for the commanding impression is that the pomegranate, whatever its true history, has taken root in the African imagination as if it really were an indigenous—or indigenized—alternative that weakens the imperial hegemony. There is a sense, both here and elsewhere, of a foreign element transformed, of the colonial impingement as an assimilation or translation into another order of experience instead of an obliteration of one culture by another. For example, although the child imagines the mysterious supernatural companions of the *oro* (spirit) as being like (or even being) the Wolf Cubs, thus taking the Western form as his yardstick, he can make sense of the stained-glass figure of St. Peter only in terms of the ancestral egungun whose strange noises penetrate the parsonage walls and whose timbre he hears in the church organ. Here the indigenous religious form, which has survived the incursions of Christian sainthood, is the point of reference and the primary reality. There is no simple, one-way hegemony at work here. Similarly, the African religious position on the abiku is not replaced by the Western skeptical-rationalist attitude but coexists with it. For the child Wole, Bukola is simultaneously an awesome supernatural figure and an interesting case study in behavioral psychology; a malevolent spirit being and a willful child who, like all children, communes with secret, imaginary friends and threatens fits and tantrums to escape discipline. Even the mother's fiery evangelicism is compounded with traditional African beliefs. She is a "Wild Christian" (the nickname Soyinka uses for her) not only because of her militant, confrontationist approach to "pagans" and her erratic discipline, coupled with a tough love and compassionate wisdom, but also in the sense that she is the "wild card" in the Christian pack. Side by side with Bible stories, she fills her children's heads with tales of forest spirits and the oro Uncle Sanya's supernatural visitors, and her story of the egungun's collapsing of the church walls is an ironic lesson in faith that both upholds and undermines Christianity since the egungun, though unable to harm the Christians, do succeed in bringing down the building. Her notion that "harmful medicines could also be passed through the head," which causes her to have her children's hair cut by a pagan neighbor, Broda Pupa, is informed by the same fear of poison and the same traditional faith in magical protective substances that prompt the ritual incisions and infusions performed by the grandfather on the young Wole in Isara.

These unreconciled contradictions between indigenous and imported beliefs are, of course, rich sources of creative conflict throughout Soyinka's work from *Camwood on the Leaves* to *The Road*, and though the child sees "the world of the parsonage and the Aafin" (the Alake's palace) as "so far apart" that they cannot "be linked in any way" (*Aké*, 205), the seasoned Soyinka reader suspects that they are connected, as indeed are the polarized worlds of Christian and pagan, father and grandfather, Abeokuta and Isara. The grandfather, significantly called "Father" throughout the Isara episode, lets slip that he has arranged the scarification rite with the boy's father (presumably, knowledge has been kept from Wild Christian), and he seems to be remarkably well informed, in his backwoods wilderness, about the pastor's educational world and the obstacles awaiting the boy at Ibadan Government College. The distance between the child's biological and spiritual parentage, between his father-in-Christ and his father-in-Ogun, does not seem to be nearly so great as his limited perspective would have us believe. Given the contradictions within the text itself, it comes as no surprise to find that in Soyinka's fictionalized persona in his subsequent memoir *Isara*, the grandfather is already a baptized Christian and a man in step with the march of the modern world, not someone easily consigned, as he is in *Aké*, to "that same province of beliefs as the *ogboni* of Aké, as the priests and priestesses of various cults and mysteries against whom Wild Christian and her co-religionists sometimes marched" (139). (A Christian version of the ogboni existed, in any case, from the turn of the century onward.) Neither is it surprising to read in James Gibbs's researches into Soyinka's family history that the social circle of the "heathen" side of the family had close political dealings with the Christian side (the Ransome-Kutis), and that, as is evident in *Isara*, the public figures in both groups straddled cultures and drew creatively upon dual traditions.[4] Clearly, things are happening here that the child does not perceive and that Soyinka is not, directly, telling us about. Somewhere in the unexplained silences, the natural lacunae of autobiography that allow the author to say things and yet leave them unsaid, a secret dialogue seems to be going on between the historical prototypes of the book's ostensibly opposed cultures.

A certain amount of autobiography is, of necessity, fictional, as a great deal of fiction is autobiographical. Memory fictionalizes, rearranging and embroidering on events, and the creative imagination, it is clear from *Aké*, shapes and orchestrates facts into significance with the aid of the devices and techniques of fiction. In the account of the women's uprising an omniscient third-person narration that affects the spurious authority of historical narrative is combined with a personally involved recital to give the writing the composed, editorial element of fiction, while, more specifically, the child's presence at the most dramatic scenes of the uprising seems to draw somewhat upon the conventions of the historical adventure novel. In the seminar on his book Soyinka claimed a near-mystical ability to reenter and reinhabit his own past, almost to the extent of being physically transported to and reincarnated in it, as in spirit possession, and giving him the faculty of total recall (Gulledge, 525). The coherent, structured dialogues presented in the uprising, however, sound like the carefully staged imaginative reconstructions of the poet-dramatist. We read of Daodu that "everything that [he] did was not merely larger than size, he made trivia itself larger than life and made a drama of every event" (*Aké*, 173), and this is what the book itself, with consummate dramatic skill, succeeds in doing. *Aké* mythologizes family members into types and larger-than-life figures, each of them magnified by memory and rescued from the diminishing effects of time. (The contemporary Aké is described as "shrunk with time.") Their speech is not verbatim quotations but, rather, typifying approximations drawn from family sayings and maternal recollections (Soyinka consulted his mother when writing the book), and as James Olney has suggested, the author tells us not so much what a "real" person once said as what a character in the world of the autobiography would have said.[5]

Moreover, as historicist approaches to the text have shown, Soyinka takes all of the historical novelist's and dramatist's liberties with facts and dates.[6] The protests against the Sole Native Authority System and the taxation of women, which took place between 1947 and 1952—during his teenage years—Soyinka moves back into his nonage. The 48-hour vigil that he describes in chapter 14 in fact took place in 1947, when he was 13 and presumably away at Government College. More seriously, the Egba Women's Movement was not a sudden impulsive response to corrupt administration, dependent upon male suggestion and support for its initiatives, but a carefully planned progress complete with printed manifestos and reports, petitions, press conferences, and legal representations; though her husband was a useful ally, "Beere" Ransome-Kuti was a largely self-motivated woman whose activities did not always accord with his ideas.[7] Within Soyinka's fictional scheme, Daodu is perhaps a necessary "device" for exercising a restraining effect on her impetuosity, but none of this matters very much, except maybe to outraged feminists and misled social historians. What makes *Aké* such a magnificent and captivating work is its richly reimagined, not its documentary quality. Its main value is as a treasure trove of anecdotes about the world Soyinka grew up in; as a quarry for the raw material of incidents and characters in the plays, poems, and novels (the abiku, the child's death on its first birthday, Egbo's refusal to prostrate himself); and as a circular re-creation of the tensions and contradictions that were the formative agents of the writer's creative vision. It has quickly become a classic of childhood literature; nostalgic without being sentimental, and never blanching from the dark and vicious side of traditional Yoruba life—as instanced in the public humiliation of the bed-wetting girl and the stoning of the pregnant madwoman—it remains to date Soyinka's most compelling and enchanting prose work.

It is a truism of autobiography that the nearer it brings the narrative to the present time of writing, and the less completely, therefore, the past has passed, the more likely it is to collapse into incoherence. Soyinka does not fall into this trap but ends his childhood memoir with the boy of 11 about to leave the primal, mythic world of Aké to go off to Government College in Ibadan. His next volume of "memorabilia," *Isara: A Voyage around "Essay"* (1989), is not the hoped-for sequel dealing with the secondary and university years—Soyinka has said that he will make no further forays into autobiography—but a kind of "prequel" that delves even further back, into the life of his father and his generation ten years before his own birth, and pursues their story up to the outbreak of World War II. The completion of *Aké*, Soyinka remarks in his prefatory note to *Isara*, did not dispense conclusively with these seminal years in the nation's life but only fueled further curiosity about them. Two years later, when he chanced upon a tin box containing his father's letters and notebooks, school reports and committee minutes, he set out to reconstruct the lives of "Essay" and his "inner sect" or "Circle" as the "representative protagonists" of that whole Western-educated generation that was at the forefront of the independence movement before and during the Second World War. The former children of Isara who style themselves "ex-Iles," indicating that they are simultaneously graduates of Ilesa Teacher Training Seminary and cultural exiles as a result of the Western ideas absorbed from it, are the provincial schoolmasters, businessmen, bureaucrats, lawyers, and trade unionists who, for better or worse, took up the white man's political and economic burdens during this epochal period. These cultural intermediaries—dandified, intellectually disputatious, aficionados of European art, music, and politics—are the familiar stereotypes of the Christianized colonial world whom we have already encountered in *Aké*, but they are brought to life here on a much broader canvas and, in Soyinka's words, "on a very different level of awareness and empathy."[8] Soyinka re-creates with a deft touch the comic traumas, confusions, and dilemmas of these insecure figures—regarded by their own parents as "the next thing to oyinbos" *(white men)* and by the colonial regime as "very well-to-do modern and professional Nigerians"—as they become increasingly sequestered from an indigenous way of life that they can neither reject nor replace (*Isara*, 187, 92). Soditan, as the father is called here, makes no secret of his preference for local glue and paint products over expensive "imported jars" sold by the

pharmacist. But his advocacy of a native-medicine store is of the devil's
kind, and in practice, he persists with European treatment of his wife's
mysteriously malady (it turns out to be pneumonia) and makes only
token gestures toward the last resort of a trip back to Isara and his father's
traditional curative magic. At the same time Soditan's mischievously
theoretical, tongue-in-cheek comparisons of the secret ministrations of
Western surgery to his father's *etutu* (ritual medicine) betray real doubts
about the superior efficacy of Western medicine: "I don't know which
ground you are standing on right now," cries his bemused wife, and in
truth, neither does he (*Isara*, 128). This halfway-house world is full of
strange contradictions. The business tycoon Sipe seeks the advice of a
medium on profits and commissions, and even Soditan consults the local
oracle to find out if he will be successful in his career. "The church bells
only sound in the ear," says his mother, "while the drums of *osugbo*
[meeting place of ogboni priesthood] resound in the pit of one's stom-
ach" (*Isara*, 94).

Isara is an openly fictional biography that uses mainly approximate
and invented names. (Thus Soyinka's father Samuel Ayodele becomes
"Soditan" Akinyode, and his mother Eniola, "Morola.") Yet, for all this,
the picture of the changing traditional world and its alumni is more
historically accurate than the one drawn in *Aké*. The new Odemo of Isara
is a far cry from the stereotype of the titled elder, steeped in ancient
tradition, out of touch with the modern world of Abeokuta, and curious
about its strange new ways, who is glimpsed by the child during his
occasional visits in the earlier volume. In *Isara*, as in history, Akinsanya
is a highly educated man, an outspoken and controversial Lagos trade
unionist and a shrewd, modern-minded politician who knows that the
nationalist cause is served not by disregarding positions of ancient power
but by filling them with enlightened people: he proceeds to use the
support of the colonial regime to maneuver himself into an obaship from
which he is then able to oppose and eventually unseat it. Neither is
Soyinka's grandfather, here called Pa Josiah, the quintessentially pagan
backwoods figure who, in *Aké*, is defined in opposition to the Christian
influences of Abeokuta. Josiah is, in fact, an opportunistic Christian who,
for politic reasons, has had himself baptized and sends his son off to a
Christian seminary to learn and to keep him informed about the ways of
the white man. At the same time he maintains several wives, continues
secretly to frequent ogboni meetings, and adheres to traditional cures.
He gives Sipe magic talismans to hang over his native-medicine store,
schemes to lure his sick daughter-in-law to Isara to practice his fetishistic

ritual etutu upon her, and, when Soditan is appointed to his first headmaster's post, "prepares the necessary protection" to guard his son, as he will later guard his grandson, from the secret charms and poisonous potions of enemies. "I knew what I was doing when I let those people baptise me," he protests. "It wasn't that I meant to turn my back on everything I knew" (*Isara*, 144). This doubleness, or duplicity, has both serious and comic repercussions. Having officially "forsworn osugbo after his baptism," he is unable to act as emissary to the ogboni to procure funeral rites for a member of the family, and the ogboni themselves have to make a special, "extraordinary" visit to his frantic senior wife, to whom the responsibility has fallen. On the other hand, his duplicity gives rise to some delicious comic ironies, as when he fixes a retaliatory "evil eye" upon the witch whom he deems responsible for Morola's sickness and then declares: "She can thank her stars we are all Christians now. If she had tried this when I was as I was, I would be doing more than just taking a look at her" (*Isara*, 146). Josiah's African-Christian and traditional-modern syntheses are carefully worked out marriages of convenience, not the anxiety-ridden spiritual conflicts of Essay's and Daodu's generation, but it is clear that Isara is less spiritually secure than is suggested by *Aké*. The grandfather lives a version of the syncretic existence that his son and grandson adopt in the earlier book, and pure paganism is now projected back onto his mother (Soyinka's great-grandmother), an eternally dying matriarch who defies him to perform any act of Christian worship over her body. Pa Josiah's generation has one foot in the modern world, and it is no accident that he is the one who brings news of the outbreak of the European war and that, in the final image of him on the last page of the book, he is standing beside a group of ex-Iles and the motor vehicle that has brought his son's American pen-friend to Isara. Thus *Isara* fleshes out some of the puzzles in *Aké* and explores its unexplained contradictions—for example, the amount of time Essay spends with the Odemo, the latter's excusing the children from the custom of prostration, the grandfather's informed knowledge of the white man's schools. The result is a more penetrating and complex, if less vividly animated and intimate portrait of a society in transition.

Not surprisingly, in the light of Soyinka's prefatory remark that the pattern of his ex-Iles' lives was set "under the compelling impact of the major events in their times, both local and global," the "voyage around 'Essay'" is a circuitous and ever-expanding one. After first doubling back into its immediate subject's boyhood and adolescence (there is a magnificent description of the 14-year-old Soditan's railway journey to the seminary), it then follows the pattern of *Aké*, opening out in the last third of the book as the collective protagonists are caught up in broad public movements and events: nationalism, war, and the indigenization of public services and utilities in preparation for independence. The local kingmakers who have Akinsanya elected to the obaship belong to the same class of people who carried B.N. Azikiwe into office as the leader of the national independence struggle, thus invalidating Sipe's opposition of "the movement" to local power struggles. "Everything is being transformed," a sneering, ultra-Westernized court official is advised. "Adjustments are being made to a new age and the obaship is only one of the institutions that are affected" (*Isara*, 216). The "purist" traditionalists and reactionaries, whose views are stated at great length in the book, resist this process—"What Isara needed was a king steeped in its oldest traditions. . . . Isara simply wished to be left alone" (*Isara*, 253)—and it is conceded that the provincial insularity that they advocate has at least preserved a sense of community and identity that Abeokuta has lost. Isara is "that mutely demanding, irritating entity from which they had all dispersed" and to which "they would massively 'return to sender'" (*Isara*, 259). But a heavy price is paid for this insularity in depopulation, unemployment, unsanitary conditions, and disease. "Isara was still backward," Soditan reflects truthfully. "Isara could not provide a living . . . he knew now, for a certainty, what made the Isara such exiles. There were no factories, not even small businesses, no institutions, nothing of note that would draw in the curious or make the existence of the indigenes a productive adventure" (*Isara*, 254, 260). The ex-Iles have a program for developing the region economically, thus countering the colonial depopulation policy, and know that only a Western-educated oba will have the knowledge to implement it. When Soditan consults the oracle about his career, he is told to "find Asabula," which he assumes to be a nonsense answer designed to tell him that he had asked the wrong question; to belong, it is implied, is better than to succeed. But that same day he arrives home to find waiting for him the first letter from his American pen-friend Wayne Cudeback, postmarked "Ashtabula, Ohio" (not quite "Asabula" but almost), and years later, when Cudeback turns up unexpectedly in Isara at the height of the kingship crisis, Soditan greets him with the words "Welcome to Ashtabula." The significance seems to be twofold: the meaning and purpose that Soditan has sought to discover in his life have been there all the time in his native world, but that world is now itself part of the larger modern order represented by the Ohioan Ashtabula. Life for the ex-Iles, says Soyinka in the preface, was marked "by an intense quest for a place in the new order" (*Isara*, vi). The oracle's instruction to Isara, to "find Asabula," is an injunction to find a niche in that order, to discover the village's place in the world, until when it will be no more than a disease-infested wilderness. Thus the "voyage" is a journey home, but the end of the voyage is to discover that "home" is now the world: it is a circular journey, but one in which the circle is always expanding and the perspectives widening. The farsighted Pa Josiah advises his son that for *his* children (meaning Wole Soyinka), study overseas will be the logical next step: "That is the way it is. We all pray that our children go farther than we did" (*Isara*, 148).

Isara is not without its flaws. The pedantic humor of nicknames is carried to excessive and confusing lengths ("Essay" has no fewer than four appellations), and the glossary of Yoruba words is erratic, explaining some words twice and others not at all. The Circle's debates, though amusing, are often sterile, serving no greater purpose than the preening of the private intellectual ego: "They returned to the same subject again and again, never resolving anything but feeling mentally elated afterwards" (*Isara*, 124). But the book's sprawling narrative, which goes on introducing new characters right up to the closing sequence, teems with life, and the exuberant portrait gallery of entrepreneurs, eccentrics, and rogues—the chance-chasing tycoon Sipe, the mail-order cowboy Wemoja, the hapless conartist Ray Gunnar—is done with great charm and care. *Isara*, though it lacks the childhood magic and charm of *Aké*, is a beautiful and evocative book, a loving reimagining of things past.

Chapter 9
Soyinka as Poet

Soyinka is Africa's finest dramatist and one of its most original prose writers, but he is not a great poet. His poetry has become notorious for its densely clotted, elided syntax and knotty grammar, its tortured diction and eccentrically overloaded metaphors, which have caused even his most idolatrous critics to falter. Some of the most imaginatively moving poems of *Idanre and Other Poems* (1967) are spoiled by an overinventive vocabulary, as in "The Hunchback of Dugbe," where the introduction of merely decorative images ("lace curtains") and gratuitous verbal wit ("pigeon eggs of light") obscures the essential human crisis of the protagonist and leaves unclear the nature of the transfiguration—madness or death—wrought by his confrontation with the cement mixer. Even in the volume's most powerfully terse emotional statements, such as "Ikeja, Friday, Four O'Clock," Soyinka dilutes sensuous particularities with incongruous abstractions: to the compelling image of soldiers offered up as an ironic harvest sacrifice he adds, in the closing couplet's gathering up of "Loaves of lead, lusting in the sun's recession," a distracting suggestion of Christ's feeding of the multitude, when the mere opposition of lead and bread is (as in the poem "Civilian and Soldier") already more than sufficient to carry the burden of meaning.[1] He does not hesitate, in the volume's title poem, to impede the most awesome and rhapsodic lyrical surges with turgid and unevocative mathematical and scientific terminology, as in "Spatials / New in symbol, banked loop of the 'Möbius Strip,'" or, "The unit kernel atomised, presaging new cohesions / Forms at metagenesis" (*Idanre*, 83, 64). As a result, "Idanre" frequently collapses into meaningless, esoteric verbiage:

> Who, inhesion of disparate senses, of matter
> Thought, entities and motions, who sleep-walk
> Incensed in Nirvana—a code of Passage
> And the Night—who, cloyed, a mote in homogeneous gel
> Touch the living and the dead?
>
> (*Idanre*, 82)

The dense little lyrics that make up the *"Other Poems"* of *Idanre* suffer, though to a much lesser extent, from a similar semantic anarchy. They have been rationalized, at various times, as syntactically wrenched English equivalents of Yoruba mythic language; as coherent embodiments, in their very indeterminacy and confusion, of the tortuously ambivalent Yoruba metaphysics that underlies the title poem; and as an expression, in their harsh disruptive, dissonant language, of the fragmented personality of the god Ogun.[2] The besetting danger on the first two scores is the tendency to overlook crucial syntactical obscurities and metaphorical puzzles in favor of broad mythographic explanations and vaguely to regard them as self-evident parts of the general poetic effect, as if verbal coherence was not to be expected or desired at the primal, mythic level. Such reductivist readings, in addition to making the poet's "ethnocentric compulsions" (Macebuh's phrase) an excuse for all manner of stylistic failure, seem to behave as if myth were somehow antithetical to and transcendent of language, inhabiting an unfathomable prelingual reality, and were not itself a linguistic construct, informed by language's historical and cultural determinants. At this level of interpretation, the lyrics cease to be dramatic poems about particular individuals coming to grips with the great life crises and dilemmas and become mere correlatives for mythic impulses or, at worst, abstract, mythopoetic exercises exploring Ogunian ambivalences and Yoruba ideas about history and the cosmos. Thus the poem "Abiku," its powerfully realized dramatic situation and sensuous particularities ignored, is valued by mythopoetic commentators chiefly as an illustration of the cyclical view of history and the forlorn hope of escape from it, and of the close interdependency, indicated by their rapid succession, of birth and death in Yoruba metaphysics. Similarly, "Season" is transformed from a simple farmers' harvest-thanksgiving, combining images of ripened corn with the faintest suggestion of fungal disease ("the germ's decay") into an evocation of the whole life cycle (*Idanre*, 45).[3] It is perhaps timely to remember at this juncture that Soyinka, in his composition of the poems in *Idanre*, was troubled by his own tendency toward a complacent cyclicization of experience and vented this fear in a written note on the original typescript": "I know nothing more futile, more monotonous or boring than a circle." He struggled to find ways "to accept Death and creativity not on that revolting cyclic level, but as incidents within occupations, the most trivial of which far exceed the *knowledge* of Death and the accident of Birth" (Priebe 1988, 116). This is, in fact, a strongly antimythographic statement: Soyinka is saying that the local experience, the dramatic incident and occasion, override and outweigh in value the knowledge that emerges from them. The joy and pain of the "Of Birth and Death" and "For Women" sections are immediately private and local in reference, their mythical dimensions secondary.

On the third score, a great deal of critical energy has been misspent on the alleged pervasiveness of Ogun and the intertextual nature of the poems in *Idanre.* It now seems unlikely that the collection was a planned volume, particularly as the shorter poems were composed separately over an eight-year period and out of diverse circumstances. The capacity of lyric poetry to sustain mythic meaning is, in any case, problematic (the "lone figures" in the section of that name are the solitaries who feature in all lyric poetry, not Ogunian prototypes), and these lyrics are not driven by the Yoruba metaphysical dynamo in quite the same way as the epic verse. They benefit little from a spurious coherence imposed, retrospectively, from the thought structures of the last and spontaneously written title poem and do not depend, for their meaning, upon juxtaposition either with the latter or with their fellow lyrics in the volume. The "rust" in "Season," for example, is, metaphorically, the color of ripened corn, not the literal result of rain on Ogun's metal, and the "lethal arc" described by Ogun's sword in the title poem clearly has nothing to do with the contracting, sperm-slaying "lethal arc" of the pregnant womb in "To One, in Labour." The volume's septuple structure is more overt than implicit, and once the allusions to the road god in "In Memory of Segun Awolowo" have been conceded ("Death the scrap-iron dealer," "Him of seven paths"), the Ogun presence is either very slight (as in the vague association of airy palm filaments with high-tension wires) or, as in the case of the road as an embodiment of Ogun's cosmic journey through chaos, an optional mythopoetic extra (*Idanre,* 14). The palm tree in "Dawn" gains nothing from the knowledge of Ogun setting out with a palm tree to embellish the world. In "Death in the Dawn" it is the road, not the god of the road in the play of that name, who "waits famished," and as Robert Fraser has argued, the carefully chosen word "Progression" most likely refers to man's uncontrollable instinct for headlong, forward motion and to his restless inventive energy rather than to the doubtful, hubristic technological "Progress" represented by Ogun (*Idanre,* 11).[4] The "suppliant snake coiled on the doorstep" in "Abiku" refers not to Ogun but to the alien malice of an otherworldly creature, beyond human appeal, and the abiku child's own unique kind of doomed repetition is quite distinct from that signified by the tail-devouring snake worn around the neck of Ogun worshipers (*Idanre,* 30). The pervasive, ashen gray of Ogun is not the only transitional color in the volume—there are also rust and indigo—and, paradoxically, it makes too many transitions in the course of the whole collection to be simply an *image* of transition or of any other single thing. It connotes, in turn, age and serene wisdom; the boredom, emptiness, and negation of the prisoner's death-in-life, slowly burning itself out "in tears and ashes" ("Prisoner," 44); and the leaden skies from which regenerative rain will fall. In the eerie, chilling "Post-Mortem" it is the grayness of disease, of earth ("his man-pike shrunk to sub-soil grub"), and of death, presented, albeit with a grim and somber grandeur, not as a transitional phenomenon but as the terminal, clinically myth-resistant reality of scooped-out brains on a surgeon's scales (*Idanre*, 31). Poems like this one and "By Little Loving" appear to have no mythical perspective at all, and few of the other lyrics in the collection benefit greatly from being cast in an Ogunian one. The sentiments "Rust is ripeness" ("Season") and "The ripest fruit was saddest" ("Abiku") have little to do with the specific creative-destructive ambivalence of Ogun but express simple universal themes: life is at its fullest, its most ripe and mature, when closest to death; destruction may have to be risked to achieve anything really creative and fulfilling; pain is closely interwoven with birth and fruition, and death with fresh beginnings (*Idanre*, 45, 30). That deep awareness of mortality is an inevitable condition and function of life and a measure of its value is an ancient, commonplace perception, as old as Shakespeare and Sophocles, the very stuff of existence. We need no god to tell us that.

In *Idanre* Soyinka places human affection, desire, and grief in the broader context of nonhuman nature, in which they are imaged in terms of plant life, tides, and seasonal change. This perspective is often portentous and obscures the human situation ("In Paths of Rain," "I Think It Rains," "Night"), but sometimes, in the more intimate poems, it is achieved in a wholly genuine, natural, and unforced way, albeit with some unavoidable loss of personal intensity. An example is the climactic flourish at the end of the beautiful prayer for his daughter, "Dedication," which places sex in an elemental context—"haste to repay / The debt of birth. Yield man-tides like the sea / And ebbing, leave a meaning on the fossilled sands"—in a way that foreshadows the epic title poem: "And earth prepare, that seeds may swell / And roots take flesh within her, and men / Wake naked into harvest-tide" (*Idanre*, 25, 62). Another example is the use of grain and harvest imagery in "Psalm" to present the woman's celebrated pregnancy as "the ruin of {her} cornstalk waist." Ripeness rubs shoulders with ruination, ripeness with rot, fruitfulness with decay:

"ivory granaries are filled / a prize of pain will be fulfilled" (*Idanre*, 34). Life is perpetually on the brink of death and vice versa, the one chasing the other in an interminable seasonal motion. Their cyclic interdependency is finely caught in "To One, in Labour," where the sacrificial wastage and deathly business of birth are conveyed by the analogy between unsurviving sperm and slain soldier ants: "Gestation is a Queen insealed / In the cathedral heart, dead lovers round / Her nave of life" (*Idanre*, 38). Some critics have been troubled by an apparently facile nature metaphysic that lets no element of our individual existence go by without subsuming it, symbolically, into a cosmic context, and by the bland cyclicization of human crises and tragedies that results. One, for example, quotes the lines from "Idanre," "growth is greener where / Rich blood has spilt," as evidence that Soyinka is really celebrating death as the key to the mysteries of human existence and expressing the belief that "society periodically needs blood sacrifice," as if slaughter were somehow conducive to creation, and destruction and creativity, death and rebirth, virtually equatable (Nkosi 1981, 159). It is important here to look at the words on the page, to unravel their local intricacies and built-in ironies, instead of simply sweeping them up into complacent Ogunian abstractions. In context, the argument is more complex:

> The weeds grow sinuous through gaunt corrosions
> Skeletons of speed, earth mounds raised towards
> Their seeming exhumation; growth is greener where
> Rich blood has spilt; brain and marrow make
> Fat manure with sheep's excrement
>
> (*Idanre*, 65)

The tone of the passage is, in fact, not approving but bleakly, bitterly mocking. The ambiguous "Rich" alludes also to the wealth of the fast-car owners, victims of their own acquisitiveness and impatient speed, and, like "expense" in Shakespeare's sonnets, carries ideas of wasteful expenditure that refer to cost and price rather than value. In this instance the price—death—is a very heavy one because the blood is "poor" in its powers of sacrificial purchase: it fertilizes not grass but weeds. Man's brain, the source of all his misapplied ingenuity, is devalued and emptied of regenerative potential by being equated with the sheep's excrement with which it finds a common end. There is no lurid celebration of sacrifice here, only an ironic exposure of its futility.

This irony, though subdued in "Idanre" itself, sets the mood for the mythopoetics of the shorter poems, which are never so governed by mythic compulsions as to refuse personal responsibility or empathy. The poems "A Cry in the Night," "A First Deathday," and "Abiku," respectively about a child born dead, one who dies on its first birthday, and a "born-to-die" spirit-child, are deeply felt, harrowing evocations of individual tragedies, in which the imagery of seedtime and harvest is bitterly ironic. In the case of the stillborn, nothing grows from the "planting," an image that echoes the earthing of the yam in "Dedication" but here does service instead for the burial: "Such tender stalk is earthed / In haste." Death in "A Cry in the Night" is final, grief inconsolable and without redress, the universe alien and indifferent—"No stars caress her keening / The sky recedes from pain." In "Abiku" the life-death continuum is abruptly and mockingly truncated in the taut last line, "Mounds from the yolk" (*Idanre*, 25, 30). In "A First Deathday" the attempt to find comfort in the belief that the child's special knowledge, brought into life from its preexistent state, will not now be dissipated is reduced by the irony of the last lines to a "last breath of mockery" (*Idanre*, 26). In "Post-Mortem," after the dissectionist's fingers have failed in their presumptuous quest "to learn how not to die," the closing mock paean implicitly recommends acceptance of the finality of death, in preference to using it to prolong life: "let us love all things of grey; grey slabs / grey scalpel, one grey sleep and form, / grey images" (*Idanre*, 31). Recent commentators have construed the poet's very syntactical and metaphoric incoherencies as expressions of unease with his mythic themes, locating "the source of Soyinka's obscurity not in incompetence, nor in mythic profundity . . . but rather in his continual struggle to create coherence out of an experience which denies it: to assert conviction in a world of doubt" (Booth 1986, 66). According to this line of thought, Soyinka is fundamentally a skeptical ironist, simultaneously mythopoeist and mythoclast.[5] The tensions between these rival impulses are nowhere more in evidence than in the brilliant and moving poems of the section "October '66" about massacre and the preparations for civil war. In "Ikeja, Friday, Four O'Clock" and "Harvest of Hate" the truckloads of soldiers bound for the front are "a crop of wrath," a mock harvest of unseasonal deaths squandered on the false altar of war (*Idanre*, 50). In "Massacre, October '66," written from Tegel in Germany, the attempt to seek refuge in European pathetic fallacies by placing the slaughtered Ibos in the context of nonhuman nature is seen, self-consciously, as an evasion of the horror—"this idyll sham." Acorns may be crunched and cropped as part of the seasonal process, but the broken skulls for which they are the distracting poetic referents (and which outnumber them, as brute fact outstrips metaphor) are a meaningless and undisguisable horror. The poet's uncertainty about his purpose in borrowing foreign seasonal patterns and literary traditions is reflected in the vibrant ambiguity of the last lines, "I borrow alien lands / To stay the season of a mind," where "stay" can mean to postpone or to prolong (mental agony), to evade or avert (as in a stay of execution), or to steady and focus the horror, therapeutically, in order to preserve sanity and prevent the mind from collapsing under its enormity (*Idanre*, 52).

In the above poems the ambiguous playing-off of irony against myth patterns produces some complex poetic effects. Sometimes, however, even the strictest mythological coherence does not make for coherent poetry, as in the much-discussed opening lyric "Dawn." There has been a great deal of superfluous debate about the gender of the sun and the lone palm tree in the poem, debate that can perhaps be short-circuited by reference to a possible prototype of Soyinka's "celebration rite" in Ifa divination verse. Noting that "it is the nature of penetration to take the shape of that which is penetrated," Judith Gleason writes of the *odu*, or ritual incantation, "Iwori Meji": "Topographically, earth's excrescences rise to meet the burning intruder from the heavens. Termite hill and tree are ambivalent symbols of this process of penetration, being both hollow containers and erect. The intruder may be regarded beneficially as fertilizing rain, destructively as searing fire."[6] The dormant generative power of the earth (female) is activated by the "intruder" sun (male), and the palm, which grows out of one toward the other, partakes bisexually of both. Soyinka's poem, in which the palm is both raped by the sun and is itself the rapist, seems to fit this pattern:

> Breaking earth upon
> A spring-haired elbow, lone
> A palm beyond head-grains, spikes
> A guard of prim fronds, piercing
> High hairs of the wind
>
> As one who bore the pollen highest
>
> Blood-drops in the air, above
> The even belt of tassels, above

Coarse leaf teasing on the waist, steals
The lone intruder, tearing wide

The chaste hide of the sky

(*Idanre*, 9)

In a poem full of calculated ambivalences (note the jarring oxymorons
"coarse teasing" and "chaste hide"), the palm tree is both vigorously
phallic ("spikes," "piercing") and seductively virginal ("guard of prim
fronds," "teasing at the waist"). Both the tree and the sun can be seen, in
their variant erections, as "tearing wide" the dawn sky, the palm piercing
the air and the sun rising on the horizon. The "high hairs of the wind"
refer at once to palm filaments and straggling clouds, and palm and sun
are contracted, in perfect integration, in the final phrase "aflame with
kernels." The poem's eccentric grammar carefully sustains this doubleness. The agentless participle "Breaking" is left deliberately loose, and
the "spring-haired elbow" disembodied, so that the reader is free to
attach them to either sun or palm or both. However, although the
long-delayed main verb "steals," unequivocally governed by "the lone
intruder," seems to make the sun the subject of the sentence, the reader
has already been lured by the deceptive syntax into allocating that
function to the "palm beyond head-grains" in the third line. Soyinka
maintains the ambiguity of the main action, and the unresolved sexual
ambivalence of his palm, only by placing the main verb at such a
confusing distance from the opening participle that we are not only
uncertain as to what it is that is "Breaking earth" but are also confronted
with a somewhat awkward image of *the sun* lifting itself over the horizon
on an elbow. (Since the sun is not normally thought to possess an elbow,
"spring-haired" or otherwise, the reader's natural and immediate instinct is to allocate the elbow to the tree.) The price of perfect ritual and
mythological coherence is, it seems, syntactical and metaphoric confusion.

Soyinka is at his best in this volume in those poems where the dance of
his brilliantly precise images—"the dognose wetness of the earth," "a
mind at silt bed"—is carefully and economically orchestrated to maintain a disciplined clarity of line (*Idanre*, 10, 51), as in the haunting,
numinous "Death in the Dawn"; the chilling dramatic monologue
"Abiku"; the narrative fragment "Civilian and Soldier," where the poet
assaults the military man, trained in his trade of death and able to offer
nothing but bullets, with the creative and fruitful things of life; and the

ingenious metaphysical poem "To One, in Labour," in which the familiar interdependency of life and death is worked into a successful analogy
of the womb and an ants' nest, with those microscopic extensions of the
lovers, the fertilized ovum and the sperm that fail to reach the egg
("Desolate wonder of you and me") represented by the queen ant and her
sacrificed, laboring "lovers" (*Idanre,* 38). The most impressive and
intricate of the lyrics, and the finest poem in the volume, is the brooding,
tormented "Massacre, October '66." Here the subtle wordplay upon
"shell," drawing on both the word's agricultural and military associations, transforms crunched acorns in a German forest into crushed Ibo
skulls—"each shell's detonation / Aped the skull's uniqueness"—and
the linking of human heads with the "favoured food of hogs," in addition
to its wanton devaluation of life, effects a sinister transference by which
the massacred Ibos themselves become, obscenely, food for the reviled
pig—"Brain of thousands pressed asleep to pig fodder"—in the Muslim
North (*Idanre,* 51–52).

The 25-page epic title poem, though it surges with the same lyrical
energy as the shorter pieces, is in a category of its own and obeys its own
mysterious laws. There is, simply, far too much in this formidable
poem—much more than there is space to discuss here and too much for
anyone to say exactly what it is or what it is all about. "Idanre" is at once
a record of a mystical ascent of the rock hills of that name undertaken, in
the words of the preface, "in company of presences such as dilate the head
and erase known worlds"; a description of a spectacular thunderstorm in
an earlier night-walk that, in the poet's mind, presaged a full harvest;
and a Yoruba creation myth, envisioning the creative union or "elemental fusion" of Ogun with Sango, whose lightning he conducts to earth "in
his three-fingered hand." But also included are Ogun's raid on the
transitional abyss to link gods with men, followed by his blood-crazed
slaughter of his own men in the battle of Ire, and, using this mythical
event as a paradigm, a philosophy of recurrence, of "the eternal cycle of
karmas that has become the evil history of man" (*Idanre,* 88). Additionally, the poem is a celebration of the artist's iconoclastic individualism by
way of Atunda, who splintered the unified godhead into a thousand
fragments; of the "virile essence" of the rebel child Ajantala; and of
various other figures from the Yoruba mythological arsenal with which
the reader needs to be equipped prior to an assault upon the poem. What
all these elements amount to, practically, is as hard to say now as when
the poem was published, and the preface and notes are more distracting
than illuminating. It does not help, for example, to learn from the notes

that the wine-girl, who is already overburdened as votary of Ogun and wife of Sango, is also "a dead girl, killed in a motor accident," since the reader cannot possibly get this information from the poem. The prefatory remark that, since the poem's composition, "the bloody origin of Ogun's pilgrimage has been, in true cyclic manner, most bloodily re-enacted," sounds like a fortuitous hindsight attempt to make Ogun's mythic carnage, and the unleashing in the god of forces that cannot be controlled, retroactively relevant to the fratricidal slaughter of the civil war. Though Soyinka's apocalyptic use of the myth might be thought ominous and prophetic, his placing of "Idanre" after the "October '66" poems and at the climax to the volume is misleading: "Idanre" was written in mid-1965, well before the October uprisings and the massacres of the following year, and its placement seems, somewhat spuriously, to claim for an essentially mythic composition a relevance of a quite different, topical-historical order.

"Idanre" is a magnificently jumbled and confused poem, full of intellectual loose ends that result from the crossing of different legends. While Ogun instigates in his pilgrimage a cyclic pattern of infraction and retribution, and as a connector of gods and men is a unifying and homogenizing agent, Atunda seeks to break, or at least to redirect, this enslaving pattern of repetition (linked to the Möbius strip, which can be twisted, circularly, into a loop and back into a straight line) and to introduce diversity and freedom in all their myriad forms. Death, the poet reflects, will soon enough restore us to the undifferentiated integration with the divine that is represented here by Ogun; he must, in the here and now, "celebrate the stray electron" that is his diverse self:

> It will be time enough, and space, when we are dead
> To be a spoonful of the protoplasmic broth . . .
> Time enough to abdicate to astral tidiness,
> The all in one, superior annihilation of the poet's
> Diversity
>
> (*Idanre*, 81–82)

Yet there is, inevitably, interference from our knowledge that Ogun in his other roles is also a daring innovator, an anarchic individualist who himself undergoes violent *dis*integration, and a cycle-breaker in the best Atunda tradition. Perhaps Atunda, in his performance of an Ogunian task, is part of—and thus simultaneously opposed to and aligned with—

Ogun, as the mathematician's strip is contained within the circle it forms. Understanding is not aided, however, by Soyinka's riddling reminder in the notes that the "evolutionary kink" in Möbius's "mathemagical ring," which seems to offer "a possible centrifugal escape from the eternal cycle," is a purely hypothetical phenomenon and a poetic illusion (*Idanre*, 87–88). Though the god may claim to have drawn "warring elements to a union of being," in a "mesh of elements," it is debatable whether the poem itself has done so. The problem is that, in the purely mythological and vaporously abstract contexts in which these symbolic beings operate, it is difficult to distinguish like from opposite, union from irreconcilable rivalry, multiform from uniform. "I earth my being," exclaims the Ogun-inspired poet, and the poem is sensuous, muscular, and visceral in its striving to register primal myth on the pulse and to make the infinite intimately personal. Yet, for all this, "Idanre" is the least "earthed" of poems, being basically a poetry of mystical (and therefore obscure) revelation. It is Soyinka's *Paradise Lost*—only its English sounds like Yoruba instead of Latin—a turbulent, furiously inspirational piece written in a kind of cosmic delirium, caught up in the "whirling incandescence" of "exploding planets" and the "crush of starlode" that it portrays. Its thunderous phrases and flashing images convey a sense of tremendous scope and energy surpassing its individual opacities, but the final effect is of a high-sounding impressiveness rather than specific meaning. Its intellectual incoherence may not, finally, matter very much. It is, after all, a breathlessly vocal poem, an essentially aural and dynamic work—originally a performance piece with music[7]— and though some degree of interpretive understanding may steal in before the music dies, it would be foreign to the nature of the poem for interpretation to make off with all the goods. But where "Idanre" really falters is in its lack of any informing, humanizing perspective and in its tendency to take refuge from the human implications of myth in its preoccupation with archetypal, elemental struggle. When all the myth-making is done, it still remains to be shown, for example, how the Möbius kink in the cycle of recurrence, signaling individualism within uniformity, fragmentation within unity, is personally indexed to Soyinka's own anarchic iconoclasm and private philosophy of risk. In the absence of this human nexus the mathematical imagery is merely intrusive. The poem is valid chiefly as a mine for images and motifs in the early plays and the first novel rather than in its own right. Nadine Gordimer wrote in a 1971 review of *Idanre*:

For myself, the voices of thunder and lightning are inclined to rant harmlessly overhead; it is the most human, the most mortal note that speaks inescapably from a poet's work, and it is the most specific and precisely local of images that succeed in conveying in one and the same flash their original uniqueness and the essence of the great abstractions which they embody. I would trade all the Wagnerian heroics of "Idanre," despite its beauty, for a few perfect lines from a short poem entitled "Grey Seasons": "I think it rains / That tongues may loosen from the parch / Uncleave the rooftops of the mouth."[8]

For the present writer, 20 years of criticism of Soyinka's first collection have not greatly improved upon this judgment.

A Shuttle in the Crypt (1972) is the bitter distillation of Soyinka's imprisonment. "It is a map of the course trodden by the mind," he says in the preface, "not a record of the actual struggle against a vegetable existence— that belongs in another place."[9] That other place is, of course, *The Man Died*, and understanding of a few—but no more than a few—of these poems is enhanced by a reading of the prison notes. The poems themselves tell us very little about the actual conditions of Soyinka's incarceration and his struggle for physical survival. The shuttle of the title is the writer's imprisoned mind and, more specifically, his entrapped poetic imagination that shunts back and forth in solitary confinement, weaving symbolic threads of meaning and fashioning sublime lyrics from the squalor and sordor that were the raw experience of his prison existence. At one polarity of the volume are those poems that are driven by the urge to communicate with the world beyond the prison walls; two of these "prisonnettes," written early in Soyinka's imprisonment, were actually smuggled out and published in 1968. "Live Burial" presents grim caricatures of his warders—a deviant, a catarrhal "lizard" with a "concrete mixer throat," a snuff-sniffing "Ghoul" fresh from a hanging—and mixes sardonic surface banter with deep simmering outrage in its official bulletin on the prisoner's health and ironic defense of his manufactured "confession":

He sleeps well, eats
Well. His doctors note
No damage
Our plastic surgeons tend his public image.

Confession
Fiction? Is truth not essence
Of Art, and fiction Art?
Lest it rust
We kindly borrowed his poetic licence.

(*Shuttle*, 60–61)

But the personal outrage, as so often in these poems, is tempered by an instinctive humanism and empathy with cosufferers that sees the harm inflicted as a general scourge: "They hold / Siege against humanity / And Truth / Employing time to drill through to his sanity" (*Shuttle*, 60). "Flowers for My Land" hauntingly weaves the 1960s antiwar protest song into a sustained amplification of floral images that takes in, in turn, the irrecoverable flower of the nation's manhood sacrificed in the civil war ("I do not / Dare to think these bones will bloom tomorrow"); the flowering bombs dropped from death-sowing "steel kites"; and "garlands of scavengers" and sycophantic "creepers, climbers." The last are the only ones who thrive in the "ordure" and "corruption" of the weed-infested national garden where "Truth" has been buried (*Shuttle*, 62–64). At the other end of the volume, and equally "public" in tone, are those poems that were evidently written after Soyinka's release and that open a window onto the outside world. "Relief: or Wedding in a Minor Key" tells of the notorious diversion of a food-relief plane to carry champagne and guests to Gowon's wedding. In "Background and Friezes," "Jacques d'Odan" (honest "Jack" Gowon from Dodan Barracks) hypocritically "whispers" to his sadists and sycophants to stop the war and, a parody of Pilate, proceeds to wash his hands "in a bowl of blood" (*Shuttle*, 72). "Future Plans" hilariously pillories the paranoia of totalitarian regimes that argue that black is really white and everything its opposite, constantly "breaking speed of the truth barrier" (*Shuttle*, 75). These are savage, stinging satires, written with all the vituperative clarity necessary to put evil opponents fairly and squarely in the wrong (Gowon is a "mud reptilean") and to express the satirist's superior contempt for the unreason and crass insensitivity of military power. Striking a much mellower note is "Apres le Guerre," a poignant elegy on Biafra that declares the losses of war to be irreparable and calls upon the younger generation to eschew "familiar opiates" and bear witness, without bitterness, to suffering: "Do not cover up the scars / In the quick distillery of blood" (*Shuttle*, 84). More wistful yet, the personal elegy "For Christopher Okigbo," in a reversal of values that reflects the moral chaos of an evil war, sings a dirge for those who remain alive, compromised by their condition as survivors. Okigbo is the purified torchbearer of absolute beliefs, faithful to the death to the distinction between "weed" and "rose"; Soyinka is the Promethean who would rather have died than remain to be slowly eaten alive in a climate of contaminated values, a leftover world of "violated visions" (*Shuttle*, 89).

It is not clear from the texts whether the "Four Archetypes" were written during Soyinka's early internment or in the postrelease period. It is likely that Soyinka used sheer technical execution in composition as an imposed discipline to help hold his mind together and keep his sensibility from running wild among discrete impressions; indeed, he refers in *The Man Died* to his "lyrical breezes," which were sufficiently short and metrical to commit to memory until such time as it was possible to write them down. The "Archetypes" also use deliberate versification and rhyme, but they are too lengthy and sustained, too methodical and studied an exercise, with too cool an air of retrospection, to belong to this order of composition. In the quartet of poems the confined scholar-poet, denied the freedom to read and write, liberates himself imaginatively into the world's literatures, where he finds analogues for the events and personalities of the civil war and famous roles for him to conceptualize himself in, with a view to universalizing and thus objectifying his personal predicament. Except in the third-person "Hamlet," in which Victor Banjo appears to serve as the analogue for the prevaricating, procrastinating prince, Soyinka systematically and correctively measures himself against his literary models. Like Joseph in Genesis, he is falsely accused and imprisoned by lying authority, but with the difference that he is a "cursing martyr" who, unlike his biblical prototype, refuses to sacrifice his sense of injustice: "A time of evils cries / Renunciation of the saintly vision / Summons instant hands of truth to tear / All painted masks" (*Shuttle*, 21). Like Gulliver, a much closer alter ego, he is a mediator and peacemaker who refuses to compromise his principles of justice and who enrages the belligerent Lilliputian government when, with wise compassion, he advocates "temperate victory" over the enemy in preference to total annihilation. In this largely self-vindicating, self-heroizing poem, Gulliver-Soyinka is an enlightened giant among benighted pygmies, an "alien hulk" in a "thumb assemblage" of small and small-minded people. When his wisdom is not heeded he crosses over to the other side (the Blefuscudians become the Biafrans), is tried for treason by a legalistic and imperialistic regime, and awaits execution of sentence: he is to be blinded so that the state may be rid of his dangerous, visionary insight and foresight (*Shuttle*, 23–26). In "Ulysses," the most abstruse of the "Archetypes," the voyage undertaken is a labyrinthine mental quest for the essence of the self that is finally abandoned for the mind's disembodied contemplation of its own workings in its lonely crypt.

"Ulysses" prefigures the mystic withdrawal that is the subject of "Animystic Spells" and parts of the sequences "Chimes of Silence" and

"Phases of Peril," a withdrawal that takes place in three stages. In
"Roots" the poet, to ward off paranoia and avoid the vain expenditure of
energy in rage and protest, first seeks to draw every available morsel of
mental sustenance and inspiration from the few square feet of earth, the
material of his degradation, that connects him with common human
reality. Secondly, in the four "Wall" sections of "Chimes of Silence," he
struggles to maintain a constant relation to the external world by turning
his cell into a microcosm of the evil state pursuing its insane war,
charging his narrow environment with larger significances. Thus he
creates a miniature infernal cosmology, hedged in by the echoing human
cries of "damned" lunatics and lepers from behind the northward "Wailing Wall," female inmates from the westward "Wall of Mists," and
beaten prisoners from the southward purgatorial "Wall of flagellation."
Counterpointing these terrors, the shouts of playing children issue from
the eastward "Amber Wall," which also supplies the redemptive vision
of a young boy, an image of effortless freedom and control, scaling a
mango tree while bathed in a symbolic rising sun. Thirdly and finally, in
"Animystic Spells" and the long "Procession" section of "Chimes of
Silence," the landmarks of being subside and material reality vanishes as
the mind, in its most desperate effort so far to stave off madness, retreats
into the remote regions and mystic inner reaches of consciousness. In
this nirvanalike state it ceases to batter itself uselessly against its prison
walls but is content to wait, observe, and simply exist, "a shawl of grey
repose" at the "still centre of our compass points"—in its obstinate
inertia, an image of death still secretly alive. The prisoner's greatest
terror in his ordeal is of negation, of discovering that nothing is happening and there is nothing for the mind to fix upon; the problem is the
perennial one, for the prison poet, of finding a language to express this
ultimate, last-ditch loneliness that can only be experienced, not imagined or communicated. Language is, finally, all he has to preserve his
sanity, to reassure himself of his continuing consciousness, for it is only
when a thought is written down or spoken that its existence is confirmed.
But in the vacuum of utter seclusion, language floats objectless and the
mind, faced with nothing to occupy it, alternatively becomes preoccupied
with itself and its own contemplation of the void. When the poet, in
"Procession," emerges briefly from his slumbering chrysalis to probe for
meaning in the death of five hanged men, he can come up with nothing
other than the guilt of their judges and executioners, and in "Purgatory"
the minds of the reprieved men are, like his own in the protracted
execution of solitary confinement, "dissolved in vagueness . . . /

Empty as all thoughts are featureless which / Plunge to the lone abyss"
(*Shuttle*, 39). And when reality is made featureless by the total sealing-off
of communication, strange things happen to language. The "Animystic
Spells" induce a state of self-hypnosis by incantatory repetition, allowing
the poet to reassure himself of the reality of his existence through the
therapy of sheer sound, the utterances of the disembodied voice: "That
mantra will serve. Utter words, order moods if thoughts will not hold"
(*TMD*, 187). The untracked images of the "Spells" are "Fragments / We
cannot hold . . . / Parings of intuition / Footsteps / Passing and
re-passing the door of recognition," without any pretension to meaning
(*Shuttle*, 68). It is, finally, as incantation, hermetically self-enclosed and
understood perhaps only by the writer himself, that the language of these
fairly impenetrable, unnegotiable compositions is valid, not as poetry.
This is the literature of survival, functional rather than meaningful, to be
judged not by any intrinsic excellence but by its practical efficacy; the
problem for the reader, therefore, lies in telling the successful "Spells"
from the failures.

After the dynamism of *Idanre, A Shuttle in the Crypt* is—inevitably,
given its prison genesis—a static, meditative volume, but its medita-
tions are anything but tranquil. On the contrary, it contains some of
Soyinka's most brittle, unbearably strained, and pun-demented verse.
Even the vintage Soyinkan themes of cyclic seasonal renewal and the
familiar imagery of bread, seeds, and kernels are here attended by
tormented, self-lacerating ironies. In "When Seasons Change" the com-
forting hope that "progression" is the "source for great truths," distilling
over the centuries "a salvaged essence / Transcending death, legacy of
seasons," is accompanied by the futile knowledge that the warmongers
have turned deaf ears to the lessons of the past, that human aspiration is
"rooted in quagmires," and that everything that has happened before on
this "old earth" will happen again: "A solemn future casts a backward
glance / Over drooped shoulders" (*Shuttle*, 15-17). The perception in
"Passage" that "Earth is rich in rottenness of things," pinning hope on
the energy of decay, is confronted by the bleak prospect of garbage pure
and simple—"the refuse heap" that knows no "festive fermentation"—
and denied the comfort of cyclic complacency (*Shuttle*, 43). In "Recession" the idea of cosmic apocalypse, which is taken from the Indian
Mahapralaya and is, in fact, but a temporary rupture in the eternal chain
of recurrence, is indexed to a dissolution of personal consciousness so
absolute (signaled by the lower case *i*) and presented in such hermetic
terms that the possibility of the poet's return to the waking world is left

in some doubt. More bitter yet, the "cockroach" who, in the powerful
"Conversations at Night with a Cockroach," represents the insidious,
time-serving corruption fostered by the new Nigeria, offers a twisted
version of Soyinka's own cyclic mythology, as presented in the introduction to his *Bacchae*, to justify the genocide of the Ibos within the
regenerative cycle of nature:

> Yet blood must flow, a living flood
> Bravely guarded, boldly split
> A potency to rejuvenate
> Mothers-of-all earth, the river's
> Endless cycle . . .
> Oh I know my lore, I've heard the poets.
>
> (*Shuttle*, 11)

The cockroach has the last word, mocking the author with the glib,
self-satisfied fatalism of the philosophy of "As" from *Madmen and
Specialists*: "All was well. All was even / As it was in the beginning"
(*Shuttle*, 13).

The intolerable strain driving this poetry frequently breaks through in
darkly humorous, almost obsessive punning. Some of the verbal twists
have an exhilarating flippancy ("The meeting is called / To odium"
[*Shuttle*, 75]), others more serious undertones, as in this from "Gulliver":

> From Us the Lillywhite King Lillypus
> To you the obfuscating Blefuscoons
> From Us the Herrenyolk of Egg
> To you Albinos of Albumen
>
> (*Shuttle*, 25)

The modification of Blefuscudians to "Blefuscoons" hints at fascist
ethnic prejudices ("coons" as against "Lillywhite"), and "Herrenyolk,"
through the idea of the master race, attributes a genocidal ideology to the
federal military regime. Sometimes, however, the wordplay is labored
and poorly integrated and makes no real connections between meanings,
as in the facetious intermingling in "Ulysses" of obscure punning words
and phrases such as "tossed thorn in matriseas" and "A sea-weed cord to
hold your breaths to mine / Prime turd among a sea of faeces" (*Shuttle*,
28). More often than not, the flashing and contrived verbal play, as C.
Tighe has suggested, serves as a half-apologetic escape therapy to keep
helplessness and frustration at bay and to harmlessly deflect traumatic

subjects: "It is as if he finds his subject far too painful to discuss seriously and dismisses it with a pun, avoiding any attempt to articulate fully what he feels."[10] The threat to health and sanity posed by the atrocious and the unbearable, of which there is plenty in this volume, is neutralized by parodic mockery and puns, as in the throwaway vaudeville theatricals used for the flogging scene in "Purgatory" or the description of the northward wall of the lunatics in "Bearings" as a "Wailing Wall" and a "Wall of prayers, preyed upon / By scavenger, undertaker" (*Shuttle*, 35). The words *pray* and *prey* are here connected by no more than the sound echo (it is not the wailers' prayers that are preyed upon), and the image of the "Wailing Wall" telescopes Jewish prayer and mental agony in a similarly arbitrary way. The confused religious conceit that is developed from this concatenation, in which crows and vultures are travesty priests before a congregation of lost souls and the "Word" of truth is broken on "altars of evil" in the place of bread, actually obscures instead of clarifying the suffering to which the poet refers. Perhaps the best example of this punning diffusion of indignation comes at the end of "Flowers for My Land":

> Come let us
> With that mangled kind
> Make pact, no less
> Against the lesser
> Leagues of death, and mutilators of the mind.
>
> Take Justice
> In your hands who can
> Or dare . . .
>
> Orphans of the world
> Ignite! Draw
> Your fuel of pain from earth's sated core.
>
> (*Shuttle*, 65)

Thomas Knipp has defended this strained language as a poetic strength: "The pun keeps the personal experience and the political issue at a manageable emotional and aesthetic distance."[11] Unfortunately, it also distances, by cheapening the call for their unity, the downtrodden, disenfranchised multitude ("the mangled kind") that is the referent of the Marxian cliche, those same oppressed masses who are being asked, in mock solemn manner, to draw their "fuel of pain" from the blood of slain innocents soaking the earth. The fact that it *is* a pun—"ignite," not unite—introduces, willy-nilly, a note of levity that weakens the seriousness of its application. It is as if the author, embarrassed by his open incitement to revolt, has to neutralize his protest once again with a self-puncturing pun, and the resulting tonal disruption leaves the poem in a joking halfway house between dignified outrage and absurdity, revolutionary fervor and cynical despair.

A Shuttle in the Crypt is the brilliantly rich testament of a poet driven to the brink of madness by the "mind-butchers" of military power. It contains, as well as a few bafflingly obscure poems in which the twisted, tangled style reaches extreme limits, a good many poems that are simply confused, either in substance or tone, as a result of overloading lines, through puns and conceits, with more meaning than they can bear. Sometimes the critic has had to do the poet's work for him, picking up trails of logical threads where none have in fact been left.[12] Some of the incoherence can, of course, be put down to the circumstances of the poems' composition, though to account for it is not the same as to value it as poetry. "How golden finally is the recovered fleece?" the narrator asks in "Ulysses," questioning the ultimate value not only of Odysseus's quest and Joyce's difficult novel but also, by implication, of his own present poetic endeavor. The answer is perhaps that ultimately *Shuttle* displays a klieg-intensity brightness rather than illumination, emits more a diamond dazzle than a golden glow. Its searing vision cannot easily be transported back into the dimness of ordinary reality; its "lighted beings" are "suspended as mirages on the world's reality" (*Shuttle*, 29).

Soyinka's next excursion into verse, *Ogun Abibiman* (1976) was inspired by the Mozambican president's virtual declaration of war against white-ruled Rhodesia in March 1976. This 22-page "epic" is at once a direct call to action, a mythologized manifesto for the liberation of the southern part of the continent, and a fantasy of moral retribution on South Africa and its allies. In a rather forced mixture of three tribal cultures that involves rapid switches from Yoruba forests to Sharpeville shanties and blends Zulu praise-poetry with Soyinka's usual Ogun imagery, the Yoruba god of war joins forces in violent, mystical union with the legendary Zulu chieftain Shaka to effect the liberation of Abibiman, the Akan word for the world's black peoples. Ogun, because of his identification with metal, is an infinitely expandable deity, equally adept with *panga* (machete), spear, or machine gun, and the title of the opening section, "Induction," seems to pun, subtextually, on the god's magnetization of steel by electrical induction and on the initiation of new combatants into the armed struggle. After carefully matching the characters of the two bellicose leaders by recounting their heroic exploits and indicting all further political negotiation and compromise as futile, the poem ends, optimistically, with a vision of massed clans, "from hill to hill / Where Ogun stood," dancing to Shaka's war cry and about to inaugurate the black millenium.[13]

Ogun Abibiman is poetry of the public voice and is passionately, glowingly committed, but like so much work of this kind, it carries no deep emotional conviction. Though refreshingly lucid and accessible after the first two volumes, its forced doggerel rhetoric is patently lacking in the inner tensions and conflicts that give the earlier poetry its personal intensity and human resonances. Soyinka's exhortative mini-epic, perhaps partly because it preaches to the converted, is curiously impersonal, emotionally unengaging stuff. Though it enjoins and celebrates swift and silent action, it is, paradoxically, the most labored and stridently declamatory of his poems, noisily elegizing the death of dialogue, speaking loudly about there being nothing left to say, and its wordplay is often merely facetious where it means to be portentous: "Ogun is the tale that wags the dog / All dogs, and all have had their day" (*OA*, 6). More seriously, the hybridization of two messianic legendary heroes produces a rather strange paradigm for collective revolutionary action and for the re creation of humane values in Africa, particularly in the presence of more readily available and suitable models such as Frelimo and in the light of the history behind the Shaka legend. In a militantly pan-African mood, Soyinka, perhaps too casually, subsumes into Ogun's divine homicidal stupor the temporary fit of mental distraction or "manic depression" that caused the historical Shaka to decimate the Zulu nation, reaping "Harvests of manhood when time wavered / Uncertainly and the mind was transposed in / Another place" (*OA*, 15). In a carelessly dissociative note to his poem, he then declares the "murderous buffoon" Amin to be an unworthy claimant to the throne of this ancestor, and the poem itself marks off the new mythified, ideological Shaka from his historical successors with a strenuous rhetoric of differentiation:

> Distance breeds ignorance, your companion host
> From far-flung lands of Abibiman may seek
> A leader in the heart of amaZulu and embrace
> A viper. Bid them beware . . .
> Make note of the dealer in death

A stink of the hyena, gorged in carrion.
Ravenous of fame—he dreams his image Shaka . . .
Shaka built nations, forged a new sense of being
But see what slinks home from the pit
Of night to sleep in Shaka's shadow—
A dank hyena, such as prowl
In execution over the condemned, proudly tearing flesh
From victims in their bonds.

                                                        (*OA*, 14-16)

In fact, the poet's historical sense is wiser than his ideology, and his poem wiser than his note, since the Zulu leader is made to remember confessionally the destruction and disintegration that followed his previous attempts to unite his people: "Where I paused, Ogun, the bladegrass reddened. / My impi gnawed the stubble of thornbushes, / Left nothing for the rains to suckle after" (*OA*, 11). But the projection of Shaka as an ordering and unifying force, whose feet are "perfumed in earth and dung of all Abibiman," rings hollow beside the warning against the megalomaniacal modern tyrannies plaguing modern Africa when we remember the murderous dementia that led Shaka to plunge his own nation into civil carnage and genocide. The images of potency and reproduction that Soyinka's Shaka opposes to impotence and destruction—"Reclaim my seeds. Restore my manhood"—appear to be innocent of any irony, even though they are applied to a leader who murdered his own children because he saw them as a weakening dissipation of his own energy, not a perpetuation of his strength (*OA*, 13).[14] "Reclaim my seeds. Restore my manhood," Soyinka's hero cries in good faith. The rehabilitation of Shaka is, of course, partly achieved by pressing him into the service of the continuing struggle against white colonialism: "The task must gain completion, our fount / Of being cleansed from termites' spittle— / In this alone I seek my own completion" (*OA*, 13). But the programmatic mythical construct has also in this respect traveled some distance from its historical prototype, who merely foresaw white expansion but died before he was able to come into active opposition to it, uttering a prophecy that his slayers would be servants, not rulers. Soyinka has, additionally, come a long way from his early vision as expressed in works like *A Dance of the Forests*, where the senseless, squandered wars of African history, the symbol of justified anti-imperialist violence in *Ogun Abibiman*, attracted only satiric praise: "The accumulated heritage—that is what we are celebrating. Mali. Chaka. Songhai. Glory. Empires" (*CP1*, 11).

Soyinka turns once more to southern Africa in his next and most recent volume of poems, *Mandela's Earth* (1988). In "Dragonfly at My Windowpane," in the final section of the new collection, he admits that his poems "yield a stark view of the world," though with the reservation that any dark distortions of "true vision" are the result of smudges on the world's windowpane, not an "inner warp." He concludes: "When darkness gathers I may dance / The world in fey reflections; or splay its truths / In a shadow play of doubts."[15] The best poems in *Mandela's Earth* are those that, in the manner of the "shadow play of doubts," refract the world through the shadowy prism of personal fears and uncertainties. The euphoria of Samora Machel's stand against Rhodesia quickly evaporated in the wake of the Nkomati nonagression pact between South Africa and the frontline states, which agreement further isolated South African blacks and their long-imprisoned leader. "Apologia (Nkomati)," more apology than defense, weighs black Africa's sluggish self-judgment against Mandela's refusal to capitulate:

> We wear our shame like bells on outcasts.
> The snail has feet—I know; our jury
> Shuffles to assemblage on the feet of snails.
> . . . An old man of sixty-five ekes out his life
> In prison slops.
>
> (*ME*, 24-25)

The poem ends with a bitterly self-deflating pun in which the primary references to verse and lifelines are tautly underlaid by the innuendo of useless, comfortless patter as a substitute for action: "The poet / Strings you these lines, Mandela, / To stay from stringing lead" (*ME*, 25). In "'No!' He Said," Soyinka marvels at Mandela's awesome ability to withstand pressure to compromise and images him as a rock of truth and faithful belief, holding firm against the dark warp of the poet's uncertainty. Perhaps most insidiously, at the end of the disturbing "Your Logic Frightens Me, Mandela," the black leader, in prison so long that he is now more symbol than man, becomes a kind of vicarious surrogate will for black Africa, suffering and expending himself on its behalf so that it need not act for itself:

> Your bounty threatens me, Mandela, that taut
> Drumskin of your heart on which our millions
> Dance. I fear we latch, fat leeches

On your veins. Our daily imprecisions
Dull keen edges of your will . . .
Feeding will-voided stomachs of a continent,
What will be left of you, Mandela?

(ME, 5)

Among the other poems in the "Mandela's Earth" section, "Like Rudolf
Hess, the Man Said!" is a pungently sardonic fantasia woven around the
statement of the South African foreign minister Pik Botha,"We keep
Mandela for the same reason the Allied Powers are holding Rudolf
Hess." Daringly crossing the frontiers of taste to exploit the howling
absurdity of such statements, Soyinka turns the regime's mendacious
rhetoric against itself by affecting to take it at its word. Mandela
becomes, through a series of verbal shifts, the Nazi doctor Mengele in
disguise: he was, it transpires, the secret orchestrator of the Sharpeville
massacre and of the deaths of Steve Biko and the Jewish activist Ruth
First, and of all those "Icarus-syndrome" defenestrations from "fifty-
story floors" while in police custody. The gold extracted from the teeth of
Auschwitz victims is succeeded by "golden eggs" dug from the earth by
the African *untermensch* in "the golden tip of the black continent" (ME,
8). After this savagely, painfully funny poem, "Funeral Sermon, Soweto"
is a somber and moving elegy on the self-multiplying dead of township
funerals. In this poem Soyinka recalls the resplendent hierarchic funeral
traditions of the Ashanti, Yoruba, and Egyptians, not forgetting the
"ancient vanities" that greased royal "tunnels of transition" with the
blood of slaves and minions, and places beside them the anonymous
mourners of Soweto. No "merchant princes, scions of titled lineage"
these, "no peerage aspirants / Nor tribal chieftains," but only

> The sludge of gold and diamond mines,
> Half-chewed morsels of canine sentinels . . .
> The butt of hippo trucks, water cannon mush . . .
> Our dead bore no kinship to the race
> Of lordly dead, sought no companion dead
> To a world they never craved.

(ME, 20)

Their "death tariffs" and "purchase rights" are merely revocable licenses
to attend, granted by white authorities on the condition of "orderly
conduct." But grief is not orderly, and the police open fire. Another

58—ironic "companion voyagers to the dead" after all—are added to the toll, and a final poignancy to the refrain "And now, we wish to bury our dead."

Mandela's earth is, however, not just the southern tip but the whole of Africa, and the "Other Poems" in the volume extend the bitter-satiric vision to the continent at large and then to the world beyond. In the section "After the Deluge" the targets are displaced dictators who in the heyday filled their private pools with bank notes and fed caviar to their dogs while their people starved, and Liberia's "Master Sergeant Doe," who follows their example with a depressing predictability. (Soyinka, in a prophetic climax, looks forward to the fitting elevation and "apotheosis" of the "Swinging Redeemer" from a lamppost.) Also pilloried are Nigeria's new post-oil boom elite, crude and graceless beside their merchant forebears ("Apollodorus on the Niger"), and in the later "My Tongue Does Not Marry Slogans," Africa's sloganeering, nirvana-seeking academics and philosophers who, with the aid of a few well-placed verbal placebos, blandly subsume the continent's ills under imaginary absolutes of universal harmony and justice. The weakest part of the book is perhaps the section "New York, U.S.A.," and particularly the prosy and overlong title poem that satirizes America's synthetic junk culture and interminable media hype without adding much in the way of fresh insights. The imperatives barked by advertisers and waiters have a sinister banality ("Enjoy your meal," "Touch someone"), and on the evening news the "most expensive anchorman in U.S.A." turns even the Bhopal and space shuttle disasters into high entertainment. The tone of amused condescension is much in the tradition of 1960s autobiographical writing about America by African visitors, and though often funny, it is easily earned satire that has been done considerably better by others. The exception is the moving tribute "Muhammad Ali at the Ringside, 1985," in which the ex-champion boxer, now a victim of Parkinson's disease as a result of his failure to quit the ring in time, is caught unguarded by the television camera in his sadly depleted condition. Soyinka finds his form again when he returns to his familiar Yoruba world in the last section, especially in the magnificent final poem, "Cremation of a Wormy Caryatid." The "caryatid" of the title is a carved Yoruba doorpost, richly decorated with an ancient culture's lords and warriors, harems and slaves, royal regalia and sacrificial animals. Worm-eaten, it is now consigned to the fire, for anything that is allowed to last too long infects new things with its decay if it is not removed from their midst. But then, reversing the motif of Keat's "Grecian Urn," the sculpted figures suddenly leap back to life in the incandescent flames of the funeral pyre, in the very death of the artwork that gives them life, and the poem becomes both a haunting elegy for a whole hierarchic culture, its high art forms and patterns of social relationships, and an expression of that culture's dynamism in decay, its flexibility even in obsolescence, its life-in-death.

Leaving aside the relatively slight *Ogun Abibiman*, a total of 16 years elapsed between *A Shuttle in the Crypt* and the next major collection of poems, and it is not surprising that Soyinka's poetic style in *Mandela's Earth* is very different from that in the early work. The professed "stark view of the world" is much in evidence in the searing clarity and directness of these poems, in their unusually crisp diction, and in the sharp scornful wit that Soyinka now prefers, as a weapon for withering opponents, to the hectoring, sermonizing habit of the prison poems. The poems in the title section of *Mandela's Earth* have been swiftly overtaken by events, as was *Ogun Abibiman*, and some of them are already starting to sound dated. Nelson Mandela is now out of jail, and his wife Winnie, eulogized in the poem "So Now They Burn the Roof above Her Head," is herself indicted for her alleged involvement with the black faction violence that, since her husband's release, has ironically divided and weakened the struggle against apartheid. There are, moreover, moments when the irreproachable and occasionally pious political sentiments expressed in these poems smack too much of the public and too little of the individual voice. Soyinka, as always, is at his best when his tongue is not marrying slogans, when his dexterous, idiosyncratic wit is puncturing individual shibboleths, and when his quirky sensibility is recording elusive insights into instants of time, moments in nature, in all their complexity. The enduring themes of *Mandela's Earth* are, accordingly, the vintage Soyinkan ones: the plague of power abuse in postcolonial Africa; the brute persistence of privation and atrocity in defiance of rhetorical mystification; and the complex ambivalence with which his own vibrant culture, unspared by "the woodworm's evenhandedness," asserts its resilience even in the throes of dissolution. It is the poems on these subjects that achieve parity with the best of the early work.

Chapter 10
Soyinka's Criticism

It is impossible to represent the substance of over 1,000 pages of critical prose in a mere dozen. As the most relevant essays have already been referred to, the author's criticism will be dealt with summarily here.

Soyinka's critical essays operate in a great variety of social and intellectual contexts and cover an extraordinary range of topics, including literary criticism and aesthetic theory, theater and cultural history, political power and ideology, and, more recently, religious extremism, nuclear pollution, and (in his Nobel speech) apartheid. They are an uneven achievement, at times crisp and incisive, at times couched in a lugubrious jargon and written in dense, intricately threaded sentences that are difficult to disentangle. In *Myth, Literature, and the African World* Soyinka is at his most lucid and revealing in his literary criticism: for example, when his Yoruba religious predilections grapple with the Igbo secular pragmatism of Chinua Achebe's *Arrow of God* (1964), or when he charts the loss of the Yoruba deities' terrestriality and anthropomorphic fallibility in their literary transposition to Brazil. (Though the non-Yoruba reader may wonder how much Soyinka's own gods have been "compromised" in his work by their cohabitation with foreigners.) He is at his most turgid and furiously complex when distilling theories of drama from religious mysteries, and at his most mystifying and obfuscatory when making sudden imaginative leaps that evaporate distinctions between "tragic drama" and festive rite, community and cosmos, stage and "chthonic space." Into the multivalent personality of Ogun, truly a demanding deity, are gathered such a confusing diversity of elements that it is not surprising when rival critics, armed with contradictory quotations from *Myth, Literature, and the African World*, produce diametrically opposed readings of Soyinka's works. Loftily verbose and impenetrably obscure phrasing are often to blame, as when, for example, in his essay "Who's Afraid of Elesin Oba?" (1979) he speaks of "catalysing the status quo into a new level of society" so that a "necessary culmination in Obatala harmony and serenity [can] vitalize society" (*ADO*, 123). The reader is hard put here to say what "catalysing" or activating a static, preexisting order of value amounts to in practical terms, or what is meant by "a new level of society," or how achieved states like harmony and serenity, or a culmination in them, can "vitalize" in any logical sense of the word. There is also much tedium and excess in this work, and Soyinka's complaint in a 1982 lecture that criticism had outrun creativity in his country is borne out by his own recent critical output. The initial ripostes to leftist and *"bolekaja"* (literally, "come down and fight") critics have been duplicated many times in the essays, and at the third or fourth time around there is a strong sense of critical overkill, of butterflies being broken on wheels, and rhetorical sledge-hammers used to crack intellectual nuts. On the other hand, when, by a kind of cosmic intertextuality, Soyinka discovers an abiku in an Australian painting and echoes of the *Islamic Book of the Dead* in Cleopatra's "mystic moment of transition" and finds a perfect African blend of the physical and metaphysical in "Eternity was in our lips and eyes, / Bliss in our brows' bent," the result is sheer wonder and delight (*ADO*, 257–58, 213–19).

The slipperiness of Soyinka's critical prose is partly a matter of content, partly of context. The essays, many of them originally lectures, were written out of diverse situations over a period of 30 years and presented to widely different audiences. For example, the early essay "The Writer in a Modern African State" (1967), in which Soyinka uncharacteristically decries "mythology" in favor of urgent contemporary relevance, came out of the national "collapse of humanity" in the Biafra crisis of 1966 (*ADO*, 17, 20), and his 1975 redefinition of the special "strong breed" of his 1963 carrier drama as "just ordinary human beings like you and me" reflects a felt need for public altruism and sacrifice during the political megalomania of the Gowon years (Gates, 41). If his discussion of "ritual," in his 1973 University of Washington lecture "Drama and the Revolutionary Ideal," as the provider of an inner formal consistency in grass-roots milieus is a far cry from the uncompromising religious esoterics of the lectures in *Myth, Literature, and the African World*, given in England in the same year, it is not surprising. There are crucial contextual differences between a highly reflective, cerebral course of lectures on African culture delivered to unreceptive Cambridge academics and an address to a predominantly black American audience in search of authentic dramatic idioms compatible with the cause of black revolution. No doubt, also, the strong anti-European polemic and refusal to accommodate Western audiences that are such marked features of both *Myth, Literature, and the African World* and *Death and the King's Horseman* were partly the fruit of Soyinka's experiences in an English cultural backwater that in 1975 had not heard of African literature and forced the visiting fellow to give his lectures in the Anthropology Department!

The slipperiness of the content of Soyinka's criticism has to do with a constant hedging of his ideas with qualifications and disclaimers in an effort not to be misunderstood or misrepresented—for example, by Western ideologues eager to exploit his antinegritude stance to further their own opposition to the idea of an authentic African worldview. Soyinka's concern throughout his essays on African writing, aesthetics, and sociopolitical ideology has been "the apprehension of a culture whose reference points are taken from within the culture itself" (*MLAW*, viii), and he has constantly urged the African's "indifferent self-acceptance" or "self-apprehension," as distinct from the self-denigration encouraged by colonial and Eurocentric views and the narcissistic self-glorifications of negritude. This self-acceptance, argues Soyinka, breaks down whenever African products, by choice or necessity, have recourse to concepts or value systems external to their own self-apprehended world in order to define, interpret, or rationalize the African experience. Among the examples taken from the art world are a South African play that resorts to an alien Christian-salvationist ethic to resolve the issue of racial division (Lewis Nkosi's *The Rhythm of Violence* [1964]), and the false magpie eclecticism of a British director who, in the 1973 National Theatre production of Soyinka's own *Bacchae*, gratuitously grafted oriental Tantric art onto the Africanization of a Greek original (*MLAW*, 70–72; *ADO*, 64–73). Soyinka adds to the list of cultural offenders "Neo-Tarzanist" critics, who project spurious Hollywood images of Africa under the guise of authenticity, and Ali Mazrui, whose television series "The Africans" implicitly denies authentic African spirituality by presenting the continent as a religious vacuum in which two alien superpowers, Christianity and Islam, fought for the indigenous soul.[1] From the political arena Soyinka cites the case of a Nigerian journalist who accounts for local student violence in the seminarist language of French and American academicians (*ADO*, 150–52), and, in East Africa, the suppression of plays about the anticolonial struggle, and hence of indigenous history, by a neocolonial regime whose official censor carried out the selfsame role during the colonial suppression of Mau Mau.[2]

Soyinka's main targets, however, lie closer to hand. Most guilty of conceptual alienation and misappropriation are the ideologues of the Nigerian left who implicitly subscribe to the Euro-Marxist view that the

African must go outside his own culture, in which he merely partici-
pates, in order to understand it. One of their expatriate allies, Geoffrey
Hunt, attacks Soyinka because "the effect of [his] rejection of external
concepts . . . of understanding is to cut off all possibility of recognizing causal determinants of social institutions and activities" (Hunt, 75).
The implications, of course, are that the West has a monopoly on
sociopolitical concepts upon which Africa, incapable of *self-*
apprehension, depends absolutely for a rational understanding of its own
social and cultural institutions, and that these "external" (meaning
European) modes of understanding have a logical purity and objectivity
unaffected by their own historical conditioning. Thus, with the aid of
Marxism, Western analysts have graduated from the assertion that Africa
has no sociocultural identity to the claim that it has a single collective
identity that only they can understand and that derives its definitions
from Africa's conjunction with Europe. Their African proselytes, locked
into false universalist assumptions, uncritically transplant the class
jargon of dialectical materialism ("masses," "proletariat") to the local
context, as if Nigerian radicalism had no indigenous roots but were
simply a subbranch of metropolitan Marxism, and notwithstanding that
to call creek fishermen and northern nomads "peasants" is neither to
describe them accurately nor to address them in a language they can
understand. Soyinka berates this new ideologue for his slavish submission to "a universalist-humanoid abstraction defined and conducted by
individuals whose theories and prescriptions are derived from the apprehension of *their* world and *their* history, *their* social neuroses and *their*
value systems," and for his failure "to consider whether or not the
universal verities of his new doctrine are already contained in, or can be
elicited from the world-view and social structures of his own people"
(*MLAW*, x, xii). The new Marxist internationalism is thus seen as
another self-negating variant upon the old liberal universalism and
Christian brotherhood, enforcing Eurocentric ideologies upon Africa
under a facade of global solidarity, and insisting upon Africa's need of
"outside help" to define and interpret itself. The first instinct of this
crude, sloganeering school of Marxists (Soyinka dubs them "vulgar" or
"superstitious Marxists") has been to reject or rewrite an African past in
which they can find nothing of ideological value. Both they and more
sophisticated left-wing theorists, such as Femi Osofisan, have attacked
the "reactionary" elitist, patrician elements in the classics of African oral
and written literature, including those in Soyinka's work, which they
find strangely inconsistent with his political activism.[3] Soyinka's re-

sponse has been to protest the critical double standard that enforces a mandate of social commitment on the artist alone, but not on the critic, and to examine the sociology of these critics, thereby exposing a basically middle-class Marxism that is morally and socially disingenuous as well as culturally inauthentic.

Some African philosophers, such as Paulin Hountondji and Kwasi Wiredu, have, of late, regarded virtually all systematizations of collective and immutable worldviews common to all Africans as essentially European inventions, or as undertaken at the dictates of European philosophy. These thinkers would most likely regard Soyinka's expounding of African gods to Cambridge academics, over the heads of Africans and in terms they might have difficulty recognizing themselves in, as an act of conceptual alienation not very different from those he condemns in others. One of Soyinka's most subtle Marxist critics, Biodun Jeyifo, has in fact accused him of smuggling into plays like *Death and the King's Horseman* "typically conventional Western notions and practices of rendering historical events into tragedy" (Jeyifo 1985, 27). Jeyifo neglects to mention, however, that Duro Ladipo's epic mythological dramas *Oba Koso* (1968) and *Oba Waja* (1964) (an earlier Yoruba version of the Elesin episode) do much the same thing, raising doubts about the very existence of exclusively Western and African categories. It has, of course, never been Soyinka's intention to shut off Western cultural legacies—"There's no way at all that I will ever preach the cutting off of *any* source of knowledge: Oriental, European, African, Polynesian or whatever"—but rather to deny Western thought systems their self-arrogated privileges as explicators and guarantors of Africa's cultural existence. Soyinka has insisted that his explorations have been neutral ones "into points of departure as well as meeting points between African and European literary and artistic traditions" (*SP*, xv), carefully avoiding the reductionist tendency to make one the reference point or yardstick for the other. He has sought always to broaden the theater of cultural debate, to keep alive the natural eclecticism and adaptability of the African spirit, and to see difference as a mark of possibility and further exploration, not of restriction and closure. Yet, as Soyinka learned in his years as coeditor of *Black Orpheus*, the desire to prevent one world from being grounded in the cultural matrix of another is frought with vexations, and his brave intellectual tightrope walk between the points of cultural convergence and departure takes him into some problematical territory, where these two foci become inextricably confused. The fourth lecture of *Myth,*

Literature, and the African World, in which Soyinka settles both old scores
with and debts to negritude, is such an area.

Soyinka's own cultural exercise in race retrieval is neither a belated
espousal nor a denial of a despised and rejected negritude but perhaps, as
Jeyifo has suggested (*ADO*, xv), a revisionary deconstruction of the same,
designed to rescue Africa's animist metaphysics from its alien primitivist
encrustations. He has always resisted the simplistic negritudinous view
of African culture as a stable or static unity of harmonious feeling and
intuition, to be placed in dialectical opposition to a mobile, modern
European rationalism. For Soyinka this culture is a complex and contradictory plurality and a fully contemporary reality, constantly added to,
modified, and diversified by the modern world. Though its intricate
network of matrices is reducible, in his own myth system, to a collection
of primal unitary essences, it partakes, through these essences and
without any loss of indigenous autonomy, of the broader conflicts in the
universe, to which no part of it can therefore be opposed. Thus he rejects
both the Cartesian dictum "I think, therefore I am" and negritude's
borrowed response, "I feel, therefore I am," because, concerned as he is
with distinguishing the conceptual "totalism" or "holism" of African
humanity from the European compartmentalist intellect that devises
these false dichotomies, he is unhappy about the reduction of human
experience to any one of the many modes of being, whether it be feeling
or the analytic thought that makes distinctions between modes. "The
principle of distinction in the African world system," he claims, "is far
more circumspect, and constantly avoids the substitution of the temporal or partial function or quality for the essence of an active or inert
socio-political totality" (*MLAW*, 136). Unfortunately, he does not define this principle of definition, and he nowhere explains how an "essence" is to be perceived except through its partial functions or qualities
(for example, the primary energy source of power through its destructive
political workings). In a 1973 interview Soyinka dismissed all movements and ideologies in European aesthetics as "itemist fallacies" and
"minute-by-minute profundisms of the universal creative essence," leaving perplexingly open the question of how this latter property is to be
experienced if not through its particular manifestations (Jeyifo 1973,
64). It is alien to the African viewpoint, he argues, to conceive the "idea
of separating manifestations of the human genius" (*MLAW*, 130), but
the assimilative capacity of this worldview, its ability to accrete new
experiences without being destroyed by or dissolved into them, has also
an obverse side, and it leads Soyinka's thought into two troubled areas.

The first concerns such different manifestations of the human genius as science and religion.

Soyinka argues, in his discussion of Sembene Ousmane's work, for the importance of a dynamic and organic traditional culture as a precondition of successful technological transformation and has often commented to the effect that "Sango now chairmans the Electricity Corporation, [and] Ogun is the primal motor mechanic" (*ADO*, 9, 185–86), thus denying "the existence of impurities or 'foreign matter' in the god's digestive system" (*MLAW*, 51, 54). In the light of these statements, Geoffrey Hunt's allegation that in Soyinka's work "technology is utterly unconnected with the ethico-religious ideas embraced by a culture" sounds, at first hearing, absurd (Hunt, 76). Yet Soyinka's mythography contrives to be at once accumulative and reductive, additive and blandly absorptive, and there is, perhaps, a sense in which modern technology in his work is unmoored and radically disconnected from culture in that little or no account is taken of its unique points of departure. "Traditional religion," asserts Soyinka in his acerbic reply to Hunt, "is inextricably bound with the technological awareness and development of the society of that religion," and he goes on to offer by way of proof the motor park (parking lot) touts of his play *The Road* and their real-life counterparts who sacrifice dogs on the hoods of cars (*ADO*, 308). For the Western skeptic this leaves unanswered the question of whether Ogun actually helps his devotees to understand motor technology, and the cynic might surmise from the number of breakdowns and wrecks on the murderous Nigerian roads that the god prefers to keep them ignorant, perhaps the better to feed off the daily carnage. There is, they argue, a world of difference between the purely internal updating of scientific facts, as when the atom was split (the example Soyinka gives of world redefinition), and the absorption of these new phenomena into a preexisting mythology. Soyinka claims that the "unscientific contradiction" of cars and canine sacrifice is perfectly in order for "as long as the churches, the mosques, the temples and synagogues remain assertive aspects of the spiritual landscape" of "progressive" societies; then he further begs the important question of whether learning painfully to live with religious-scientific contradictions is quite the same thing as dissolving them at the outset by subsuming scientific phenomena into animist metaphysics. And this—the question of whether Soyinka has provided a definition or a mythologizing mystification of technology—is the real burning issue behind Hunt's crude controversialist tactics. It is perhaps a sign of the obtuse egocentricity that mars so much of Soyinka's critical writing, and of the predominance of "outrage" over "dialogue," that, given a hapless opponent and an elephantine 40 pages in which to demolish him, he never really comes to grips with the source of his disputant's objections.

The second murky area in Soyinka's arguments concerns negritude's European-African poles of definition. The desire for restoration with some primal cosmic unity or pristine wholeness and the belief in creativity as a single "smooth-flowing source of human regeneration," without "watertight categories," are characterized by Soyinka as "fundamental to African thought" (MLAW, 130), but they are also at the metaphysical core of European romanticism.[4] Soyinka's idea of the cyclic release of energies through periodic hubristic violations of nature, though it has currency in a number of African cosmogonies, has its immediate source in Nietzsche, leading to a double paradox in his antinegritude polemic. On the one hand, he uses "undialectical," "un-Manichean" European thinkers like Nietzsche, who collapsed conventional Apollonian and Dionysian categories, to criticize the so-called European habit of dialectical thinking and to uphold a (presumably undialectical) opposition between African unitarism and European dualism. Meanwhile, with a similar paradoxical irony, he selects certain features of the European civilization that he is dissociating Africa from, such as the "scapegoat idea" (Gates, 36), and proceeds to valorize them by giving them superior African origins and credentials. This is a two-way interaction, so Europe is not seen, solely and negritudinously, as the reference point for, and the mentor and guarantor of, African values. And yet Soyinka does appear to have argued himself back into a dialectical progression of the kind he is decrying in negritude concepts, only with a new dichotomy of "European compartmentalism" and "African holism" replacing the old one of European intellect and African emotion. The paradox is a fine, and perhaps a quibbling one. The African quality of *not* being dualistic or "Manichean"—that is, not being an "either-or" culture—is opposed to a Western categorism that does produce precisely that kind of culture, and this opposition then poses a new either-or binarism in which the choice is between an African "totalist essentialism" and a divisive European "itemism." Moreover, Soyinka's claim for the indivisibility of African culture—"the very idea of *separating* the manifestations of the human genius is foreign to the African world-view" (MLAW, 130)— takes him perilously close to negritude's racist syllogism of Western rationalism and African "mystic-intuitionism." Separation and demarcation are, after all, hallmarks of definitional, analytic thought, which in the scheme of negritude the African is incapable of and to which

Soyinka's own refusal to differentiate in this instance also seems to be opposed. The subsequent retreat from intellectual analysis, using Ogun as the gulf-bridging or separateness-removing agent, traps Soyinka in the same magical, Manichean circle of radical oppositions. One way out of this vicious circle would be to drop the Western-African opposition altogether. Another way past the impasse would be to outrightly condemn Western culture and disclaim any African connection. In *Myth, Literature, and the African World*, however, Soyinka is too torn between the conflicting impulses of cultural authenticity and a freewheeling eclecticism to opt unequivocally for either of these. Ultimately he draws a generally unsatisfactory, highly speculative, and not very reliable picture of a continental "worldview" refracted through the narrow ethnic prism of Yoruba culture, while at the same time making nebulous references to a wide range of non-African touchstones, including Greek myth, Jungian psychology, and Nietzschean aestheticism.

Soyinka is on firmer ground in his long acrimonious debate with the so-called *bolekaja* critics, in which the issues are predominantly literary and aesthetic, the field narrower, and the boundaries more clearly marked. For Soyinka, African poetic and artistic traditions exist not in purist terms but as a dynamic flux that is constantly being created, and even new additions that appear to break with these traditions are part of an interactive process that renews them by infusing them with new energy. For Chinweizu and his two coauthors of *Toward the Decolonization of African Literature*, these same traditions, particularly the oral tradition, seem rather to constitute an immaculate, petrified bloc of immutable wisdoms, a cultural museum of poetic exotica walled off from the modern world in which most Africans now live, and to tamper with them is to attract the charge of "Euromodernization" or "Westernization." They condemn Soyinka's own tortuous, often bafflingly obscure poetry, accordingly, as "obscurantist" and "Euroassimilationist," using arguments that are based on a naive conception of oral and traditional poetic forms as simple and instantaneous in effect. The gnomic, oracular qualities of Ifa divination verse and the deliberate ambiguity of much oriki praise-chant, not to mention the intricate, richly ornamental oral poetry of Somalia, are all left out of account by the bolekaja critics, who also do not consider the many extraverbal forms, such as drama, by which modern African artists have rediscovered and sustained indigenous traditions. In his essay "The External Encounter" (1988) Soyinka notes astutely that "it is invariably the uprooted, the culturally alienated who turn back to the roots with the fierceness of the long-deprived—and with

its corresponding ignorance" (*ADO*, 235). Indeed, the decolonization
troika's own misty, misinformed vision of indigenous African culture is
essentially that of the nostalgic expatriate (they are all American-
educated), and it is no accident that they have continued to champion
negritude as a force for cultural liberation long after it has been abandoned, by writers and intellectuals across the continent, as a mystifying,
European-sponsored opiate that has little to do with the reality of
modern Africa. Ignoring the inescapable hybridization and syncretiza-
tion of Africa's cultural heritage by Western technology and education
systems (for example, by foreign study like their own), they cling to an
image of the African poet as a town crier calling to a hypothetical villager
across an exotic, superstitious-primitivist landscape of "elephants, beggars, and calabashes, serpents, baskets . . . a landscape portrayed with
native eyes to which aeroplanes naturally appear as iron birds."[5] "My
African world," Soyinka responds, "is a little more intricate and embraces precision machinery, oil rigs, hydro-electricity, my typewriter,
railway trains (not iron snakes!)" (*ADO*, 316). This more comprehensive
picture of Africa's complex cultural matrices runs through the whole of
Soyinka's criticism, from the 1963 essay "From a Common Back Cloth,"
in which he defends Amos Tutuola's modern "shotgun image-
weddings" from "the diminishing minority of African primevalists," to
the following 1975 statement from the Neo-Tarzanism essay: "Sango is
today's god of electricity, not of white-man's magic light. Ogun is
today's god of precision technology, oil rigs and space rockets, not a
benighted rustic cowering at the 'iron bird'" (*ADO*, 9–10, 329).

In addition to their fallacious equation of orality with simplicity, the
new "primevalists" argue from a number of false premises: namely, that
African art is essentially communal and functional rather than individ-
ually expressive, and that African poetry is literalist and empirical rather
than symbolic and mystical. Soyinka's challenging responses not only
reveal Chinweizu's to be a crudely materialistic and, therefore, highly
un-African view of African literature (insofar as it instinctively outlaws
the numinous), but also demonstrate that African art, far from upholding
a collective, anonymous heritage, has always celebrated outstanding
individual talents in all creative forms.[6] It is, however, in his function-
alist, utilitarian view of poetry that Chinweizu is at his most absurd.
Operating as a sort of self-appointed time-and-motion-man of African
literature, he advises the reader that attention given to the "unfinished
explorations" of poets like Soyinka, and of oversubtle critics like D. I.
Nwoga, is "wasted work"; he proceeds to extol a trite and artless piece of

prosification, Matei Markwei's "Life in Our Village" (quoted in Chin-weizu, 186, 224) as "simple and vivid, without surface complexity or clutter." Markwei's language, he adds revealingly, "does not get in the way" (Chinweizu et al., 214, 227, 187). In such moments Chinweizu, who is a mathematician and philosopher by training, betrays a ridicu-lously simplistic notion of poetry as a reductive, one-for-one translation of idea into meaning, of prelingual thought into image, or, in his own words, of "medium" and "message." His constant talk of "surface lucidity" and "surface complexity" presents the poem as a box and its language as a removable lid that admits the reader to its inner contents, after which the vessel can be thrown away—as if language were not itself the meaning and poems were constituted of statable "messages," addi-tional to and separable from it. Chinweizu's notion of the almost ma-chinelike separability of form and content is itself, of course, impeccably located in Eurocentric praxis ("What oft was thought but ne'er so well expressed"), and his poetic education, as Soyinka observes, and as is indicated by his obsession with "smooth flow," is "largely Tennysonian" (*ADO*, 90). Chinweizu is, in fact, not anti-Western at all but simply antimodern. His chief enemy is complexity, as represented by the Hopkins-Eliot-Pound syndicate, and he pins charges that could have been leveled at any number of modern African writers upon a handful of poets who are thought specially prone to its baneful influence. The troika's English, premodern governing criteria let it down badly in the modern context. For example, after belaboring the reader with artificial, watertight oppositions of private opacity and public clarity that deny the possibility of complex public poems or transparent personal ones, they then allege that the "private obscurantism" of "imperialist" critics "limits the impact of whatever treatment of such [public] matters still manages to slip into the poetry, since only a few hard-working initiates would be able to decipher whatever political messages are coded into obscurantist poems" (Chinweizu et al., 160). Obscurity is thus blamed for preventing the decoding of what privacy should already have ex-cluded: for keeping secret what isn't there. The non sequiturs result from imprecise and obsolete intentionalist terms ("decipher," "treatment," "message") quite inappropriate to the kind of poetry being discussed.

Toward the Decolonization of African Literature is crude and at times hysterical polemic, full of groundless allegations, hysterical, anti-African conspiracy theories, and irresponsible misrepresentations of opponents' arguments. Soyinka has labored long over what should have been given short shrift, and justification may be found in both a belief that self—

definition comes through controversy and a genuine fear of the harm done by the duplicities of ostensibly "reformist" critics. But a more convincing explanation is that he recognizes important and familiar ideas buried beneath the tirade. Both Soyinka and this "Simple Simon" school of critics are, after all, engaged in rival modes, respectively sophisticated and crude, of the same pursuits: the recovery of an authentic cultural essence and the unshackling of African creative and critical practice from foreign ideologies, causes that are not well served by the projection of Neo-Tarzanist images that play into the enemy's hands. The term *bolekaja* was borrowed from the touts of Nigerian passenger-lorries and in the language of *The Road*, the critics of this school and Soyinka are really touting for the same vehicle. They are trying to steer African literature in the same general direction, though Soyinka's is the richer, more select cargo, his the more circuitous and labyrinthine route, and along the journey his tires (to take a phrase from *The Interpreters*) perform some "cruel arabesques" of style and technique. His vehicle is an alloy of many metals, a mixture of raw, inchoate ore not yet hammered into shape (pure Ogun, as in "Idanre") and of scrap iron well past its best (the later satires). But in the 1990s it is still roadworthy. The outrageous bolekaja touts are perhaps able to pack more passengers in with a great deal of empty persuasive noise, but they seem to have little idea of how to drive the wagon, except in reverse. Their representatives, in Soyinka's play *The Road*, are the naive pretender Salubi (exuding, appropriately, a pungent critical effluvium) and the overexuberant Samson, neither of whom inspire a great deal of confidence. Meanwhile, the lorry seems in danger of being hijacked by any number of foreign-mouthing Say Tokyo Kids (the neo-Marxists) who, though alert to the authentic quality of what they carry, would like to overhaul the vehicle entirely and drive it in a different direction. The Kotonu in the model, the numinous figure who has the most sensitive touch and exact judgment, but who is reluctant to drive, is, of course, Soyinka himself, and it is still Soyinka who is at the wheel, steering the juggernaut into whatever future there is. In today's busy traffic he is being overtaken by younger and faster drivers—Femi Osofisan, Kole Omotoso, Festus Iyayi, Ben Okri. But it is largely thanks to him—and they have all been quick to admit the debt—that they are on the road at all.

Notes and References

Chapter 1

1. John Agetua, "Interview with Wole Soyinka in Accra, Ghana, 1974," in *When the Man Died*, ed. John Agetua (Benin City, Nigeria: Bendel Newspaper Corp., 1975), 42, hereafter cited in the text.

2. Wole Soyinka, *Myth, Literature, and the African World* (Cambridge: Cambridge University Press, 1976), 61, hereafter cited in the text as *MLAW*.

3. Wole Soyinka, "Class Discussion," in *In Person: Achebe, Awoonor, and Soyinka at the University of Washington*, ed. Karen L. Morell (Seattle: University of Washington, Institute of Comparative and Foreign Area Studies, 1975), 113–14, hereafter cited in the text as Morell.

4. Speaking of his play *The Strong Breed* in 1962, Soyinka said: "The moment I realize I'm pursuing a theme again, it seems to ring a bell warning that I have preceded myself somewhere." Ezekiel Mphahlele, Lewis Nkosi, and Dennis Duerden, " Wole Soyinka" (interview), in *African Writers Talking*, ed. Dennis Duerden and Cosmos Pieterse (London: Heinemann, 1972), 173, hereafter cited in the text as Duerden and Pieterse except in references where more than one work is listed, that is, in multiple references. See also Wole Soyinka, *The Man Died: Prison Notes of Wole Soyinka* (London: Rex Collings, 1972; Harmondsworth, England: Penguin, 1975), 88, hereafter cited in the text as *TMD*.

5. See Wole Soyinka, "Neo-Tarzanism: The Poetics of Pseudo-Tradition," in *Art, Dialogue, and Outrage: Essays on Literature and Culture* (Ibadan, Nigeria: New Horn Press, 1988), 315–29, hereafter in the text as *ADO*.

6. Biodun Jeyifo, "Wole Soyinka: A *Transition* Interview," *Transition* 42 (1973): 62, hereafter cited in the text except in multiple references.

7. Jeremy Harding, "Interview: Wole Soyinka," *New Statesman* (27 February 1987): 22. To the appeal to the author as savior, "Lead us, writer, lead us," Soyinka has elsewhere responded, "Lead us, paid ideologues, paid socio-economic theorists, paid philosophic carpers, lead us" (*ADO*, 301). He has also said, "I believe very much in social problems being solved by social action." Interview at University of Leeds, 10 May 1973, videotape no. 1053, Commonwealth Literature Series no. 15.

8. Wole Soyinka, Introduction, *Soyinka: Six Plays* (London: Methuen, 1984), xv, hereafter cited in the text as *SP*.

9. Jo Gulledge, ed., "Seminar on *Aké* with Wole Soyinka," *Southern Review* 23, no. 3 (Fall 1987): 515, 518, hereafter cited in the text.

10. Material relevant to this paragraph can be found in Joel Adedeji, "The

Literature of the Yoruba Opera," in *Essays in African Literature*, ed. W. William Ballard (Atlanta: Spectrum, 1973), 56–77; Karin Barber, "Yoruba *Oriki* and Deconstructive Criticism," *Research in African Literatures* 15 (Winter 1984): 497–518, hereafter cited in the text; Ulli Beier, *Yoruba Myths* (Cambridge: Cambridge University Press, 1980); K. Carroll, "God in Yoruba Belief," *Ibadan* (October 1962): 26–27; Oyekan Owomoyela, "Tortoise Tales and Yoruba Ethos," *Research in African Literatures* 20 (Summer 1989): 165–80; Peter Morton-Williams, "Yoruba Responses on the Fear of Death," *Africa* 30, no. 1 (1960): 34–40.

11. George Steiner, *The Death of Tragedy* (London: Faber, 1961), 194, hereafter cited in the text.

12. See, in particular, Geoffrey Hunt, "Two African Aesthetics: Soyinka vs. Cabral," in *Marxism and African Literature*, ed. Georg M. Gugelberger (Trenton, N.J.: Africa World Press, 1985), 64–93, hereafter cited in the text.

13. Wole Soyinka, "And after the Narcissist?" *African Forum* 1, no. 4 (Spring 1966): 59, hereafter cited in the text.

14. The Yoruba believe either that the soul's fate, or *ori* (literally, "head") is sealed by Olodumare (the supreme deity), or that it is free to choose its own fate before it reenters the world but ceases to be free once the choice has been made. In the latter case, moreover, it makes its choice when it is still a spirit and not yet a wholly responsible being, and then has no memory of its chosen destiny. Though basically unchangeable once selected, this fate can be modified by prayer and constant consultation of the Ifa oracle. See J. O. Awolalu, *Yoruba Beliefs and Sacrificial Rites* (Harlow, England: Longman, 1979), 23, hereafter cited in the text except in multiple references; Beier, *Yoruba Myths*, 61; interviews with Soyinka, Olatunde Olatunji, and Oyin Ogunba at the universities of Ife and Ibadan, October-November 1980, reprinted in Ketu H. Katrak, *Wole Soyinka and Modern Tragedy: A Study of Dramatic Theory and Practice* (Westport, Conn.: Greenwood Press, 1986), 115–16, hereafter, except in multiple references, cited in the text.

15. Wole Soyinka, *Collected Plays,* vol. 2 (London: Oxford University Press, 1974), 225, hereafter cited in the text as *CP2*.

16. Question-and-answer session with Wole Soyinka at the African Studies Association Conference, Los Angeles, California, November 1979, reprinted in Katrak, *Wole Soyinka and Modern Tragedy*, 43.

17. Dennis Duerden, *African Art and Literature: The Invisible Present* (London: Heinemann, 1975), 1–35.

18. See especially the plays *Kongi's Harvest* (1967), *The Trials of Brother Jero* (1964), and *Madmen and Specialists*, in *CP2*, 131, 167, 269–70. Although the stage directions of the 1964 text of *Trials* state that we do not hear the "fire-breathing speech" rehearsed by the politician in the last scene, a fully audible speech full of hilarious references to the Rhodesia crisis of that year was added in a 1966 production of the play by Athol Fugard at the Hampstead

Theatre Club, London, and is quoted in James Gibbs, "The Masks Hatched out," *Theatre Research International* 7, no. 3 (October 1982): 196.

19. Victor Turner, *The Forest of Symbols* (Ithaca, N.Y.: Cornell University Press, 1970), 93–110.

20. Wole Soyinka, "Salutations to the Gut," in *Reflections: Nigerian Prose and Verse*, ed. Frances Ademola (Lagos, Nigeria: African Universities Press, 1962), reprinted in *Africa in Prose*, ed. O. R. Dathorne and Willfried Feuser (Harmondsworth, England: Penguin, 1969), 360. This balance of pleasure and pain is also evident in the scene in *The Lion and the Jewel* in which Baroka's favorite wife plucks hairs from his armpit. *CP2*, 25–26.

21. Wole Soyinka, "This Past Must Address Its Present," (Nobel Prize speech, 10 December 1986), reprinted in *Black American Literature Forum* 22, no. 3 (Fall 1988): 448.

22. Sandra T. Barnes points out that Ogun is linked with fertility and fecundity mainly in the northernmost parts of Yorubaland and in minority cult groups such as that of Offa. In Awolalu's account Ogun plays a very limited role in the New Yam Festival, even when, as at Ondo, the festival takes place at the local Ogun shrine. The god of farmers is, in fact, not Ogun but Oko (they sing *ijalas* to Ogun only in a hunting context), and the use of palm fronds in Ogun ceremonies does not signify a fertility dimension but has to do with the god's fondness for palm wine. See Sandra T. Barnes, *Ogun: An Old God for a New Age*, ISHI Occasional Papers on Social Change no. 3 (Philadelphia: Institute for the Study of Human Issues, 1980), 23, hereafter cited in the text; Awolalu, *Yoruba Beliefs*, 33, 150. For more traditional interpretations of the role of Ogun in the Yoruba pantheon, see E. B. Idowu, *Olodumare: God in Yoruba Belief* (New York: Praeger, 1963), 71–89; Awolalu, *Yoruba Beliefs*, 20–32.

23. Ulli Beier, ed., *Yoruba Poetry* (Cambridge: Cambridge University Press, 1970), 33–35.

24. Lewis Nkosi, *Home and Exile* (London: Longman, 1983), x; James Gibbs, review of *A Writer and His Gods* by Stephan Larsen, *Research in African Literatures* 15 (Winter 1984): 615.

25. See Abiola Irele, *The African Experience in Literature and Ideology* (London: Heinemann, 1981), 210–11; Biodun Jeyifo, *The Truthful Lie: Essays in a Sociology of African Drama* (London: New Beacon Books, 1985), 27–35, 42; Gerald Moore, *Twelve African Writers* (London: Hutchinson, 1980), 218, 224–35; Lewis Nkosi, *Tasks and Masks: Themes and Styles of African Literature* (London, England: Longman, 1981), 188–91; all cited hereafter in the text except in multiple references. See also Femi Osofisan, "Ritual and the Revolutionary Ethos" (paper presented at the University of Ibadan, 1976), quoted in Gerald Moore, "Against the Titans in Nigerian Literature," *Afriscope* (July 1977): 19. Soyinka's reply to Osofisan and others can be found in his essay "Who's Afraid of Elesin Oba?" *ADO*, 110–31.

26. In 1973 and 1983 interviews, Soyinka spoke of the "depressing . . .

wearisomely familiar patterns" and the "repetitiousness of history" and its "recurrent cycle of stupidities," though in his original use of the latter phrase, in the 1967 essay "The Writer in a Modern African State," his emphasis fell on "what alone can be *salvaged* from the recurrent cycle of human stupidity." See Jeyifo, "Wole Soyinka," 63; *SP*, xviii; *ADO*, 20.

27. Peter Nazareth, "An African View of Literature (Evanston, Ill.: Northwestern University Press, 1974), 65–66.

28. Chidi Amuta, "The Ideological Content of Wole Soyinka's War Writings," *Commonwealth* 8, no. 2 (Spring 1988): 111; Biodun Jeyifo, "Some Corrective Myths for the Misguided Native and Arrogant Alien," review of *Myth, Literature, and the African World* by Wole Soyinka, *Positive Review* (Ile-Ife) 1 (1978): 15–16; Jeyifo, *Truthful Lie*, 32, 35.

29. James Gibbs, ed., "Soyinka in Zimbabwe: A Question-and-Answer Session" (29 November 1981), *Literary Half-Yearly* 28, no. 2 (July 1987): 72, hereafter cited in the text except in multiple references.

30. James Booth, "Myth, Metaphor and Syntax in Soyinka's Poetry," *Research in African Literatures* 17, no. 1 (Spring 1986): 58, hereafter cited in the text.

31. Quoted from Wole Soyinka, *Culture in Transition* (transcript), Esso World Theatre, 1963, reprinted in Ann Dundon, "Soyinkan Aesthetics in *Culture in Transition*: An Essay on Film" (paper presented at the First Ibadan Annual African Literature Conference, 6–10 July 1976), 14, hereafter cited in the text.

Chapter 2

1. The following articles are useful sources of information about the two phases of the egungun: Ulli Beier, "The Egungun Cult," *Nigeria Magazine* 51 (1956): 380–92, and "Yoruba Theatre," in *Introduction to African Literature*, rev. ed., ed. Ulli Beier (London: Longman, 1979), 269–80; Joe de Graft, "Roots in African Drama and Theater," *African Literature Today* 8 (1976): 1–26; Oyin Ogunba, "Traditional African Festival Drama," in *Theater in Africa*, ed. Oyin Ogunba and Abiola Irele (Ibandan, Nigeria: Ibadan University Press, 1978), 3–26, hereafter cited in the text; Ola Rotimi, "Traditional Nigerian Drama," in *Introduction to Nigerian Literature*, ed. Bruce King (London: Evans, 1971), 36–49.

2. The consensus of opinion among African dramatists and theater scholars about the ritual origins of African drama is perhaps best represented in de Graft, "Roots in African Drama and Theater," 5–10. A dissenting view is expressed by Oyekan Owomoyela in his article "Folklore and Yoruba Theater," in *Critical Perspectives on Nigerian Literatures*, ed. Bernth Lindfors (Washington, D.C.: Three Continents Press, 1975), 27–29.

3. The dramatist Femi Osofisan underlines Soyinka's kinship with traditional artists by tentatively dividing his plays into twin categories that have loose affinities with both the split-level performance of festival drama and the two stages of the egungun. The Marxist critic Biodun Jeyifo polarizes contem-

porary Nigerian theater along the same figurative "cultic" and "popular" lines: the university playwrights and their literary drama, performed before elite audiences of educated initiates far from the popular arena, constitute the new cult "priests" and practice; the indigenous folk theaters are the modern masquerade revelers, providing lighthearted entertainments in the Yoruba vernacular for the masses. In Jeyifo's opinion, Soyinka's work continues to express the ruling cosmology, theocratic ethos, and animist-pantheism of Yoruba cultdrama. See Femi Osofisan, "Tiger on Stage: Wole Soyinka and Nigerian Theatre," in Ogunba and Irele, *Theatre in Africa*, 156–57, 163; Jeyifo, *Truthful Lie*, 113–17, and Jeyifo, *The Yoruba Popular Travelling Theatre of Nigeria* (Lagos: Nigeria Magazine, 1984), 120–21, 126–27.

4. In this essay Soyinka follows the Yoruba theater historian Joel Adedeji in tracing Yoruba drama to a form of masque theater that allegedly emerged not from the sacral rites but broke away from the secular masquerade of egungun funeral obsequies at the Oyo royal court in the early seventeenth century. By the midnineteenth century, it is claimed, the splinter movement had ramified into traveling troupes of performing masqueraders such as the Alarinjo. Adedeji's argument has been contested by Oyekan Owomoyela. See Joel Adedeji, " 'Alarinjo': The Traditional Yoruba Travelling Theatre," in Ogunba and Irele, *Theatre in Africa*, 27–32, hereafter cited in the text except in multiple references; Oyekan Owomoyela, "Creative Historiography and Critical Determinism in Nigerian Theater," *Research in African Literatures* 17 (Summer 1986): 249–50; Gibbs, "Soyinka in Zimbabwe," 57–58.

5. At the same time Soyinka is aware that his close derivation of tragic drama from religious ritual follows certain currents of Western thought, notably Aristotle's and Nietzsche's reading of the Greek dithyramb, and he acknowledges his debt to Nietzsche at the outset in "The Fourth Stage" (*MLAW*, 140). See Aristotle, "On the Art of Poetry," in *Classical Literary Criticism*, trans. T. S. Dorsch (Harmondsworth, England: Penguin, 1965), 32–33, 36–37; Friedrich Nietzsche, *The Birth of Tragedy* [1872], trans. Francis Golffing (New York: Doubleday/Anchor, 1956), 27–28.

6. For an example of this view of masquerade dramaturgy, see John Ferguson, "Nigerian Drama in English," *Modern Drama* 11 (May 1968): 10.

7. For some examples of the complex circular interactions between folk theater and traditional mask drama, and of the feedback from modern literary theater into both folk and festival forms, see Joel Adedeji, "Oral Tradition and the Contemporary Theater in Nigeria," *Research in African Literatures* 2 (Summer 1971): 135–39, 143–47, Adedeji, "The Literature of the Yoruba Opera," 73–74, and Adedeji, " 'Alarinjo,' " 49–50; Austin Asagba, "Roots of African Drama: Critical Approaches and Elements of Continuity," *Kunapipi* 8, no. 3 (1986): 88–89; Jeyifo, *Yoruba Popular Travelling Theatre*, 15–22, 39–41, 98–105, 128–29; Oyin Ogunba, "Theatre in Nigeria," *Présence Africaine* 58 (1966): 70–73; Owomoyela, "Folklore and Yoruba Theater," 33.

8. On the Alarinjo troupes, see chapter 2, note 4. There is also a clear line of development from Kola Ogunmola's popular satiric entertainment medlies to Soyinka's revue sketches and to *Opera Wonyosi* and the *Jero* plays, as is evident in a number of features: for example, the episodic structures and the anti-illusionist acting styles, moving actors back and forth between character and choric roles and having them directly address the audience. (Folk theater is inherently Brechtian.)

9. Kofi Awoonor, *The Breast of the Earth* (New York: NOK, 1975), 323.

10. Critics seem to be some uncertain as to whether Soyinka's Rockefeller research, which in fact extended beyond Nigeria to Ghana and Ivory Coast, covered traditional festivals or modern (folk) theater or both, and whether Soyinka's unpublished paper "The African Approach to Drama," presented at the International Symposium on African Culture in Ibadan in December 1960, was drawn from his empirical research or academic reading. The relevant files in the University of Ibadan library, containing Soyinka's personal correspondence and comments on the future of West African theater prepared for his Rockefeller sponsors, are not generally available. See Gerald Moore, *Wole Soyinka*, rev. ed. (London: Evans, 1978), 9; Bernth Lindfors, "The Early Writings of Wole Soyinka," in Lindfors, *Critical Perspectives on Nigerian Literatures*, 184; Robert W. July, "The Artist's Credo: The Political Philosophy of Wole Soyinka," *Journal of Modern African Studies* 19 (September 1981): 448; James Gibbs "Soyinka's Drama of Essence," *Utafiti* 3, no. 2 (1978): 427–40; Katrak, *Wole Soyinka and Modern Tragedy*, 25–30.

11. Soyinka's intimacy and childhood encounters with the egungun and masquerades are documented in his autobiography, *Aké: The Years of Childhood* (London: Rex Collings, 1981), 6–12, 30–35, hereafter cited in the text.

12. Wole Soyinka, *Collected Plays*, vol. 1 (London: Oxford University Press, 1973), 5, hereafter cited in the text as *CP1*.

13. Victor Turner, *The Ritual Process* (Harmondsworth, England: Pelican, 1974), 82.

14. Oyin Ogunba, "The Traditional Content of the Plays of Wole Soyinka," *African Literature Today* 5 (1971): 106.

15. Soyinka uses as his model for this conjunction the play *The Imprisonment of Obatala* (1966) by Obotunde Ijimere, which is the pseudonym of the German scholar Ulli Beier.

16. In the first category, see Ann Davis, "Dramatic Theory of Wole Soyinka"; in the second, see Andrew Gurr, "Third-World Drama: Soyinka and Tragedy"; both essays appear in *Critical Perspectives on Wole Soyinka*, ed. James Gibbs (Washington, D.C.: Three Continents Press, 1980), 139–57.

17. In a 1975 interview Soyinka noticed the tendency in Western dramatic thinking to turn the defeated challenger or failed revolutionary into a tragic hero. Mistrusting this transposition of terminologies, he compressed the alternatives into the unitary concept of the sacrificial revolutionary, remarking

that "inherent in all struggle on behalf of society is always the element of self-sacrifice." See Louis S. Gates, "An Interview with Wole Soyinka," *Black World* 24, no. 10 (August 1975): 37, hereafter cited in the text.

18. See, for example, Nkosi, *Tasks and Masks*, 190.

19. See Gurr, "Third World Drama," 142–44; Obi Maduakor, *Wole Soyinka: An Introduction to His Writing* (New York: Garland Press, 1986), 299–305. The motif of recovered universal harmony and of the withdrawal from action into the sphere of consciousness that is implicit in the Ogun-Obatala paradigm has led to comparisons between Soyinka and romanticism. See Brian Crow, with S. Abah and S. T. Balewa, "Soyinka and the Voice of Vision," *Journal of Commonwealth Literature* 17 (August 1982): 107–22, and Crow, "Soyinka and the Romantic Tradition," in *Before Our Very Eyes: Tribute to Wole Soyinka*, ed. Dapo Adelugba (Ibadan, Nigeria: Spectrum, 1987), 147–69.

20. See Osofisan, "Ritual and the Revolutionary Ethos," quoted in *ADO*, 123; Richard Priebe, "Demonic Imagery and the Apocalyptic Vision in the Novels of Ayi Kwei Armah," *Yale French Studies* 53 (1976): 105.

21. The echo is of Albany's words: "It will come, / Humanity must perforce prey on itself, / Like monsters of the deep." *King Lear*, act IV, scene ii, lines 47–49.

22. The Ghanaian playwright Joe de Graft has also written of acting in terms of risk and possession. The actor, he says, is always in danger of being "carried away on the uncertain currents of hysteria and ecstasy . . . acting is most electrifying when it dares to go as close as possible to the psychological safety point, the farthest limit within control—the brink of possession." The idea of acting as controlled hysteria has been stated in secular terms by Stanislavsky as the subjection of the inhibitive forces of the personality to deep psychic resources (the god inside), followed by the retrospective presentation of this subjection in performance: the actor must "experience the agony of his role, and weep his heart out at home or in rehearsals, that he can then calm himself [and] convey . . . in intelligible and eloquent terms what he has been through." This twofold process corresponds loosely with Nietzsche's Dionysian-Apollonian polarity, with "tragic" and "Brechtian" styles of acting, and with the two theatrogenic Yoruba gods Ogun and Obatala, who represent, respectively, the traumatic turmoil of the creative process and the aesthetic calm of the finished achievement. See Joe de Graft, "Roots in African Drama and Theater": 6; Konstantin Stanislavsky, *Building a Character*, trans. Elizabeth R. Hapgood (London: Max Reinhardt, 1950), 72.

23. In his essay "Theatre in African Traditional Culture" Soyinka observes that the pure ritual activities of male initiation societies contain rudimentary performance elements but no finished and fully rounded artistic form (*ADO*, 193). In a reply to criticism of an Afro-American choreographer working in Nigeria in the early 1960s he argues that "authentic" dances do not come ready-made for theater performance but have to go through a "necessary

transition" to be shaped into a "conscious art form." By the same rule, the ritual dramaturgy of transition should itself go through a process of transition and adaptation in its passage into stage drama. Wole Soyinka, "Five Minutes of Our Dances in a Theatre Will Chloroform You," *Daily Times*, 7 July 1962, quoted in James Gibbs, "Tear the Painted Masks, Join the Poison Stains," *Research in African Literatures* 14 (Spring 1983): 5, hereafter cited in the text except in multiple references.

24. Soyinka had a live goat sacrificed on stage in his "1960 Masks" open-air production of J. P. Clark's *Song of a Goat* at the Mbari Club in Ibadan, Nigeria, 1962. See Moore, *Wole Soyinka*, 40.

25. Schematic readings along these lines can be found in Joel Adedeji, "Aesthetics of Soyinka's Theatre," in Adelugba, *Before Our Very Eyes*; Katrak, *Wole Soyinka and Modern Tragedy*; Stephan Larsen, *A Writer and His Gods: A Study of the Importance of Yoruba Myths and Religious Ideas to the Writings of Wole Soyinka* (Stockholm, Sweden: University of Stockholm, Department of the History of Literature, 1983); and Maduakor, *Wole Soyinka*.

26. See Katrak, *Wole Soyinka and Modern Tragedy*, 136; Larsen, *Writer and His Gods*, 42.

27. Adedeji reads *The Strong Breed* in terms of the Obatala Festival; "Aesthetics of Soyinka's Theatre," 109–10. Ann Dundon also points out similarities between the roles of Obatala and Ifada in "Soyinkan Aesthetics in *Culture in Transition*," 23–24.

28. Annmarie Heywood, "The Fox's Dance: The Staging of Soyinka's Plays," in Gibbs, *Critical Perspectives of Wole Soyinka*, 131.

Chapter 3

1. Soyinka's other radio play, "The Detainee," a moving account of a visit to a political prisoner by a former comrade, is a less ambitious but a more economical and technically accomplished piece of writing. This short play, broadcast by the BBC African Service in 1965, exists only in unpublished playscript form.

2. James Gibbs, who takes a much more moralistic view of *Camwood* than I do, multiplies Isola's blasphemies by the addition of the slaying of a "sacred python." The python, however, is sacred to no one in the play and is not a communal religious symbol, as in Chinua Achebe's *Things Fall Apart* (1958); it is Isola's personal image for his father and his parochial religious creed. It was, perhaps, to avoid confusion with "sacred pythons" that Soyinka called the snake a "boa." See James Gibbs, "Grafting Is an Ancient Art: The Relationship of African and European Elements in the Early Plays of Wole Soyinka," *World Literature Written in English* 24 (Summer 1984): 95–96; and Gibbs, *Wole Soyinka* (London: Macmillan, 1986), 62, hereafter cited in the text.

3. It has been pointed out that *jero* is Hausa prison slang for criminal. Oyin

Ogunba, *The Movement of Transition: A Study of the Plays of Wole Soyinka* (Ibadan, Nigeria: Ibadan University Press, 1975), 65, hereafter cited in the text.

4. Richard K. Priebe, *Myth, Realism, and the West African Writer* (Trenton, N.J.: Africa World Press, 1988), 127–38, hereafter cited in the text.

5. Various critics have offered the eponymous hero of Joyce Cary's 1939 novel *Mister Johnson* as a model for Lakunle, but a likelier and closer source, particularly for his vacuous grandiloquence, is the bombastic schoolteacher, Bambulu, who is used to sing the virtues of progress by J. E. Henshaw in his play *This Is Our Chance* (London: University of London Press, 1956).

6. The interplay between "traditional" and "modern" modes of behavior in *The Lion and the Jewel* is explored by J. Z. Kronenfeld in his essay "The 'Communistic' African and the 'Individualistic' Westerner: Some Comments on Misleading Generalizations in Western Criticism of Soyinka and Achebe," in Lindfors, *Critical Perspectives on Nigerian Literatures*, 237–64.

7. In the early years of independence Soyinka's suspicions of Nigeria's traditional rulers increased. See his comments on "polygamous elders" in his 1963 essay "From a Common Backcloth" (*ADO*, 13) and his letters to the Nigerian press criticizing the opportunistic and obscurantist tactics of the Obas during the Biafra crisis (quoted in Gibbs, "Tear the Painted Masks," 6, 21).

Chapter 4

1. The red-and-white dye used for Jaguna's carrier in *The Strong Breed* points to the Yoruba akogun, as described by Soyinka in a 1962 interview. The conveyance of pollutions to the river in a miniature wooden boat by Eman's father in the ancestral village appears to be based on the Eyo Adimu, discussed by Soyinka in a 1975 interview, and on the Ijaw Amagba, as described by the anthropologist Robin Horton. See Duerden and Pieterse, *African Writers Talking*, 171; Gates, "Interview with Wole Soyinka," 40–41; and Robin Horton, "New Year in the Delta" *Nigeria Magazine* 67 (1960): 256–74.

2. The Ijaw Amagba rite was founded by a doctor, however, and Eman's tree death, though untypical of African carriers, has an African prototype in the Akan Apo Festival, in which the personal slave to the king was sacrificially hanged in a tree to rebuild the waning spirit of both the king and his community at year's end. See Horton, "New Year," 259; and Eva Meyerowitz, *The Akan of Ghana* (London: Faber, 1958), 52–53.

3. For elaboration of the distinctions between carriers and scapegoats, see Derek Wright, "Scapegoats and Carriers: New Year Festivals in History and Literature," *Journal of African Studies* 14 (Winter 1987): 183–89.

4. Soyinka observes that "the individuals who carry, who serve as carriers for the rest of the community, are not expected to survive very long. The whole demand, the stress, the spiritual tension, as well as the forces of evil which they trapped into their own person are such that after a few years they either go

insane, or they catch some mysterious disease, or they simply atrophy as human beings and die." Gates, "Interview with Wole Soyinka," 40–41.

5. Katrak (*Wole Soyinka and Modern Tragedy,* 52–55) deems the bequests for the community built into Eman's death to be so definite as to constitute a firm option in the Brechtian manner.

6. Wole Soyinka, *The Bacchae of Euripides: A Communion Rite* (London: Methuen, 1973), vii, hereafter cited in the text.

7. In a 1966 essay on Nkrumah, published just before *Kongi,* Soyinka observes that "society has, from the earliest primitive beginnings, incorporated into its code for healthy functioning processes for a change in the leadership," but the "modern autocrat" refuses to give up power, so that "the hemlock has always to be forcibly administered." "Of Power and Change," *African Statesman* (Lagos, Nigeria) 1, no. 3 (July-September 1966): 18–19.

8. Although Soyinka has discouraged any narrow identification of Kongi with Nkrumah, the origins of "positive scientificism" are probably to be found in Nkrumah's equally uneuphonious and unpronounceable "Consciencism."

9. These continuities, which to some degree run counter to the ritual paradigms of the New Yam Festival, have been traced to the complex radial patterns of parallels and incremental repetition found in the Obatala festival. See 'Ropo Sekoni, "Metaphor as Basis of Form in Soyinka's Drama," *Research in African Literatures* 14 (Spring 1983): 45–57.

10. Wole Soyinka, quoted in David Atilade, "*Kongi's Harvest* and the Men Who Made the Film," *Interlink* (Lagos, Nigeria) (October-December 1970): 4.

11. Alan Akaraogun, "Interview with Wole Soyinka," *Spear* (Lagos, Nigeria) (May 1966): 18.

12. Annemarie Heywood advises a highly formal, "narrated" style of acting for *Kongi.* See Gibbs, *Critical Perspectives on Wole Soyinka,* 135.

13. In the first of these categories, see D. S. Izevbaye, "Mediation in Soyinka: The Case of the King's Horseman," in Gibbs, *Critical Perspectives on Wole Soyinka,* 116–25; Jasbir Jain, "The Unfolding of a Text: Soyinka's *Death and the King's Horseman,*" *Research in African Literatures* 17 (Summer 1986): 252–60. In the second category, see Mark Ralph-Bowman, "Leaders and Leftovers: A Reading of Soyinka's *Death and the King's Horseman,*" *Research in African Literatures* 14 (Spring 1983): 81–97.

14. See, for example, Jeyifo, *Truthful Lie,* 26–35. See also James Booth, "Self-Sacrifice and Human Sacrifice in Soyinka's *Death and the King's Horseman,*" *Research in African Literatures* 19 (Winter 1988): 529–50.

15. See, for example, Moore, *Twelve African Writers,* 225–26; Booth, "Self-Sacrifice and Human Sacrifice," 545–47.

16. See, for example, Paulin Hountondji, *African Philosophy: Myth and Reality* [1976], trans. Henri Evans (London: Hutchinson, 1983), 161–66.

17. According to Soyinka's 1975 interview discussion, the carrier "is doing nothing special" and is not taken from "artists or teachers or any of these

special classifications of society" but from "ordinary human beings like you or me." In *The Strong Breed* Eman's father, a perennial carrier of 20 years, refers to this ordinary figure but only to distinguish his own special "breed" from it: "Other men would rot and die doing this task year after year. . . . Our blood is strong like no other." See Gates, "Interview with Wole Soyinka," 41; *CP1*, 134.

18. In this first production Soyinka isolated Elesin on a wide and largely empty stage, distancing him both from the audience and from the choruses of market women and praise-singers, who were confined to side balconies. See Moore, *Wole Soyinka*, 159–60.

Chapter 5

1. Anon. "Nigeria's Bernard Shaw" (interview with Wole Soyinka), *Drum* (Lagos, Nigeria) (March 1961): 27.

2. Soyinka entitled his translation of D. O. Fagunwa's Yoruba novel *Ogboju Ode Ninu Igbo Irunmale, The Forest of a Thousand Daemons* (London: Nelson, 1968).

3. *Ampe* means "Do as I do, we are the same." See Ogunba, *Movement of Transition*, 92.

4. The emphasis on communal recovery at the end of *A Dance of the Forests* is much stronger in Soyinka's original manuscript version of the play. See Robert Fraser, "Four Alternative Endings to *A Dance of the Forests*," *Research in African Literatures* 10 (Winter 1979): 373.

5. Alternative readings of the Half-Child along the lines sketched here can be found in Ulli Beier, *A Dance of the Forests*: A Play by Wole Soyinka," *Black Orpheus* 8 (1960): 57–58; John Ferguson, "Nigerian Drama in English," *Modern Drama* 11 (May 1968): 23–24; Una Maclean, "Soyinka's International Drama," *Black Orpheus* 15 (1964): 49; Ogunba, *Movement of Transition*, 87–95; Nick Wilkinson, "Demoke's Choice in Soyinka's *A Dance of the Forests*," in Gibbs, *Critical Perspectives on Wole Soyinka*, 69–73.

6. In a 1988 essay Soyinka described the abiku, rather abstractly, as both "a metaphor for the phenomenon of creativity" and "an expression of doom" and stated that the ability of the "creative hand" of the artist to "earth Abiku once and for all" was dependent upon the suitability of historical conditions (*ADO*, 258). Forest Head's closing remarks in *A Dance of the Forests* seem to suggest that none of the human and spirit beings present can be entrusted with the future of the new nation, which will therefore have to wait for a more auspicious historical moment to be born (*CP1*, 71).

7. Soyinka said in a 1987 interview that audiences "even empathize in those moments when they do not fully understand because theatre is not all literal, one to one understanding, word by word, phrase by phrase." By "sensing" and "absorbing," "they have understood this theatre in its fullest sense." If the dramatist's remarks at the time of the production are to be trusted, it was the

"illiterates" of the community, not the intellectuals, who in October 1960 came back night after night to see *A Dance of the Forests*. See *ADO*, 330–31; Mphahlele, et al., "Wole Soyinka," 176–77.

8. See James Booth, *Writers and Politics in Nigeria* (London: Hodder and Stoughton, 1981), 130–31.

9. Parts of *A Dance of the Forests* were adapted, with few changes, from an unpublished play about South Africa; there are four extant versions of its conclusion; and as if there were not already enough role-playing and confusion, Soyinka, who, metatheatrically, played the part of Forest Head in the 1960 Yaba (Lagos) production, anagrammatized his first name in the cast list to arrive at one "Elow Gabonal." See James Gibbs, "The Origins of *A Dance of the Forests*," *African Literature Today* 8 (1976): 66–71; Fraser, "Four Alternative Endings," 359–74; *CP1*, 3.

10. Nick Wilkinson discusses the many confusing levels of existence in *A Dance of the Forests*, and Bernth Lindfors notes amusingly: "One has to struggle to remember that X in one context is equal or analogous to Y in another and that either or both may be reincarnations of Z in another world." A kind of identification parade, no doubt to dispel some of this confusion, apparently preceded a production of an extract from the play in Paris in April 1972. See Nick Wilkinson, "Literary Incomprehension: Wole Soyinka's Own Way with a Mode," *Nsukka Studies in African Literature* 1, no. 1 (1978): 46–49; Bernth Lindfors, "Wole Soyinka, When Are You Coming Home?" *Yale French Studies* 53 (1976): 200; Femi Osofisan, "Soyinka in Paris," *West Africa* (21 July 1972): 935.

11. For examples of the "socio-historical" and "metaphysical" extremes of interpretations of *The Road*, see Biodun Jeyifo, "The Hidden Class War in *The Road*," in *Truthful Lie*, 11–22; Elaine Fido, "*The Road* and Theatre of the Absurd," *Caribbean Journal of African Studies* 1 (Spring 1978): 75–94.

12. Soyinka referred, in a program note to the 1984 Goodman Theater production of *The Road* in Chicago, to "the very indeterminacy of Truth" in which the Yoruba worldview is rooted and against which Professor's pursuit of categoric certainty is vain (15).

13. These latter aspects of *The Road* are discussed by Jeyifo in *Truthful Lie*, 14–15.

14. In the agemo cult of the Ijebu Yoruba, from which Soyinka comes, leadership among the priesthood is deliberately confused partly to prevent the god from becoming the personal property of any individual. See Oyin Ogunba, "The Agemo Cult in Ijebuland," *Nigeria Magazine* 86 (1965): 181

15. Since Professor is a necromancer, it is likely that the climactic appearance of the egungun in *The Road* is in its fiercest and most dreaded form, that of the punitive Executioner of Witches, who expressed the moral anger of both the living community and the ancestors at broken taboos. See Morton-Williams, "Yoruba Responses to the Fear of Death," 37.

16. Soyinka's recommendation that a film be made of "this edifying aspect of Northern culture" perhaps convinced a few readers, as well as the censor, that the outrage was being upheld instead of censured. "Flogging Women Offenders," *Daily Express*, 4 November 1963, quoted in Gibbs, "Tear the Painted Masks," 6, 19.

Chapter 6

1. This sketch was originally published in *Before the Blackout* (Ibadan, Nigeria: Orisun Acting Editions, 1971) but is now published separately as *Childe Internationale* (Ibadan, Nigeria: Fountain Publications, 1987).

2. Soyinka has said, in connection with these satiric sketches, that "the cosy, escapist air of formal theatres tends to breed amnesia much too quickly" (preface to *Before the Blackout*, 4), and that the script was a starting point rather than an end. Yemi Ogunbiyi has said of Soyinka's production of *Opera Wonyosi*: "The text of the play was never completely written as it was ever being rewritten and reshaped during rehearsals. Nothing was finally arrived at until the play closed. . . . For him [Soyinka] the text, even his own text, was merely a map with many possible routes." "A Study of Soyinka's *Opera Wonyosi*," *Nigeria Magazine* 128–29 (1979): 13, hereafter cited in the text.

3. Quoted in Bernth Lindfors, "Begging Questions in Wole Soyinka's *Opera Wonyosi*," *ARIEL* 12 (July 1981): 32, hereafter cited in the text.

4. Wole Soyinka, "Before the Blow-out" (1978 mimeo), consisting of the sketches "Home to Roost" and "Big Game Safari." The "big game" hidden in the jungle and hunted down by metal detectors in the second sketch is the murderous domesticated animal that feeds on humans, the motorcar.

5. *Opera Wonyosi* was criticized by Ogunbiyi for its failure " to lay bare unambiguously the causal historical and socio-economic network of society," and by Jeyifo for its lack of "a solid class perspective." See Ogunbiyi, "Study of *Opera Wonyosi*," 12; Biodun Jeyifo, "Drama and the Social Order: Two Reviews," *Positive Review* (Ile-Ife, Nigeria) 1, no. 1 (1978): 22.

6. *Unlimited Liability Company*, featuring Tunji Oyelana and His Benders, with music and lyrics by Wole Soyinka, EWP 001 (Ewuro Productions, 1983), side 2.

7. *Requiem for a Futurologist* (London: Rex Collings, 1985) began as a much shorter radio play, "Die Still, Rev. Dr. Godspeak!," which was broadcast by the BBC in 1982 and first performed in 1983. At the climax of the original radio play Godspeak does not pretend to lie in state but dies for real, by jumping off the window ledge.

8. Wole Soyinka, *A Play of Giants* (London: Methuen, 1984), vii, hereafter cited in the text.

9. Wole Soyinka, interview in the *Guardian* (Manchester, England), quoted in Albert Hunt, "Amateurs in Horror," in Gibbs, *Critical Perspectives on Wole Soyinka*, 14.

10. Art Borreca, "'Idi Amin Was the Supreme Actor': An Interview with Wole Soyinka," *Theater* 16, no. 2 (Spring 1985): 32, hereafter cited in the text.

11. For a full exposition of this theory of African dictatorship, see James W. Fernandez, "The Shaka Complex," *Transition* 29 (1967): 11–15.

Chapter 7

1. Wole Soyinka, *The Interpreters* [1965] (London: Heinemann, 1970), 114, hereafter cited in the text as *TI*.

2. Though cast as both Barrabas and Christ, Noah does not escape death like the former, and his sacrifice is not willing like the latter's. Neither does he make connections or covenants like the rainbow spirit or motif in Yoruba and Christian lore. In fact, his blankness suggests the white that the rainbow's colors combine to produce, thus denoting, after the pattern of his albino master, the absence of pigment. Even as plain Noah in Lazarus's scheme, his presence does not protect the sect's church from floods.

3. Shatto Arthur Gakwandi, *The Novel and Contemporary Experience in Africa* (London: Heinemann, 1977), 82–83.

4. In this matter I disagree with Richard Priebe's argument that "to the extent they have characteristics of the gods, they [the interpreters] may also be seen as priests who have the responsibility of serving the gods that possess them." See *Myth, Realism, and the West African Writer*, 82.

5. These aspects of the novel are dealt with lucidly by Mark Kinkead-Weekes in his essay "*The Interpreters*: a Form of Criticism," in Gibbs, *Critical Perspectives on Wole Soyinka*, 232–36.

6. It has been suggested that the drunken Sagoe, the art theorist Kola, and the rebellious technologist Sekoni represent, respectively, the Dionysian, Apollonian, and Promethean aspects of Ogun. In *The Interpreters* Ogun appears to be a composite of selves whose characteristics are almost infinitely distributable. See Kathleen Morrison, "To Dare Transition: Ogun as Touchstone in Wole Soyinka's *The Interpreters*," *Research in African Literatures* 20 (Spring 1989): 60–71.

7. Wole Soyinka, *Season of Anomy* (London: Rex Collings, 1973), 6, hereafter cited in the text as *SOA*.

8. In his acerbic reply to Gerald Moore's criticism of *Season of Anomy*, Soyinka points out that Aiyero is not a model for the "cellular mobilization of the country" but an agent of transformation, though he gives little indication, either in the novel or in the essay, of the directions this transformation is to take. See *ADO*, 166–68; Moore, *Twelve African Writers*, 226–29, and *Wole Soyinka*, 134.

Chapter 8

1. There is an astute reading of these passages of *The Man Died* in Booth, *Writers and Politics in Nigeria*, 143–46.

2. See the contribution by Kole Omotoso in Agetua, *When the Man Died*, 19; Irele, *African Experience in Literature and Ideology*, 205.

3. Soyinka said in an interview not long after the publication of the book that *The Man Died* is "very pointedly political and . . . geared towards re-educating the minds of Nigerians by relating things which they thought they knew about and shaping their ways of looking at so-called public leaders and figures" (Agetua, "Interview with Soyinka," 34). In a later essay, however, he insisted that he was not writing "a political salvationary tract" (*ADO*, 288).

4. James Gibbs, "Biography into Autobiography: Wole Soyinka and the Relatives Who Inhabit *Aké,*" *Journal of Modern African Studies* 26, no. 3 (1988): 520–22, 535–36.

5. James Olney, "*Aké*: Wole Soyinka as Autobiographer," *Yale Review* 73, no. 1 Autumn (1983): 78.

6. 'Molara Ogundipe-Leslie, [review of *Aké*], *African Literature Today* 14 (1984): 144–45.

7. Ibid., 145; Gibbs, "Biography into Autobiography," 542.

8. Wole Soyinka, *Isara: A Voyage around "Essay"* (New York: Random House, 1989), v, hereafter cited in the text.

Chapter 9

1. Wole Soyinka, *Idanre and Other Poems* (London: Methuen, 1967), 49, hereafter cited in the text.

2. See, for example, Stanley Macebuh, "Poetics and the Mythic Imagination," and Robin Graham, "Wole Soyinka: Obscurity, Romanticism, and Dylan Thomas," in Gibbs, *Critical Perspectives on Wole Soyinka*, 200–12, 213–18.

3. See Eldred Jones, *The Writing of Wole Soyinka* (London: Heinemann, 1973), 129.

4. Robert Fraser, *West African Poetry: A Critical History* (Cambridge: Cambridge University Press, 1986), 235–36.

5. See also Thomas R. Knipp, "Irony, Tragedy, and Myth: The Poetry of Wole Soyinka," *World Literature Written in English* 21, no. 1 (Spring 1982): 5–26; Biodun Jeyifo's introduction to Soyinka, *Art, Dialogue, and Outrage*.

6. Judith Gleason, *A Recitation of Ifa, Oracle of the Yoruba* (New York: Grossman, 1973), 65–66.

7. Soyinka's recitation of the poem at the Commonwealth Arts Festival in London in 1965 was accompanied by a percussion orchestra.

8. Nadine Gordimer, [review of *Idanre*], *African Studies* 30, no. 1 (1971): 64–65.

9. Wole Soyinka, *A Shuttle in the Crypt* (London: Rex Collings/Methuen, 1972), vii, hereafter cited in the text.

10. C. Tighe, "In Detentio Preventione in Aeternum: Soyinka's *A Shuttle in the Crypt*," in Gibbs, *Critical Perspectives on Wole Soyinka,* 192.

11. Knipp, "Irony, Tragedy, and Myth," 20.

12. For example, Ken Goodwin assumes that the old women weaving at the loom and the reference to "Floating on lakes to cries of drowning," in the

"Passage" verses of "Procession" refer, respectively, to childhood memories and Lake Tegel, but nowhere are these things suggested by the poem itself (*Shuttle*, 46). Ken Goodwin, *Understanding African Poetry: A Study of Ten Poets* (London: Heinemann, 1982), 131.

13. Wole Soyinka, *Ogun Abibiman* (London: Rex Collings, 1976), 22, hereafter cited in the text as *OA*.

14. For this and other atrocities committed by Shaka in his mental decline, see the last six chapters of Mofolo's *Chaka*, in which the Zulu leader's case history reads much like a psychopathological blueprint of a modern African dictator. Thomas Mofolo, *Chaka* [1925], trans. Daniel P. Kunene (London: Heinemann, 1981), 142–68.

15. Wole Soyinka, *Mandela's Earth and Other Poems* [1988] (London: André Deutsch, 1989), 59, hereafter cited in the text as *ME*.

Chapter 10

1. Wole Soyinka, "Religion and Human Rights," *Index on Censorship* (May 1988): 83.

2. Wole Soyinka, "Twice Bitten: The Fate of Africa's Culture Producers," *PMLA* 105, no. 1 (1990): 114–16.

3. Femi Osofisan, one of the writer's more sophisticated left-wing critics, claims that "Soyinka has consistently subsumed history with the apparatus of ritual, while his public utterances and behaviours are an advocacy of social revolution." One such public utterance was Soyinka's recommendation, in a 1972 interview, of a takeover by workers' cooperatives. See Osofisan, "Ritual and the Revolutionary Ethos," quoted in Gerald Moore, "Against the Titans in Nigerian Literature," *Afriscope* (July 1977): 19; Wole Soyinka, [interview], *Militant* (Ibadan, Nigeria) 2, no. 1 (December 1972): 5.

4. Soyinka's affinities with the romantics are explored by Brian Crow, "Soyinka and the Romantic Tradition," in Adelugba, *Before Our Very Eyes*, 147–69.

5. Chinweizu, Onwuchekwa Jemie, and Ihechukwu Madubuike, *Toward the Decolonization of African Literature* [1980] (London: Kegan Paul International, 1985), 235, hereafter cited in the text.

6. Soyinka's argument here is in line with those of recent African philosophers, such as Paulin Hountondji in *African Philosophy: Myth and Reality* (Paris, 1976; trans. Henri Evans, London: Hutchinson, 1983), and of "alternative" ethnologists, such as Paul Radin in his *Primitive Man as Philosopher* [1927] (New York: Dover, 1947). He read the latter's *Primitive Religion: Its Nature and Origins* (New York: Dover, 1937) during his imprisonment when a copy was smuggled into his cell (*TMD*, 9).

Selected Bibliography

PRIMARY SOURCES
(excludes Soyinka's juvenilia)

Plays

The Bacchae of Euripides: A Communion Rite. London: Methuen, 1973; New York: Norton, 1974.

Before the Blackout (revue). Ibadan, Nigeria: Orisun Acting Editions, 1971 (republished with *Camwood on the Leaves*); New York: Third Press, 1974.

Camwood on the Leaves. London: Methuen, 1973 (see *Before the Blackout*).

Childe Internationale (originally part of *Before the Blackout*). Ibadan, Nigeria: Fountain Publications, 1987.

Collected Plays, vol. 1 (*A Dance of the Forests, The Swamp Dwellers, The Strong Breed, The Road, The Bacchae of Euripides*). London: Oxford University Press, 1973.

Collected Plays, vol. 2. (*The Lion and the Jewel, Kongi's Harvest, The Trials of Brother Jero, Jero's Metamorphosis, Madmen and Specialists*). London: Oxford University Press, 1974.

A Dance of the Forests. London: Oxford University Press, 1963.

Death and the King's Horseman. London: Methuen, 1975; New York: Norton, 1975.

Five Plays (A Dance of the Forests, The Lion and the Jewel, The Swamp Dwellers, The Trials of Brother Jero, The Strong Breed). London: Oxford University Press, 1964.

The House of Banigeji (extract). In *Reflections: Nigerian Prose and Verse,* edited by Frances Ademola, 96–101. Lagos, Nigeria: African Universities Press, 1962.

The Jero Plays (The Trials of Brother Jero, Jero's Metamorphosis). London: Methuen, 1973.

Kongi's Harvest. London: Oxford University Press, 1967.

The Lion and the Jewel. London: Oxford University Press, 1963.

Madmen and Specialists. London: Methuen, 1971; New York: Farrar, Straus & Giroux, 1971.

Opera Wonyosi. London: Rex Collings, 1981; Bloomington: Indiana University Press, 1981.

A Play of Giants. London: Methuen, 1984; Portsmouth, N.H.: Heinemann, 1988.

Requiem for a Futurologist. London: Rex Collings, 1985.
The Road. London: Oxford University Press, 1965.
Six Plays (The Trials of Brother Jero, Jero's Metamorphosis, Camwood on the Leaves, Death and the King's Horsemen, Madmen and Specialists, Opera Wonyosi). London: Methuen, 1984. See Jeyifo, "Soyinka at 50."
The Strong Breed. Ibadan, Nigeria: Orisun Acting Editions, 1970.
Three Plays (The Swamp Dwellers, The Trials of Brother Jero, The Strong Breed). Ibadan, Nigeria: Mbari Publications, 1963; republished as *Three Short Plays*, London and New York: Oxford University Press, 1969.
The Trials of Brother Jero. Nairobi, Kenya: Oxford University Press, 1969.

Poetry

Idanre and Other Poems. London: Methuen, 1967; New York: Hill & Wang, 1968.
Mandela's Earth and Other Poems. New York: Random House, 1988; London: André Deutsch, 1989.
Ogun Abibiman. London: Rex Collings, 1976.
Poems from Prison. London: Rex Collings, 1969.
Poems of Black Africa (edited). London: Heinemann, 1975.
A Shuttle in the Crypt. London: Rex Collings/Methuen, 1972; New York: Hill & Wang, 1972.

Uncollected Poems

"Audience to Performer." *Horn* (Ibadan, Nigeria) 4, no. 1 (1960):4.
"Committee Man." *Horn* (Ibadan) 4, no. 3 (1961): 10–11.
"The Dancer." *Nigeria* (October 1960): 222.
"Epitaph for Say Tokyo Kid." *Horn* (Ibadan) 4, no. 5 (1962): 10–11.
"For Three Children." *Ibadan* 12 (June 1961): 28.
"General Franco's Condition." *Transition/Ch'Indaba* (Accra, Ghana) 50, no 1. (December 1975): 9.
"The Ghoul Flushed," "The Meeting Is Called . . . ," and "Sixteen Places." *Anvil* (Ibadan) 1, no. 1 (21 February–6 March 1970): 3.
"Insulation." *Ibadan* 5 (February 1959): 24.
"Poisoners of the World Unite" and "Proverb: Okonjo de Hunter." *Horn* (Ibadan) 3, no. 3 (1960): 4–7, 9.
"Stage." *Horn* (Ibadan) 4, no. 1 (1960): 1.
"Telephone Conversation" and "Requiem." In *Modern Poetry from Africa*, edited by Gerald Moore and Ulli Beier. Harmondsworth, England: Penguin, 1963.
"Two in London," "The Immigrant," and "The Other Immigrant." In *An African Treasury*, edited by Langston Hughes. New York: Crown, 1960; London: Gollancz, 1961.

Novels

The Interpreters. London: André Deutsch, 1965; London: Heinemann, 1970; New York: Collier, 1970; New York: Holmes & Meier, 1972.
Season of Anomy. London: Rex Collings, 1973; New York: Third Press, 1974; London: Nelson, 1980.

Autobiographies

Aké: The Years of Childhood. London: Rex Collings, 1981; New York: Random House, 1982.
Isara: A Voyage around "Essay." New York: Random House, 1989; London: Methuen, 1990.
The Man Died: Prison Notes of Wole Soyinka. London: Rex Collings, 1972; New York: Harper & Row, 1973; London: Penguin, 1975; New York: Farrar, Straus & Giroux, 1988.

Translation

The Forest of a Thousand Daemons (translation from the Yoruba of D. O. Fagunwa, *Ogboju Ode Ninu Igbo Irunmale*). London: Nelson, 1968; Atlantic Highlands, N.J.: Humanities Press, 1969; New York: Random House, 1983.

Criticism

Art, Dialogue, and Outrage: Essays on Literature and Culture. Ibadan, Nigeria: New Horn Press, 1988 (distributed in England by Hans Zell, Oxford).
Myth, Literature, and the African World. Cambridge: Cambridge University Press, 1976.

Uncollected Essays

"Amos Tutuola on Stage." *Ibadan* 16 (June 1962): 23–24.
"And after the Narcissist?" *African Forum* 1, no. 4 (Spring 1966): 53–64.
"Bangs Big and Small." *Weekend Guardian* (Manchester, England) 21–22 October 1989, 21, 23.
"The Choice and Use of Language." *Cultural Events in Africa* 75 (1971): 3–6.
"Cor, Teach." *Ibadan* 7 (November 1959): 25–27.
"Ethics, Ideology, and the Critic." In *Criticism and Ideology,* edited by Kirsten Holst Petersen, 26–51. Uppsala, Sweden: Scandinavian Institute of African Studies, 1988.
"The Future of African Writing." *Horn* (Ibadan, Nigeria) 4, no. 1 (June 1960): 10–16.
"Gbohun-Gbohun—The Nigerian Playwright Wole Soyinka on His Dealings with the BBC." *Listener* (London) (2 November 1972): 581–83.

"The Nigerian Stage: A Study in Tyranny and Individual Survival." In *Colloquium on Negro Art*, 538–49. Paris: Présence Africaine, 1968.

"Nigeria's International Film Festival 1962." *Nigeria Magazine* (Lagos) 79 (December 1963): 307–10.

"Of Power and Change." *African Statesman* (Lagos, Nigeria) 1, no. 3 (July–September 1966): 17–19.

"Power and Creative Strategies." *Index on Censorship* 7 (July 1988): 7–9.

"Religion and Human Rights." *Index on Censorship* 5 (May 1988): 82–85.

"Salutations to the Gut." In *Reflections: Nigerian Prose and Verse*, edited by Frances Ademola, 109–15. Lagos, Nigeria; African Universities Press, 1962; reprinted in *Africa in Prose*, edited by O. R. Dathorne and Willfried Feuser; 355–64. Harmondsworth, England: Penguin, 1969.

"The Terrible Understanding." *Atlas* (New York) 15 (January 1968): 36–39.

"This Past Must Address Its Present" (Nobel Prize speech). *Black American Literature Forum* 22, no. 3 (Fall 1988): 429–46.

"Twice Bitten: The Fate of Africa's Culture Producers." *PMLA* 105, no. 1 (1990): 110–20.

Unpublished Material

"The African Approach to Drama," presented at the International Symposium on African Culture in Ibadan in December 1960.

"Before the Blow-Out" (revue). Mimeo, 1978. Includes "Home to Roost" and "Big Game Safari."

Blues for a Prodigal (film). Ewuro Productions, 1984.

Culture in Transition (film). Esso World Theatre, 1963. Includes adaptation of *The Strong Breed*.

"The Detainee" (radio play). BBC London (mimeo), 1965.

"Die Still, Rev. Dr. Godspeak!" (radio play). BBC London (mimeo), 1982.

"The Invention" (one-act play). Royal Court Theatre, London (mimeo), 1959.

"The Republican" (satirical review). 1963.

"The New Republican," a revision of "The Republican," with new material (satirical review). 1964.

"Priority Projects" (satirical review). 1983.

"Proceedings of the First Rites of the Harmattan Solstice" (eight poems). (mimeo), 1966.

"Rice Unlimited" (satirical review). 1981.

Unlimited Liability Company (record). Ewuro Productions, 1983.

SECONDARY SOURCES

There is now an enormous critical industry devoted to Soyinka's writings, and it cannot be represented here. I have listed all complete books on Soyinka, but material listed under the other headings is very selective. Only critical material that is directly about the author's works is included. For details of background studies on Yoruba religion, culture, and drama, readers should refer to the chapter notes.

Selected Interviews

Agetua, John, ed. *Interviews with Six Nigerian Writers*. Benin City, Nigeria: Bendel Newspaper Corp., 1973.

————. "Interview with Wole Soyinka in Accra, Ghana, 1974." In Agetua, *When the Man Died*, 31–46.

Akarogun, Alan. "Interview with Wole Soyinka." *Spear* (Lagos, Nigeria) (May 1966): 16–19, 42.

Borreca, Art. "'Idi Amin Was the Supreme Actor': An Interview with Wole Soyinka." *Theater* 16, no. 2 (Spring 1985): 32–37.

[Interview] "Conversations with Chinua Achebe" (discussion by Soyinka, Achebe, and Lewis Nkosi). *Africa Report* (July 1964): 19–21.

Gates, Louis S. "An Interview with Wole Soyinka." *Black World* 24, no. 10 (August 1975): 30–48.

Gibbs, James, ed. "Soyinka in Zimbabwe: A Question-and-Answer Session" (29 November 1981). *Literary Half-Yearly* 28, no. 2 (July 1987): 50–110.

Gulledge, Jo, ed. "Seminar on *Aké* with Wole Soyinka." *Southern Review* 23, no. 3 (1987): 511–26.

Harding, Jeremy. "Interview: Wole Soyinka." *New Statesman* (27 February 1987): 21–22.

Jeyifo, Biodun. "Wole Soyinka: A *Transition* Interview." *Transition* 42 (1973): 62–64.

————. "Soyinka at 50." *West Africa* (27 August 1984): 1728–31. Parts of this interview are reprinted as the introduction to *Six Plays*, xi–xxi.

Katrak, Ketu H. "Question-and-Answer Session with Soyinka at the African Studies Association Conference, Los Angeles, November 1979," and "Interview with Soyinka at the University of Ife, November 4, 1980." Extracts printed in Katrak, *Wole Soyinka and Modern Tragedy*, 19, 20, 43, 68, 87.

[Interview] *Militant* (Ibadan, Nigeria) 2, no. 1 (December 1972): 3–7.

Mphahlele, Ezekiel, Lewis Nkosi, and Dennis Duerden. "Wole Soyinka." In *African Writers Talking*, edited by Dennis Duerden and Cosmo Pieterse, 169–80. London: Heinemann, 1972.

Stotesbury, John A. "Wole Soyinka." *Kunapipi* 9, no. 1 (1987): 59–64. Reprinted as "The Reader, the Regime, and the Writer," in *African Voices: Interviews with Thirteen African Writers*, edited by Raoul Granqvist and John Stotesbury, 67–73. Sydney: Dangaroo Press, 1989.

"Televised Discussion," "Penthouse Theater," and "Class Discussion." In *In Person: Achebe, Awoonor, and Soyinka at the University of Washington*, edited

by Karen L. Morell, 89–130. Seattle, Wash.: University of Washington, Institute of Comparative and Foreign Area Studies, 1975.
"The Writer in Africa Today." *Africa Currents* 7 (Autumn 1976–Winter 1977): 26–29.

Books

Adelugba, Dapo. *Before Our Very Eyes: Tribute to Wole Soyinka.* Ibadan, Nigeria: Spectrum, 1987. A collection of personal reminiscences and critical essays originally assembled for Soyinka's fiftieth birthday and revised after the Nobel Prize award. The criticism section contains illuminating essays by Adelugba and Dan Izevbaye on Soyinka's phonograph recordings and a penetrating essay by Brian Crow on Soyinka and romanticism.

Agetua, John. *When the Man Died.* Benin City, Nigeria: Bendel Newspaper Corp., 1975. A short survey of responses to Soyinka's controversial prison autobiography. Contains an interview with Soyinka, who at the time was in Accra, Ghana, in "exile" from the Gowon regime, which was still in power in Nigeria. See Agetua, "Interview with Wole Soyinka in Accra, Ghana, 1974."

Dunton, C. P. *Notes on Three Short Plays.* Harlow, England: Longman/York Press, 1982. An excellent commentary, far in excess of the usual plot summaries and character outlines required by the format of these study guides. Particularly good on *The Strong Breed.*

Gibbs, James. *Study Aid to "Kongi's Harvest."* London: Rex Collings, 1973. This booklet contains useful background information on the play together with a letter from Soyinka and a long extract from his 1966 political essay, "Of Power and Change."

————, ed. *Critical Perspectives on Wole Soyinka.* Washington, D.C.: Three Continents Press, 1980; London: Heinemann, 1981. This is by far the best critical anthology on Soyinka, covering all aspects of his work and ideas. Excellent contributions all around, but those by D. S. Izevbaye and Mark Kinkead-Weekes are particularly fine.

————. *Notes on "The Lion and the Jewel."* Harlow, England: Longman/York Press, 1982. A useful commentary on the play and its traditional backgrounds.

————. *Wole Soyinka,* Modern Dramatists Series. London: Macmillan, 1986. A fine condensed study of the drama, its formative influences, and historical backgrounds. The most comprehensive account to date, taking in Soyinka's most recent plays and revues.

Gikandi, Simon. *Wole Soyinka's "The Road."* Nairobi, Kenya: Heinemann Educational Books, 1985. A lively, if overcompressed discussion of the play. Rather thin on its Yoruba origins and political dimensions.

Jones, Eldred. *The Writing of Wole Soyinka.* London: Heinemann, 1973, 1983, 1988; Boston: Twayne, 1973. This is still the best full-length introduction to Soyinka, containing much lucid and intelligent criticism of the poetry, the early plays, and the first novel. The material on the later plays and prose added in the second and third editions, however, is not up to the standard of the first edition and is erratically proportioned, with some odd and conspicuous omissions, notably *A Play of Giants.*

Katrak, Ketu H. *Wole Soyinka and Modern Tragedy: A Study of Dramatic Theory and Practice.* Westport, Conn.: Greenwood Press, 1986. A very scholarly and often brilliant but overschematic reading of seven plays in terms of alternative tragic paradigms drawn from classical and Yoruba tragedy, and from Nietzsche and Brecht. In the process some unlikely protagonists, such as Igwezu in *The Swamp Dwellers,* are pressed into the role of transitional hero.

Larsen, Stephan. *A Writer and His Gods: A Study of the Importance of Yoruba Myths and Religious Ideas to the Writings of Wole Soyinka.* Stockholm: University of Stockholm, Department of the History of Literature, 1983. An occasionally insightful but somewhat labored and repetitive, published doctoral thesis that, in its effort to relate everything to its chosen topic, finds the presence of Ogun almost everywhere in Soyinka's writing and, as if the god of transition were not himself transitional, tends to treat him as a static and unitary, not an evolving and eclectic phenomenon.

Maduakor, Obi. *Wole Soyinka: An Introduction to His Writing.* New York: Garland Press, 1986. Not really a general introduction but an indecisive mixture of commentary and overselective analysis, narrowly representing Soyinka's dramatic output by five "metaphysical dramas of essence." Like Katrak and Larsen, though more crudely, Maduakor tends to view the characters of the plays, baldly, as "exponents of transition" and to render the human action, abstractly, into the familiar Ogunian mythology. Contains some perceptive comments on the poetry, however, and a good summary account of Soyinka's criticism.

Moore, Gerald. *Wole Soyinka.* 1971; revised and expanded edition, London: Evans, 1978. The best short study of Soyinka's work in different genres, though going only as far as 1976. Moore's vigorous and eloquent criticism has to date not been surpassed in monographs on Soyinka.

Ogunba, Oyin. *The Movement of Transition: A Study of the Plays of Wole Soyinka.* Ibadan, Nigeria: Ibadan University Press, 1975. Though it stops at *Madmen and Specialists,* this is still the best full-length study of the drama, containing long and densely analytical chapters on each of the major plays and a wealth of background and material on Yoruba culture, language, and religion.

Probyn, Clive. *Notes on "The Road."* Harlow, England: Longman/York Press, 1981. An excellent commentary and condensed analysis by a subtle and perceptive critic, sharply illuminating one of Soyinka's most difficult metaphysical dramas.

Sotto, Wiveca. *The Rounded Rite: A Study of Wole Soyinka's Play, "The Bacchae of Euripides."* Malmö, Sweden: CWK Gleerup/Lund, 1985. Another published doctoral thesis, in this case researching the backgrounds to a single play. Scholarly and well documented but, at 176 pages, an overlong and heavily specialized work. Not for the general reader or newcomer to Soyinka studies.

Parts of Books

Arnold, Stephen, ed. *African Literature Studies: The Present State.* Washington, D.C.: Three Continents Press, 1985. Contains stimulating material by Richard Priebe on *Aké* and by Jonathan Ngate on *The Road.*

Booth, James. *Writers and Politics in Nigeria.* London: Hodder and Stoughton: 1981. An incisive discussion of the political dimensions of Soyinka's plays and novels.

Etherton, Michael. *The Development of African Drama.* New York: Africana Publishing Co., 1982. A lucid analysis of Soyinka's tragedies and later satires.

Fraser, Robert. *West African Poetry: A Critical History.* Cambridge: Cambridge University Press, 1986. One of the best accounts of Soyinka's poetry; particularly good on the composition of the poems in *Idanre* and the musicological aspects of its title poem.

Gakwandi, Shatto Arthur. *The Novel and Contemporary Experience in Africa.* London: Heinemann, 1977. The chapter on *The Interpreters* contains some discriminating criticism.

Gikandi, Simon. *Reading the African Novel.* London: James Currey, 1987; Portsmouth, N.H.: Heinemann, 1987. Contains a short but astute discussion of Soyinka's two novels.

Goodwin, Ken. *Understanding African Poetry: A Study of Ten Poets.* London: Heinemann, 1982. A sensible and informative commentary on Soyinka's poetry up to *Ogun Abibiman.*

Griffiths, Gareth. *A Double Exile: African and West Indian Writing between Two Cultures.* London: Marion Boyars, 1978. A stimulating account of the relationships between myth and reality, and between traditional ritual practices and contemporary concerns, in *The Road* and *Madmen and Specialists.*

Irele, Abiola. *The African Experience in Literature and Ideology.* London: Heinemann, 1981. Provides a lucid account of the Yoruba background to Soyinka's writing.

Jeyifo, Biodun. *The Truthful Lie: Essays in a Sociology of African Drama.* London: New Beacon Books, 1985. Contains trenchant discussion of the "hidden" politico-historical dimensions and shortcomings of *The Road* and *Death and the King's Horseman.*

King, Bruce. *The New English Literatures: Cultural Nationalism in a Changing*

World. London: Macmillan, 1980. Has a comprehensive chapter on Ogun themes in Soyinka's writing.

Laurence, Margaret. *Long Drums and Cannons: Nigerian Dramatists and Novelists, 1952–1966.* London: Macmillan, 1968. Pioneering criticism of Soyinka's early work that still reads well today.

Lindfors, Bernth, ed. *Critical Perspectives on Nigerian Literatures.* Washington, D.C.: Three Continents Press, 1975; London: Heinemann, 1979. Contains an interesting essay by Lindfors on Soyinka's early writings and a penetrating discussion by J. Z. Kronenfeld of the complex relations of modern and traditional elements in *The Lion and the Jewel.* The volume also has useful background articles on Yoruba folklore and theater.

McEwan, Neil. *Africa and the Novel.* Atlantic Highlands, N.J.: Humanities Press, 1983. Has a lively chapter on satiric form in *The Interpreters.*

Moore, Gerald. *Twelve African Writers.* London: Hutchinson, 1980. Contains some provocative criticism of Soyinka's mythic consciousness and idealizing cast of mind.

Palmer, Eustace. *The Growth of the African Novel.* London: Heinemann, 1979. A detailed and painstaking descriptive account of Soyinka's two novels by a generally unsympathetic critic.

Peters, Jonathan A. *A Dance of Masks: Senghor, Achebe, Soyinka.* Washington, D.C.: Three Continents Press, 1978. Excellent coverage of the mask and other traditional ritual elements in Soyinka's plays.

Priebe, Richard A. *Myth, Realism, and the West African Writer.* Trenton, N.J.: African World Press, 1988. Has three chapters on Soyinka and contains trailblazing discussion of mythic dimensions in the poetry, *The Interpreters,* and *The Trials of Brother Jero.*

Roscoe, Adrian. *Mother Is Gold: A Study in West African Literature.* Cambridge: Cambridge University Press, 1971. Clear and concise criticism of Soyinka's early plays and poetry.

Journal Special Issues

Black American Literature Forum 22, no. 3 (Fall 1988). Includes essays on all aspects of Soyinka's work and the text of his Nobel Prize speech.

Commonwealth: Essays and Studies, no. SP1 (1989). Special issue edited by Jean-Pierre Durix, on *A Dance of the Forests.* A comprehensive but very specialized anthology of essays, mainly by French critics, on a single play, occasioned by its inclusion in the *Agregation* syllabus at French universities.

Literary Half-Yearly 28, no. 2 (July 1987). Special issue on Wole Soyinka, edited by James Gibbs. A useful collection of essays and tributes (despite some appalling copyediting) following the award of the Nobel Prize. Its main attraction is the long question-and-answer session with Soyinka, recorded at the University of Zimbabwe (see Gibbs, "Soyinka in Zimbabwe: A Question-and-Answer Session.")

Research in African Literatures 14, no. 1 (Spring 1983), Special issue on Wole Soyinka, edited by James Gibbs. The best journal issue on the author, containing probing and illuminating essays on the poetry and plays and a long piece by Gibbs on Soyinka's journalistic writings.

Research in African Literatures 21, no. 4 (Winter 1990). Contains three challenging essays on Soyinka, by Stewart Crehan, William S. Haney, and Ruth H. Lindeborg, including Haney's on ritual drama and Lindeborg's on *Aké.*

Southern Review 23, no. 3 (1987). Includes the transcript of a seminar on *Aké* with Soyinka and a perceptive essay on the book by James Olney.

Journal Articles and Chapters in Books

Amuta, Chidi. "The Ideological Content of Wole Soyinka's War Writings." *Commonwealth* 8, no. 2 (Spring 1988): 102–12. A critical sociohistorical reading of Soyinka's civil war "quartet" of writings.

Attwell, David. "Wole Soyinka's *The Interpreters:* Suggestions on Context and History." *English in Africa* 8, no. 1 (1981): 59–71. A discerning account of the novel's social and mythological contexts.

Berry, Boyd M. "On Looking at *Madmen and Specialists.*" *Pan-African Journal* no. 4 (Winter, 1972): 5, 461–71. A lively and sophisticated account of the play's complexities and convolutions.

Booth, James. "Myth, Metaphor, and Syntax in Soyinka's Poetry." *Research in African Literatures* 17, no. 1 (Spring 1986): 53–72. The best article on Soyinka's poetry; Booth keeps myth and metaphysics at their proper distance and concentrates upon the words on the page.

Brockbank, Philip. "Blood and Wine: Tragic Ritual from Aeschyllus to Soyinka." *Shakespeare Survey* 36, no. 1 (1983): 11–19. Places *The Strong Breed* and *The Bacchae* within the perspectives of Greek and Shakespearean tragedy.

Crow, Brian. "Soyinka and His Radical Critics: A Review." *Theatre Research International* 12, no. 1 (Spring 1987): 61–73. A comprehensive survey of Soyinka's recent reactions, in plays, revues, and essays, to criticism from the Nigerian left.

Fiebach, Joachim. "Wole Soyinka as Director." In *Forty Years of Mise en Scene,* edited by Claude Schumacher, 245–50. Dundee, Scotland: Lochee Publications, 1986. An interesting short account of Soyinka's direction of his own plays, revues, and street-theater in the 1980s.

Gates, Henry Louis, Jr. "Being, the Will, and the Semantics of Death." *Harvard Educational Review* 51, no 1 (February 1981): 163–73. A reading of *Death and the King's Horseman* within the context of Soyinka's dramatic work.

Gibbs, James. "Soyinka's Drama of Essence." *Utafiti* 3, no. 2 (1978): 427–40. A sensible account of the limited input from empirical festival research into the early plays.

————. "The Masks Hatched Out." *Theatre Research International* 7, no. 3 (October 1982): 180–206. A meticulous account of the production histories of the plays and revues inside and outside of Africa.

————. "Biography into Autobiography: Wole Soyinka and the Relatives Who Inhabit *Aké.*" *Journal of Modern African Studies* 26, no. 3 (1988): 517–48. An engaging account of *Aké* in the light of available historical and biographical information.

Knipp, Thomas R. "Irony, Tragedy, and Myth: The Poetry of Wole Soyinka." *World Literature Written in English* 21, no. 1 (Spring 1982): 5–26. A comprehensive discussion of the many dimensions of Soyinka's poetry.

Lindfors, Bernth. "Wole Soyinka, When Are You Coming Home?" *Yale French Studies* 53 (1976): 197–210. Sharply criticizes the esoteric plays.

————. "Begging Questions in Wole Soyinka's *Opera Wonyosi.*" *ARIEL* 12, no. 3 (1981): 21–33. A lucid account of the play's relations to the Gay and Brecht originals.

Maugham-Brown, David. "Interpreting and *The Interpreters:* Wole Soyinka and Practical Criticism." *English in Africa* 6, no. 2 (1978): 51–62. A demystificatory account of the novel from a sociopolitical angle, stressing its elitist tendencies.

Ogunba, Oyin. "The Traditional Content of the Plays of Wole Soyinka." *African Literature Today* 3 (1969): 2–18; and 5 (1971): 106–15. An indispensable study of the early plays in their traditional Yoruba ritual, festival, and mythological contexts.

Ogunbiyi, Yemi. "A Study of Soyinka's *Opera Wonyosi.*" *Nigeria Magazine* 128–29 (1979): 3–14. An informative account of the play in its performance context.

Ogungbesan, Kole. "Wole Soyinka and the Poetry of Isolation." *Canadian Journal of African Studies* 11, no. 2 (1977): 295–312. A detailed survey of the poems in the first two collections.

Osofisan, Femi. "Tiger on Stage: Wole Soyinka and Nigerian Theatre." In *Theatre in Africa,* edited by Oyin Ogunba and Abiola Irele, 151–75. Ibadan, Nigeria: Ibadan University Press, 1978. A wide-ranging and farsighted account of the drama that, intriguingly, traces its alternating popular and hermetic modes to the bipartite models of festival dramaturgy.

Osundare, Niyi. "Words of Iron, Sentences of Thunder: Soyinka's Prose Style." *African Literature Today* 13 (1983): 24–37. A systematic examination of the novel's rhetorical devices and effects.

Pollard, Phyllis. "Myth, Literature and Ideology—A Reading of Wole Soyinka's *Season of Anomy.*" *Journal of Commonwealth Literature* 19, no. 1 (1984): 74–85. An astute account of the conflicting currents of myth and ideological commitment in the novel.

Probyn, Clive. "Waiting for the Word: Samuel Beckett and Wole Soyinka." *ARIEL* 12, no. 3 (1981): 35–48. Relates *The Road* to absurdist drama.

Weales, Gerald. "Wole Soyinka: Yoruba Plays for All Tribes." *Hollins Critic* 11, no. 5 (December 1974): 1–13. A useful survey of the plays for newcomers to Soyinka's work.

Wilkinson, Nick. "Literary Incomprehension: Wole Soyinka's Own Way with a Mode." *Nsukka Studies in African Literature* 1, no. 1 (1978): 44–53. Examines the creative use of bafflement in the esoteric plays.

Wright, Derek. "The Ritual Context of Two Plays by Soyinka." *Theatre Research International* 12, no. 1 (Spring 1987): 51–61. An explication of the carrier ritual in *The Strong Breed* and *The Bacchae*.

Bibliographies

Gibbs, James, with Ketu H. Katrak and and Henry Louis Gates, Jr. *Wole Soyinka: A Bibliography of Primary and Secondary Sources.* Westport, Conn.: Greenwood Press, 1986. The most exhaustive and up-to-date (to 1984) of the bibliographies devoted exclusively to Soyinka.

Lindfors, Bernth. *Black African Literatures in English* (to 1976). Detroit: Gale Research Co., 1979. *1977–1981 Supplement.* New York: Africana Publishing Co., 1986. *1982–1986 Supplement.* London and New York: Hans Zell, 1989. This three-volume bibliography contains large reference sections on secondary material on Soyinka.

"Wole Soyinka: A Selected Bibliography." In Gibbs, *Critical Perspectives on Wole Soyinka,* 253–72. London: Heinemann, 1981. Very comprehensive, including Soyinka's juvenilia and reviews of play productions.

Index

The Author

Derek Wright has degrees in English and American literature from the universities of Reading and Keele in England and a Ph.D. in African literature from the University of Queensland, Australia. He has taught at the University of Queensland and at the University of Sierra Leone, West Africa, and is currently senior lecturer in English at the Northern Territory University, Darwin, Australia, where he teaches courses in nineteenth- and twentieth-century literatures. He is the author of *Ayi Kwei Armah's Africa: The Sources of His Fiction* (1989) and has edited *Critical Perspectives on Ayi Kwei Armah* (1992). He has published widely, in academic journals over five continents, in the areas of African, post-colonial, and American literature.